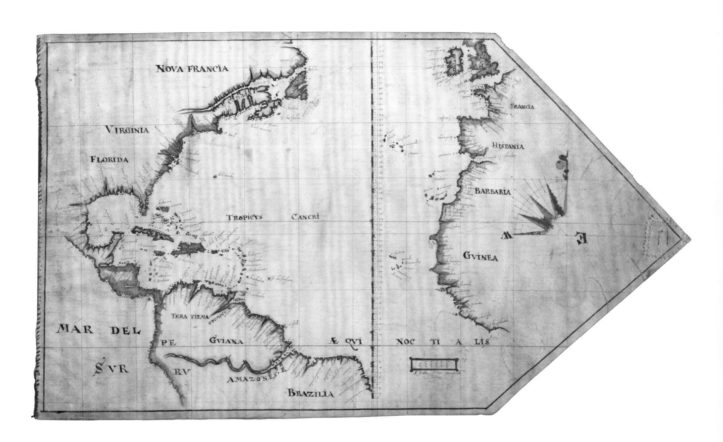

LandAmerica Financial Group is proud to present this special edition
of *Jamestown, Québec, Santa Fe: Three North American Beginnings*
in commemoration of the four-hundredth anniversary of the cities from which
English, French, and Spanish influence radiated throughout North America.

Jamestown · Québec · Santa Fe

Three North American Beginnings

James C. Kelly and Barbara Clark Smith

with contributions by Warren M. Billings, Gilles Proulx, and David J. Weber

Foreword by Charles F. Bryan, Jr., and Brent Glass

SMITHSONIAN BOOKS · WASHINGTON AND NEW YORK

This book accompanies the exhibition *Jamestown, Québec, Santa Fe: Three North American Beginnings.* The Organizing Partners are the Virginia Historical Society and the National Museum of American History, Smithsonian Institution. The Contributing Partners are the Canadian Museum of Civilization and The Palace of the Governors, The New Mexico History Museum, Museum of New Mexico, Department of Cultural Affairs.

© 2007 Smithsonian Institution
All rights reserved
Distributed by HarperCollins Publishers

Copy Editor: Nancy Eickel
Designer: Robert L. Wiser

Library of Congress Cataloging-in-Publication Data

Kelly, James C., 1949–
    Jamestown, Quebec, Santa Fe : three North American beginnings / James C. Kelly and Barbara Clark Smith ; with contributions by Warren M. Billings, Gilles Proulx, and David J. Weber ; foreword by Charles F. Bryan, Jr., and Brent Glass.
        p.   cm.
    "This book accompanies the exhibition Jamestown, Quebec, Santa Fe: three North American beginnings."
    Includes bibliographical references and index.
    ISBN -13: 978-1-58834-241-6 (alk. paper)
    1. North America—History—Colonial period, ca. 1600–1775.
2. North America—Colonization. 3. Colonization—Social aspects—History. 4. Colonies—History. 5. Jamestown (Va.)—History—17th century. 6. Québec (Québec)—History—17th century. 7. Santa Fe (N.M.)—History—17th century. I. Smith, Barbara Clark. II. Billings, Warren M., 1940– III. Proulx, Gilles. IV. Weber, David J. V. Title.
E46.K45 2007
970.02—dc22   2006033153

Printed in China

14   13   12   11   10   09   08   07   5   4   3   2   1

Page 1. The Virginia Company of London commissioned this map about 1607 to 1609. It shows the Atlantic world of English, French, and Spanish colonies in the New World, although New Mexico is out of view. England's claim to Virginia extended from present-day Maine to North Carolina and west to the Pacific Ocean. The Virginia Company of Plymouth planned to settle the northern part of the claim, but its colony at Popham, Maine, lasted only a few months in 1607 and 1608.

Pages 2–3. Made by Matthäus Greuter in Italy about 1632, this globe is one of the first to show the location of Québec City.

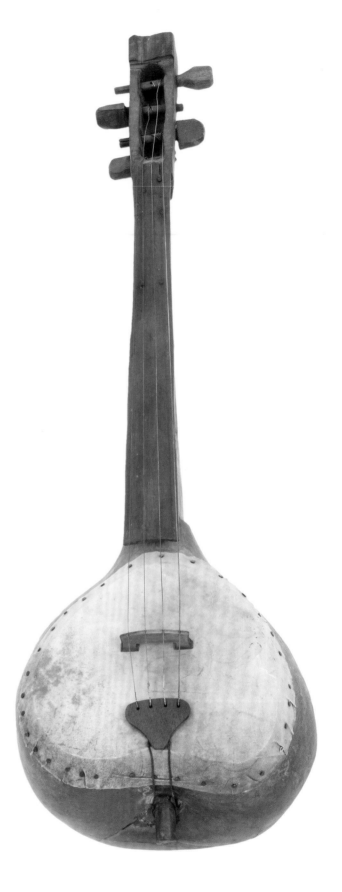

Contents

Opposite. West Africans introduced the banjo to North America. While the violin, or fiddle, was of European origin, stringed instruments made from gourds were common in many parts of West Africa. In the Chesapeake region, African Americans fashioned instruments from gourds, as was done with this nineteenth-century example.

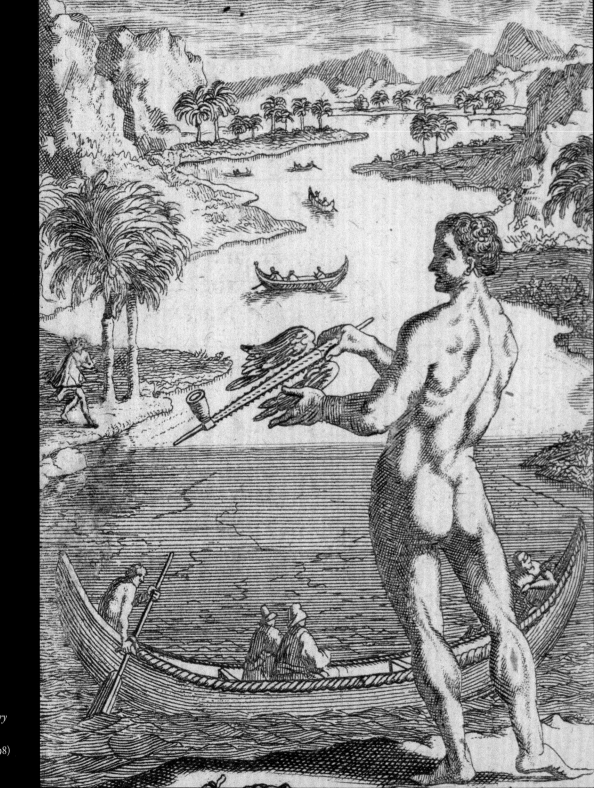

Foreword

Detail of frontispiece
from *A New Discovery
of a Vast Country in
America* (London, 1698)
by Louis Hennepin,
a Franciscan friar,

THIS OPENING DECADE of the twenty-first century is the occasion of the four-hundredth anniversaries of three important European settlements in the territory that became Canada and the United States.

As Organizing Partners, the Virginia Historical Society and the Smithsonian National Museum of American History are pleased to mark those anniversaries with the exhibition *Jamestown, Québec, Santa Fe: Three North American Beginnings.* This landmark effort brings together artifacts and images from English, French, and Spanish projects of colonization and takes a multicultural approach to a milestone in world history: the virtually simultaneous introduction of English, French, and Spanish cultures into the vast area north of Mexico. It examines the establishment of Jamestown, Québec, and Santa Fe in 1607, 1608, and 1609, respectively, and it traces the societies that emerged out of those settlements to about 1700.

By bringing these three histories together, the exhibition offers museum visitors at venues in Canada and the United States an opportunity to compare and contrast three founding stories. The comparison suggests new perspectives on a century of colonization. These stories assume added dimension when viewed in the context of the others. This broader perspective, and an appreciation of the concurrence of English, French, and Spanish colonization, might be more important than any particular set of facts visitors may acquire in the exhibition.

A second shift in outlook is also central to this exhibition and its accompanying book. Incorporating new insights from historians' study of indigenous North American societies, it views Native peoples and their experiences and aspirations as critical factors in the era of colonization. To describe that period as one of *international* encounters is to realize the essential agency of numerous *American* nations—Powhatans, Hurons, Pueblos, and many more—as well as European ones. The exhibition thus encourages museum visitors to consider the "new world" that the continent's indigenous peoples faced in the context of European projects of colonization and conquest.

The exhibition could not have been successful without the active participation of our Consulting Partners—the Canadian Museum of Civilization in Gatineau, Québec, and the Palace of the Governors (The New Mexico History Museum) in Santa Fe. They not only contributed objects and graphics, but they also directed us to other sources. They provided invaluable counsel, information, review, and constructive criticism, and the resulting book and exhibition are much the stronger for their involvement. We also are grateful to the Missouri Historical Society for agreeing to host the exhibition.

There would be no exhibition without the willingness of lenders to part for a considerable space of time with inestimable seventeenth-century treasures of Americana and Canadiana. Their names are found in the Acknowledgments.

A major and complex exhibition such as this also depends on generous financial support, which we have received from The Robins Foundation, LandAmerica Financial Group, Jamestown 2007, and the Virginia Department of Historic Resources. Without their interest, we could not have made this historic endeavor a reality, and we thank them for their participation.

Finally, we congratulate the exhibition curators, Dr. James Kelly and Dr. Barbara Clark Smith, for bringing an ambitious conception to elegant fruition. We believe this presentation provides visitors with engaging new insights and answers numerous questions about the seventeenth century.

Charles F. Bryan, Jr., Ph.D.
President and Chief Executive Officer
Virginia Historical Society

Brent Glass, Ph.D.
Director
National Museum of American History
Smithsonian Institution

Introduction

James C. Kelly and Barbara Clark Smith

Captain John Smith, English colonist,
explorer, and military adventurer.

In 2007, 2008, and 2009, the towns of Jamestown, Québec, and Santa Fe, respectively, are marking the four-hundredth anniversaries of their establishment by European colonists.[1] These towns were among the earliest lasting European settlements on the continent north of Mexico.[2] Far apart geographically, these outposts of England, France, and Spain had very close beginnings in time. Were there significant common goals, experiences, or developments among these three settlements? Do their different experiences, viewed side by side, suggest new questions or insights? The exhibition that this catalogue accompanies arose from just that possibility: the hope that bringing together these histories through surviving artifacts and images would yield some thought-provoking contrasts and comparisons. What might we learn about this distant era when Europeans colonized North America?

If this is a good time for revisiting these early settlements, it is not only because their anniversaries provide the occasion but also because a wealth of new scholarship has challenged old assumptions and revised old narratives. Three approaches are currently creating

striking insights into this era of early colonization. First, new ideas and questions arise from taking a longer view. As historian Alan Taylor points out, from 1492 to 1776 the human population of the North American continent did not increase but instead declined. (This can be particularly surprising to U.S. readers, who might have learned that the nation's colonial period was a time of growth.) In our area of focus, the 1600s, tens of thousands of Europeans came to settle, and thousands of Africans were forcibly brought to this continent. That trickle of Old World immigration became a flood in the 1700s, yet the loss of Native peoples to the deadly diseases and deep disruptions of the Columbian encounter more than offset the addition of newcomers.[3] Although the seventeenth-century establishment of lasting settlements by Europeans was momentous in its consequences, it is not correctly understood as the "peopling" of North America. Historians are finding more accurate terms to characterize the era—as a time of conquest or invasion, certainly, but also as an era marked by new interactions in diplomacy, warfare, trade, and cultural exchange that defy simple description. At the least, given the era's shocking losses of life and the dramatic destruction of established ways of living, we might rethink a basic assumption: the seventeenth century saw not the *settling* of the North American continent so much as its *unsettling*.[4]

A second approach views events of the early 1600s in the context of a broader geographical scope. Many scholars now see early European settlements in North America as small outposts in a vast and interconnected Atlantic world. Embracing all four continents that border the Atlantic—Europe, Africa, South America, and North America—this approach traces the extraordinary movement of people, products, and ideas that reshaped cultures and lives in both Eastern and Western Hemispheres. This perspective puts the little settlements of Jamestown, Québec, and Santa Fe in their humble place. Since the fifteenth century, Portuguese ships had plied the seas off the coast of Africa. Soon they were joined by Danish, Spanish, French, Dutch, and English traders. For their part, African coastal villages grew into trading towns, and many of their inhabitants learned new languages, developed new practices of trade,

Samuel de Champlain may have lost this mariner's astrolabe, dated 1603 and found in the Ottawa Valley in 1867, when he first visited the region in 1613. Navigators used astrolabes to determine latitude by measuring the altitude of the sun at noon or the meridian altitude of a known star. The instrument consisted of a simple brass ring graduated in degrees with a rotating alidade (to measure angles) for sighting the sun or a star.

Opposite. Bartholomew Gosnold was captain of the *Godspeed*, one of the Virginia Company's three ships. Theodor de Bry's *America* shows him trading with Native people of New England in 1602 during an expedition in which he gave English names to Cape Cod and Martha's Vineyard (for his daughter).

These crossbow bolt heads were found near Albuquerque, New Mexico, at the archaeological site of Puaray, the winter campsite of Coronado's expedition in 1540–41.

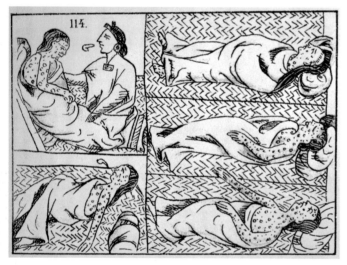

Infectious diseases from the Old World, such as smallpox, influenza, and measles, inevitably traveled to the Americas, devastating many Native societies in New France, Virginia, New England, and New Mexico in the 1600s and after. An Aztec artist documented Aztec people suffering with smallpox about 1577.

Opposite. *Nova Britannia* promoted Virginia as an "earthly paradice" and exhorted planters to "hold and keep conformity with the laws, language, and religion of England."

and acquired a new sense of cosmopolitanism.[5] In the 1500s Europeans also fished the waters off the American coast in the North Atlantic. From the European viewpoint, however, the New World *colonies* that mattered were in South America, Mexico, and the Caribbean. Spanish conquerors, especially in Peru and central Mexico, seized gold and other wealth from Native peoples. Their conquests brought untold wealth to the Spanish crown and to fortunate adventurers, and those successes fanned the rivalry among the great powers of Europe. A century after Columbus, those nations were just beginning to turn significant attention to the possibilities of exploiting the resources of the continent north of Mexico. Indeed, for decades after the establishment of Jamestown, Québec, and Santa Fe, most Europeans dismissed these towns as minor outposts on the northern rim of the far more significant Caribbean world. Santa Fe was less a project of the Old World than the extension of a colony, a new *Mexico*.

Locating those outposts in the Atlantic context also emphasizes that they were affected by developments in many other places. Scholars have suggested, for example, that England's recent subjugation of Irish peoples surely informed policies adopted toward Powhatans in the Chesapeake region. Beginning in Ulster in 1603, English "planters" established a system of "plantations," two terms that soon would be associated with Virginia society as well.[6] Equally fascinating, African Creoles— cosmopolitan, often multilingual people from the growing entrepôts along the coast of Africa—were among the earliest generation of Africans brought to labor in the Chesapeake. Their skills helped some of them achieve a modicum of security and freedom as farmers and craftsmen in the New World.[7] When looking through this broad lens, we are similarly reminded that European markets for furs and tobacco, African trade, and extraordinary demands for labor on the sugar plantations of the Caribbean all affected the lives of the disparate historical actors who would come together in North America. Distant events would limit their choices, inform their aspirations, and sometimes subvert their best-laid plans.

Nova Britannia.

OFFERING MOST

Excellent fruites by Planting in VIRGINIA.

Exciting all such as be well affected to further the same.

LONDON
Printed for Samvel Macham, and are to be sold at
his Shop in Pauls Church-yard, at the
Signe of the Bul-head.
1609.

The St. Lawrence Iroquois were an agricultural people at the time of Cartier's expeditions in the 1530s. When French explorers re-entered the St. Lawrence area in 1603, they found the local Iroquois had dispersed due to European diseases and warfare, particularly with the Huron from north of Lake Ontario. This pot was made about 1550.

A Huron wampum belt records a treaty concluded with the Iroquois at the headwaters of the Ottawa River in 1612. The square signifies the constituent units of the Huron. White generally represented peace while purple had more somber connotations. This pattern apparently indicates that these two peoples are no longer at war. The Huron had long battled with the Iroquois, but this belt may have sealed a peace made necessary by the arrival of the French.

A third perspective centers on Native peoples of the continent as active and vital agents in seventeenth-century encounters and transformations. North America was inhabited by many different peoples whose specific cultures, alliances, and immediate situations shaped their reactions to European arrivals. These groups lived in a changing, not static, world with histories of their own. In the northeastern region, for example, disparate groups had been joining together for some centuries to form larger social and political entities. Southeastern tribes were also undergoing changes in political institutions, as many chiefdoms waned in authority and power. Everywhere, different Native groups negotiated relationships of exchange, alliance, rivalry, and conflict with neighboring peoples.[8] They drew on those longstanding and familiar modes of interaction when they encountered Europeans.

By 1607 many indigenous groups had had sporadic contact with European explorers, fishermen, and traders for decades. Even that limited exposure produced extraordinary effects—most devastatingly by introducing infectious Old World diseases—and those changes had already shaped Native societies in powerful ways. In the St. Lawrence Valley, for example, sedentary Native peoples, ravaged by disease, withdrew from the area in the decades before Frenchmen established Québec. New, permanent settlements established by Europeans unleashed even more powerful economic, cultural, ecological, and epidemiological forces. As a result, historian James Merrell asserts, the seventeenth century was a "new world" for Native people as well as for British, French, Spanish, and African arrivals.[9] We see and appreciate that new world when we adopt a fresh perspective—to paraphrase historian Daniel Richter, when we "face east from Indian country." "Facing east" here provides a metaphor for facing south, north, and west as well, taking the viewpoint of Native peoples in all parts of the continent to survey the coming of Europeans.[10]

Taken together, these approaches make the story of seventeenth-century North America more complex and multifaceted than ever. The essays that follow, written by

An embroidered Huron or Iroquois moccasin from the upper St. Lawrence region can be dated to circa 1721.

leading specialists in the histories of Jamestown, Québec, and Santa Fe, offer short narratives of these three settlements. Our contribution in these introductory pages is modest. We offer brief and tentative remarks on six topics: European purposes and priorities in initiating North American settlements; Native purposes and experiences in the years of early contact; the unforeseen terms in which each settlement found a measure of stability during the century; the outbreak of significant military conflict in the latter decades of the century in some, but not all, areas of European settlement; the creation of new identities and statuses, most potently those built on a premise of slavery and race; and finally, the expansion of these settlements as rival empires seeking to control the continent.

IN LOOKING at European origins, we begin with a prosaic fact: the cost of the endeavor was in every case forbidding. Historian Karen Kupperman has suggested that we might think of the settlement of Jamestown, purely as a financial project, as needing investment capital somewhere on the scale of that required by space exploration in the late twentieth century.[11] Such settlements were extraordinary ventures, then, and what motivated their funders was the possibility of great gain.

To one degree or another, each settlement drew on earlier Spanish experiences in the Caribbean and South America. The Spanish crown—and a host of adventurers and plunderers—became rich from encounters with large sedentary Native populations, such as the Aztecs and the Incas. They seized the Native peoples' gold and silver and forced them to labor in mines and fields. The prospect of similar discoveries of precious metals and prosperous tribes encouraged explorers to move into the northern reaches of New Spain. When Juan de Oñate led a colonizing expedition to the northern frontier, it was privately funded. Oñate and some of his men invested their own fortunes in order to invade the land of the Pueblo peoples. Like Francisco Vásquez de Coronado, who had traveled the area sixty years earlier, they expected to find wealthy inhabitants living in cities, as well as mineral riches and perhaps passage to the Pacific and even Atlantic oceans.[12]

These hand-forged iron shears from the seventeenth century were collected in New Mexico.

Opposite. Made by Matthäus Greuter in Italy about 1632, this globe is one of the first to show the location of Québec City.

Clearly dated 1645, this English hand-forged anvil was excavated at Falling Creek in Chesterfield County, Virginia. When repairing weapons and tools, blacksmiths sometimes inserted such anvils into the hole of a tree stump to form a workbench.

Jordan's Journey, where this English breastplate was found, was a settlement upriver from Jamestown that existed from 1620 to 1635.

English army sergeants carried halberds, such as this one found at Jamestown, as symbols of rank and to signal troop movements.

Both Spaniards and indigenous people in New Mexico utilized shields made of buffalo or bison hides. Called *adargas*, shields such as this eighteenth-century example were used into the next century.

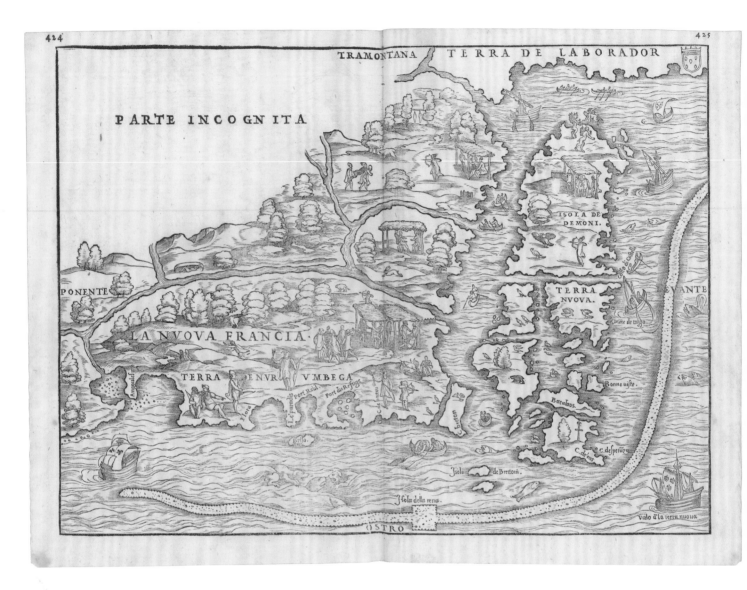

The English also hoped to gain wealth in North America. The Virginia Company of London, a joint-stock company formed in 1606, sent settlers to establish a fort the next year. The stockholders envisioned Jamestown as a base from which settlers would travel outward to discover and appropriate the natural riches of the continent. The English did not necessarily anticipate finding gold or silver, but they did expect to enjoy a relatively easy livelihood and find marketable resources to send back for the investors' profit. Thus, many of the English who arrived in Jamestown in 1607 were gentlemen and their servants, not yeomen farmers or husbandmen. They did not come for land per se but for the resources of the country, and they expected to survive by trading copper for the food cultivated by Native peoples. When they did not find valuable resources for easy export, and when seasons of unprecedented drought made the Algonquian-speaking people in the area unwilling to trade away their scarce foodstuffs, the English settlers reacted as the gentlemen and military men they were: rather than planting, fishing, or hunting, they took what they needed at gunpoint.[13]

Québec similarly originated as a business venture. Beginning in 1599, Henry IV of France decided to establish permanent French settlements in Canada.

Native people frequently decorated their clothing and hair with brass bells. These common trade items (circa 1654–81) are from a Native settlement in Onondaga, New York.

The earliest trade beads were large and worn on necklaces such as this one used in New France. Later, smaller beads that could be sewn onto clothing became more common in the fur trade.

Opposite. This map is based on the French-sponsored voyage of Giovanni Verrazzano in 1524. Ten years later Jacques Cartier began a series of expeditions that explored the St. Lawrence River, shown at the center of the map. The failure of either Verrazzano or Cartier to find a route to the Pacific or to discover local riches curtailed French exploration for the next sixty years.

A Pawtucket artist in or near Nahumkeke (now Salem, Massachusetts) made this bear sculpture, probably in the late 1500s. In 1605 and 1606 Samuel de Champlain stopped on the Massachusetts coast, but he decided not to build a French outpost because the area was heavily populated. Epidemics greatly reduced the Native population in 1616 and 1617, however, and England's Pilgrims established their Plymouth settlement at a former Native village when they landed in 1620.

Opposite, left. John Winthrop not only was instrumental in organizing the Massachusetts Bay Colony, but he also served as its first governor and was re-elected eleven times. He tried to balance church and state, freedom and responsibility, confederation and local autonomy, and executive power and a popular franchise. An anonymous artist painted this portrait some time between 1630 and 1691.

Opposite, right. *A True Discourse* touts the conversion of Pocahontas on its cover. She accepted Christianity after being kidnapped and was virtually the only Indian convert of the early period. Ardor for missionary work perished with the Anglo-Powhatan War of 1622–32.

He awarded a fur trade monopoly to a succession of private companies, granting them the authority to found a colony and to send settlers to populate it. Henry thus helped to make New France a reality without having to finance it from the royal treasury. Unlike the Spanish and the English, the French who sailed up the St. Lawrence River did not need to make contact with prosperous sedentary civilizations. They sought instead to develop a lucrative trade in furs, building on exchanges that had taken place along the St. Lawrence and northern areas in previous decades. Accordingly, they established their settlement at a site where Algonquins and Montagnais people gathered to trade in the summers, and where Hurons and Nipissings brought pelts of beaver, moose, and bear for exchange. As long as Native traders carried valuable beaver pelts to these sites, there was little need for the French to expand their settlements.[14]

Not all European settlers were interested in profits. Protestants and Catholics alike believed themselves to be blessed with knowledge of the true religion, a fact that both motivated and rationalized colonization. Devout Anglicans imagined bringing Protestant Christianity to the indigenous peoples of the New World, while Puritans and other fervent English dissenters established colonies in New England in the 1620s and 1630s. Yet even in New England, efforts to convert Natives were limited, and initiatives such as John Eliot's promotion of "Praying Towns" among the Nipmuc people were largely private in nature. Although the Virginia Company embraced the intention of bringing indigenous peoples to Christianity, settlers in the Chesapeake actually expended little effort toward that end. Pocahontas was virtually their only convert, and their Christianizing spirit largely disappeared once the Powhatans replied to English intrusions with a concerted military attack in 1622.[15]

By contrast, the Catholic powers, at the height of Counter-Reformation enthusiasm, took the challenge of converting Native peoples more seriously. Several Franciscan missionaries, called Récollets, arrived in Québec in 1615 to minister to French settlers and claim new souls. They were followed by Jesuit priests, hospital nuns, and Ursuline sisters, who taught and cared for the Native peoples. When they met with only limited success at winning converts, many Jesuits moved out to live with various tribes, learning new languages in which to preach and translate the Bible.[16]

Religion also played a crucial role in New Mexico. Oñate found no vast riches in those northern lands, and disappointed adventurers soon urged the Spanish crown to abandon the struggling colony. Franciscan friars managed to forestall that decision. Claiming to have already converted thousands of Natives in the villages

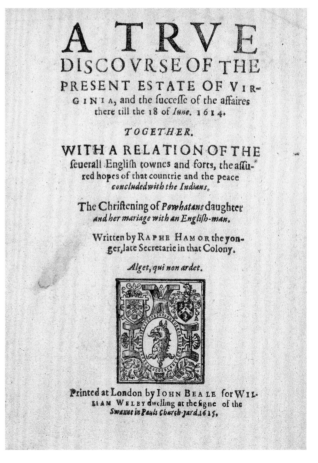

A TRVE
DISCOVRSE OF THE
PRESENT ESTATE OF VIR-
GINIA, and the successe of the affaires
there till the 18 of *Iune.* 1614.

TOGETHER.

WITH A RELATION OF THE
seuerall English townes and forts, the assured hopes of that countrie and the peace
concluded with the Indians,

The Christening of *Powhatans* daughter
and her mariage with an English-man.

Written by RAPHE HAMOR the yon-
ger, late Secretarie in that Colony.

Alget, qui non ardet.

Printed at London by IOHN BEALE for WIL-
LIAM WELBY dwelling at the signe of the
Swanne in Pauls Church-yard.1615.

THE INCONVENIENCIES
THAT HAVE HAPPENED TO SOME PER-
SONS WHICH HAVE TRANSPORTED THEMSELVES

from *England* to *Virginia*, vvithout prouisions necessary to sustaine themselues, hath
greatly hindred the Progresse of that noble Plantation: For preuention of the like disorders
heereafter, that no man suffer, either through ignorance or misinformation; it is thought re-
quisite to publish this short declaration: wherein is contained a particular of such necess-
saries, as either priuate families or single persons shall haue cause to furnish themselues with, for their better
support at their first landing in Virginia: whereby also greater numbers may receiue in part,
directions how to prouide themselues.

Apparrell.

Apparrell for one man, and so after the rate for more.

	li.	s.	d.
One Monmouth Cap	00	01	10
Three falling bands	—	01	03
Three shirts	—	07	06
One waste-coate	—	02	02
One suite of Canuase	—	07	06
One suite of Frize	—	10	00
One suite of Cloth	—	15	00
Three paire of Irish stockins	—	04	00
Foure paire of shooes	—	08	08
One paire of garters	—	00	10
One doozen of points	—	00	03
One paire of Canuase sheets	—	08	00
Seuen ells of Canuase, to make a bed and boulster, to be filled in *Virginia* 8.s.			
One Rug for a bed 8. s. which with the bed seruing for two men, halfe is	—	08	00
Fiue ells coorse Canuase, to make a bed at Sea for two men, to be filled with straw,			
One coorse Rug at Sea for two men, will cost vj, s. is for one	—	05	00
	04	00	00

Victuall.

For a whole yeere for one man, and so for more after the rate.

	li.	s.	d.
Eight bushels of Meale	02	00	00
Two bushels of pease at 3.s.	—	06	00
Two bushels of Oatemeale 4.s. 6.d.	—	09	00
One gallon of *Aquauitæ*	—	02	06
One gallon of Oyle	—	03	06
Two gallons of Vineger 1.s.	—	02	00
	03	03	00

Armes.

For one man, but if halfe of your men haue armour it is sufficient so that all haue Peeces and swords.

	li.	s.	d.
One Armour compleat, light	—	17	00
One long Peece, fiue foot or fiue and a halfe, neere Musket bore	01	02	00
One sword	—	05	00
One belt	—	01	00
One bandaleere	—	01	06
Twenty pound of powder	—	18	00
Sixty pound of shot or lead, Pistoll and Goose shot	—	05	00
	03	09	06

Tooles.

For a family of 6. persons and so after the rate for more.

	li.	s.	d.
Fiue broad howes at 2.s. a piece	—	10	00
Fiue narrow howes at 16.d. a piece	—	06	08
Two broad Axes at 3.s. 8.d. a piece	—	07	04
Fiue felling Axes at 18.d. a piece	—	07	06
Two steele hand sawes at 16.d. a piece	—	02	08
Two two-hand sawes at 5. s. a piece	—	10	00
One whip-saw, set and filed with box, file, and wrest	—	10	00
Two hammers 12.d. a piece	—	02	00
Three shouels 18.d. a piece	—	04	06
Two spades at 18.d. a piece	—	03	00
Two augers 6.d. a piece	—	01	00
Six chissels 6.d. a piece	—	03	00
Two percers stocked 4.d. a piece	—	00	08
Three gimlets 2.d. a piece	—	00	06
Two hatchets 21.d. a piece	—	03	06
Two froues to cleaue pale 18.d.	—	03	00
Two hand-bills 20. a piece	—	03	04
One grindlestone 4.s.	—	04	00
Nailes of all sorts to the value of	02	00	00
Two Pickaxes	—	03	00
	06	02	08

Houshold Implements.

For a family of 6. persons, and so for more or lesse after the rate.

	li.	s.	d.
One Iron Pot	—	07	00
One kettle	—	06	00
One large frying-pan	—	02	06
One gridiron	—	01	06
Two skillets	—	05	00
One spit	—	02	00
Platters, dishes, spoones of wood	—	04	00
	01	08	00
For Suger, Spice, and fruit, and at Sea for 6.men	—	12	06

So the full charge of Apparrell, Victuall, Armes, Tooles,
and houshold stuffe, and after this rate for each person,

	li.	s.	d.
will amount vnto about the summe of	12	10	00
The passage of each man is	06	00	00
The fraight of these prouisions for a man, will bee about halfe a Tun, which is	01	10	00
So the whole charge will amount to about	20	00	00

Nets, hookes, lines, and a tent must be added, if the number of people be greater, as also some kine.
And this is the vsuall proportion that the *Virginia Company* doe
bestow vpon their Tenants which they send.

Whosoeuer transports himselfe or any other at his owne charge vnto *Virginia*, shall for each person so transported before Midsummer 1625.
haue to him and his heires for euer fifty Acres of Land vpon a first, and fisty Acres vpon a second diuision.

Imprinted at London by Felix Kyngston. 1622.

of the region, they argued that withdrawing Spanish settlers and priests would amount to abandoning Christian souls. King Philip III of Spain accepted the obligation of maintaining a Catholic and royal presence in New Mexico, though it was clear that doing so would cost far more than it would bring into his coffers. He conceived his authority as entailing responsibility for souls in the New World.

Besides profits and religion, Europeans settled North America out of considerations that a later age would call geopolitics. Well aware of Spain's presence in Florida and anxious about the growing power of the Spanish crown, English statesmen hoped a foothold in Virginia would counter Spanish dominance. Imperial rivalries made military capacity—and defensible location—a significant part of the colonizing project everywhere. With military considerations in mind, English settlers placed their town on an island, the French set Québec on a bluff, and the Spanish built Santa Fe at a dominating height. The settlers' concern for security was well warranted, as Old World conflicts frequently spilled over into the New World. English forces took control of Québec from 1629 to 1632, only to yield to a body of Frenchmen led by Samuel de Champlain. It was the first of many contests between the English and the French.

All three settlements, originating partly as private ventures, sooner or later came under direct royal authority. King Philip III took governmental control of New Mexico just after Captain Juan Martínez de Montoya began to establish the village of Santa Fe. In 1624 the English crown took over Virginia when the Virginia Company proved scandalously unable to provide supplies or to organize colonial life to prevent numerous deaths by famine, disease, and warfare. The French monarch assumed complete control of Québec in 1663, when the decline of the settlement's Huron allies made the presence of French soldiers necessary for combating the Iroquois. After that, Québec became a political project of the resurgent French crown. Each settlement played a critical role in the imperial politics of the age. Over time, each national power sought to control what regions it could. This geopolitical logic

Found in Cayuga County, New York, this Jesuit medal of circa 1650 to 1700 probably came from New France. Missionaries also distributed so-called Jesuit rings, which were sometimes strung on a necklace and used as a trade good.

Opposite. "Inconveniencies that have Happened to Some Persons" warned of the dangers that befell those who traveled ill-equipped to the New World. In 1622 the Virginia Company published this broadside listing necessities for immigrants to take to Virginia.

In 1673 La Salle was sent on a mission to convince Iroquois leaders to allow the French to build a fort on the shores of Lake Ontario. His success won him a title of nobility and the right to take possession of the region between Florida and Mexico. Accompanied by twenty-three Frenchmen and eighteen Native people, he canoed down the Mississippi in 1682, naming the river basin Louisiana and claiming it for France. This circa 1850 lithograph shows La Salle taking possession of Louisiana.

spurred the French to found Louisiana late in the sixteenth century, with the aim of forestalling English domination, while the Spanish formed the province of Texas to preempt the French. Throughout the period, authorities in London, Paris, and Madrid often viewed affairs in the New World chiefly as an aspect of the balance of power in Europe.[17]

FOR THEIR PART, Native peoples faced their own geopolitical, economic, social, and cultural realities. Seen from the standpoints of Montagnais, Hurons, and Iroquois in New France; Powhatans and Pamunkeys in Virginia; and Pueblos and Apaches in New Mexico, how might these first meetings with new settlers be characterized? The answer varies from group to group

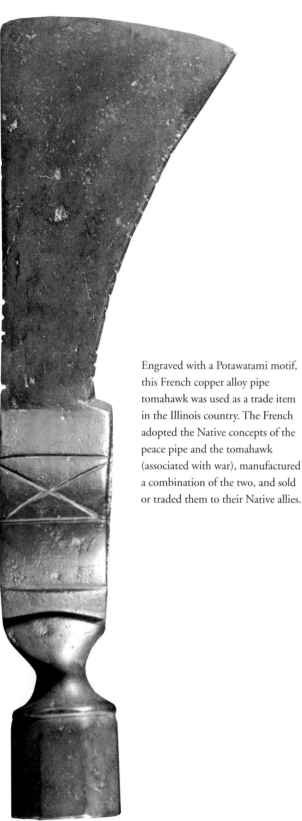

Engraved with a Potawatami motif, this French copper alloy pipe tomahawk was used as a trade item in the Illinois country. The French adopted the Native concepts of the peace pipe and the tomahawk (associated with war), manufactured a combination of the two, and sold or traded them to their Native allies.

and from place to place. The precise intentions of the Europeans mattered a great deal. It made a difference that the Spanish intended to subjugate and rule, while the French in Québec sought to trade. The precise needs and situation of the indigenous groups equally played a role. To each Native group, these Europeans might at once represent another tribe to fit into existing patterns of alliance and rivalry, a new source of goods and cultural resources, or a powerful rival seeking control and dispossession. At the time of first encounter, it was most likely clear to Native groups that the survival of the small bands of French and English depended on their support and indulgence. Many tribes were able to influence the terms of exchange and establish diplomatic practices through which the two groups negotiated. In later years, as Europe's New World empires expanded in geographic scope, some well-placed Native groups played European rivals against one another in order to secure trading terms to their own advantage.[18]

In several respects, French settlements on the St. Lawrence seem to have created the least disruption in Native peoples' lives. The French provided a wider market for furs, and they offered exotic trade goods in exchange. Native people particularly valued copper pots, iron implements, woolen cloth, and glass beads. Anemic immigration from the Old World placed little pressure on the area's agricultural land. Nonetheless, change was substantial. The French introduced diseases and pests along with opportunities to trade. As the Huron shifted their energies from agriculture to hunting, established ways of life altered. Intensive hunting put pressure on the region's fur supply and aggravated conflicts with the Iroquois over territory. New goods also introduced changes as they became part of Native life. In the long run, access to firearms had particular consequences. In 1609 the Montagnais called on the French to join them in waging war on the Iroquois Five Nations. French matchlock muskets contributed to the victory. For their part, the Iroquois turned to the Dutch, and then to the English in New York, to gain firearms of their own as it became clear that any group wishing to prevail or even survive would need access to guns. French religious authorities also pressed Natives to replace their old beliefs and practices with the Catholic religion and to adopt new family structures and mores.[19]

Of all the groups that faced European settlers, Pueblo peoples most immediately became subordinate to the newcomers. The sedentary people of the area lived in independent villages; they did not all share a single political authority, identity, or even language. The Spanish called them "Pueblos" for their villages, and over time those Native peoples forged a new identity based on common circumstances. Among the newcomers some priests and officials came from Spain, but most were from Mexico, itself an established colony populated by a culturally and ethnically mixed people under Spanish political rule. Unlike the English and the French, these newcomers brought with them from Mexico a working system for dominating New World peoples. They were Spanish in a cultural sense, although some were indigenous. The fact that these Hispanos used Native servants indicated the sorts of relationships they thought appropriate. The Spanish established authority over the Pueblos through the *encomienda* system, in which individual, elite Hispanic men held claim to particular settlements. Local inhabitants were required to pay an annual tribute in corn, cloth, and hides in return for protection and to support churches. In practice, many Pueblos often found they owed labor to two authorities, one civil and one religious, as Franciscans and the *encomenderos* each laid claim to their labor and goods.

This type of wheel-lock pistol, made in Suhl, Germany, about 1620, has been found in trash pits at Jamestown. Although Europeans had the advantage of firearms, this particular pistol's mechanism was so complicated that it was difficult to repair.

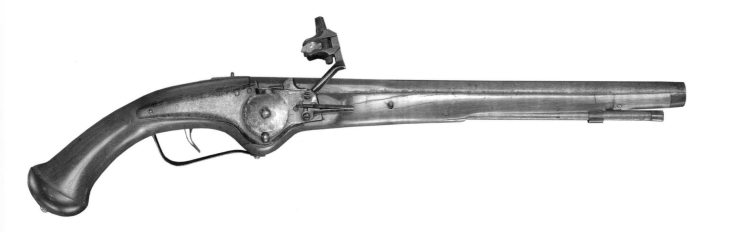

Assessing the influence of Christianity on various Native groups is difficult. Historians note that the military success of the Europeans, and especially their apparent greater immunity to the diseases that devastated Native societies, made their spiritual resources seem powerful and attractive. Their own spiritual leaders' failure to fend off the deadly diseases may have influenced some people's willingness to adopt new ways. And many no doubt recognized the genuine sacrifice, belief, and spirituality of some of the friars, priests, and—in Québec—nuns who ventured overseas. Yet, we can only surmise the meanings of baptism, conversion, and Christian worship to Native peoples by examining the accounts of non-Natives, especially reports from the Jesuits and Franciscans to authorities elsewhere. Surely some supposed converts were pragmatically performing the rituals but interpreting them in light of older beliefs. Others expressed outright disbelief in the new Christian ideas. In New Mexico, where the Spanish forcibly suppressed the Pueblos' religious ceremonies, those practices persisted underground. While some Natives found solace and meaning in Christianity, others saw that worshiping the Christian god also failed to stem epidemics of smallpox, influenza, and measles, and the coming of missionaries was itself associated with the arrival of disease. Although missionaries hoped to eliminate every aspect of what they saw as paganism, many Native people mixed new Christian beliefs with older Native ones. In every area, reserves of older spiritual traditions provided a continuing resource for cultural identity and resistance.[20]

Native societies were soon beset by a fatal dependency on European firearms, such as this seventeenth-century French matchlock musket. Once European firearms began to circulate in a region, any group without them could be enslaved or exterminated by traditional foes with guns. To obtain firearms, Native groups forged alliances with European powers and became involved in their wars.

Cowboy spurs evolved from sixteenth-century iron spurs like this one made in Spain or Mexico.

on donne la confirmation la iii.e fois

Opposite. Claude de Chauchetière, a Jesuit who learned the Huron language in France, produced this drawing, "Confirmation is given for the first time," about 1680. He arrived in New France in 1677 and began preaching at the Iroquois mission of Saint-François-Xavier at Sault-Saint-Louis (Kahnawake, near Montréal).

Right. Only fragments survive of seventeenth-century Spanish mission bells from New Mexico. This is an eighteenth-century example.

Above. In 1608 Wahunsonacock, whose
title was Powhatan, sent food to Jamestown in exchange for a grindstone,
some guns, copper and beads, a cock
and hen, men to build him an English-
style house, and fifty swords similar
to this one found at Jamestown.

Right. Captain John Smith wrote,
"Copper carrieth ye price of all." The
Virginia Company's plan was to trade
copper for food while the colonists sought
to profit in nonagricultural pursuits.
Jamestown craftsmen cut copper sheets to
make ornaments for trade.

Opposite. John Smith learned the local
Algonquian language and extensively
explored the Chesapeake Bay in a small
boat in 1608 and 1609. His 1612 map of
Virginia is one of the few early maps
explicitly to credit information received
from Native people, indicated here
by a Maltese cross.

For their part, Virginia Natives encountered Europeans who were significantly less intent on building missions or interested in their spiritual lives. For Powhatan, the most significant tribal leader in the region, the English newcomers were possible allies to bolster his power against his Siouan- and Iroquoian-speaking rivals. The English were the source of goods with both material and spiritual value: copper, mirrors, axes, beads, and other items. Many of these were prestige goods, important for their ability to symbolize the holders' access to sources of distant power. Such ability bespoke the reach of a political leader's connections, and

by giving these prestigious items as gifts, the donor might create reciprocal obligations that would enhance his influence. Aware that the English depended on his corn and other foodstuffs simply to avoid starvation, Powhatan hoped to incorporate the English into his world.

Soon, however, the relationship radically changed. Although the English wrote about providing kinder treatment than they believed the Spanish meted out, such intentions came to little. Nor were the English strong enough to take over the network of subordinate indigenous groups that paid tribute to Powhatan, as some had hoped. Whatever the English settlers' original plans,

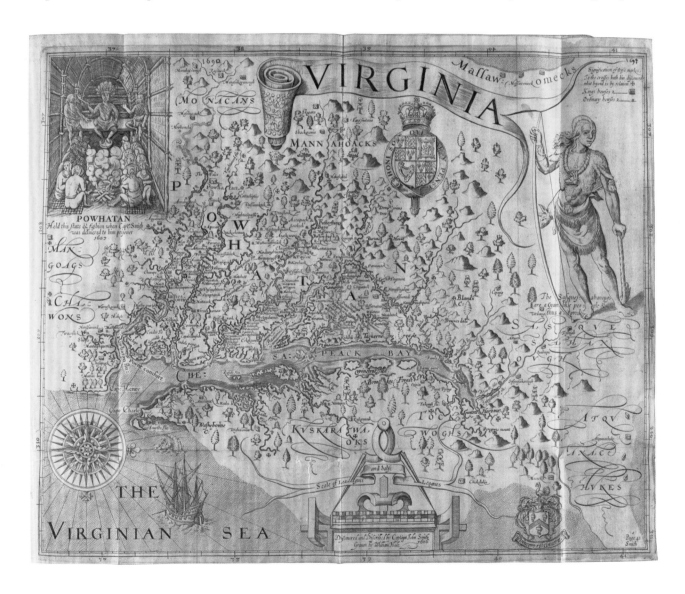

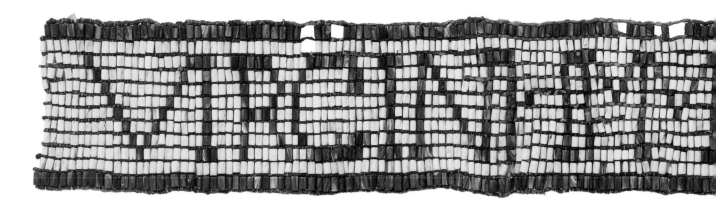

a tobacco boom in the 1620s introduced a tremendous desire for land. Although the deerskin trade remained important to the fortunes of some English households, for the vast majority trade with the Natives was insubstantial when compared to tobacco production. In stark contrast to what happened in Québec and New Mexico, indigenous people in Virginia became marginal to the emerging economy. Seeking fertile soil for their monoculture, and without regard to the many uses Natives had for these lands, the English rapidly established twenty-three "particular plantations" that reached fifty miles along the James River. In response to that expansion and to the violent forays of English settlers, Chief Opechancanough led a surprise attack on the colonists in 1622, killing a quarter of them. In 1644 he headed a last effort to expel the English. By then, the numerous English settlers were building a society with little space for Native peoples unless, as in South Carolina especially, they might serve as slave labor.[21]

EVERYWHERE, and for everyone, life in the New World took unexpected turns. When Hispano colonists failed to find precious metals, they exported wool and hides instead of silver back to Mexican centers in long treks on the *camino real*. The northern outpost attracted few settlers from established Mexico, let alone from Spain itself. Although the Pueblo population declined precipitously in the 1600s, they always outnumbered the Hispanos in New Mexico society. The colony also suffered from unforeseen disputes between civil and religious authorities, who contested whether New Mexico was principally an imperial outpost or a missionary base.

Although it was closer to its mother country, New France similarly attracted relatively few immigrants from the Old World. Some came temporarily as migrant labor. Those who held monopolies in the fur trade, however, were not anxious to face other Frenchmen who might compete for the trade and hasten the decline of the beaver population. When France banned Protestants from the colony in 1632, it stemmed one potential source of immigrants to New France. One possible solution to the population problem—and to the stark imbalance between men and women among French immigrants—was to turn Native men into settled farmers and Native women into wives. In the words of Samuel de Champlain, "Our young men will marry your daughters, and we shall be one people."[22] This project of transformation had limited success. The Jesuits established a settlement at Sillery, where households of Montagnais who had converted to Christianity might live as farmers. Ursulines and Jesuits set up boarding schools where Native children learned the Catholic religion and aspects of French culture. Godly French families served as godparents for some Montagnais children. Few Natives, however, found a life of sedentary farming or European family patterns to their liking.

Ironically, many French settlers in the New World dramatically altered their own lives. While some found work as farmers and tradesmen, called *habitants*, others took up lives as *coureurs des bois*, traveling long distances to trade and spending months in the backcountry, where they learned Native languages and sometimes married Native women. Much like the English, the French assumed Native people would wish to imitate

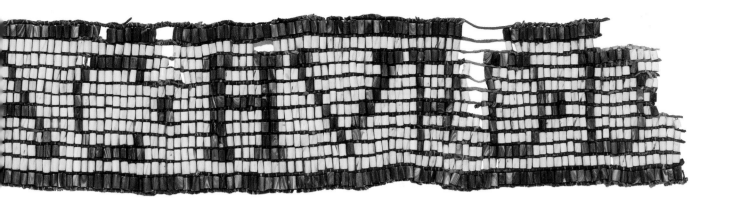

civil Europeans. Instead, some Frenchmen born in the New World—perhaps they are better called Canadians—chose to adopt the ways of the Natives. However much French authorities in Québec would have preferred to preside over a tightly controlled, hierarchical community, the *coureurs des bois* forged an independent way of life.

In the earliest years at Jamestown, authorities noted that Englishmen were also attracted to the indigenous culture. Some feared "that the colony would, because of the transformation of the English therein, become not a new England but a new Virginian Indian nation, containing and transforming the English themselves."[23] When the Virginia colony did gain greater stability, it was through the intense cultivation of a single cash crop—tobacco. King James I lamented that he would rule an empire based "on smoak," although he accepted the impressive profits from the tobacco trade that poured into his treasury. Other English colonies relied chiefly on smaller farms dedicated to mixed agriculture, but the Chesapeake area became a landscape of plantations that created a high demand for labor. The plantation system developed, in part, because England was willing and able to ship many of its poor, voluntarily or not, to work in New World tobacco fields. In contrast to France, indeed, England proved happy to dispatch many of its poor and disorderly.

To control such people, elite colonists aspired to set up familiar institutions modeled on those in England. Longtime governor Sir William Berkeley, for one, envisioned a hierarchical society in which leading gentlemen owned many acres and presided over a stable order, with tenants and servants working their lands.

Formerly in the French royal collection, this Christian devotional belt in a pattern of cylindrical shell beads, or wampum, originated in the upper St. Lawrence or Great Lakes region of New France. In the seventeenth century wampum became an accepted medium of exchange in northeastern North America.

This sickle was used to harvest grain at Kingsmill, a Virginia settlement, after 1641.

Opposite. James Revel, a convicted thief in England, was sentenced to fourteen years of labor in Virginia. Arriving between 1656 and 1671, Revel describes servants being examined "like horses" and reported working alongside enslaved Africans. His account of life in the New World was published a century later.

Below. The Mohawks were one of the Iroquois Five Nations (along with the Seneca, Oneida, Onondaga, and Cayuga), traditional enemies of the Huron, who were allied to the French. This Mohawk leader from upstate New York visited London in 1710 to strengthen the Anglo-Iroquois alliance. The bear symbolizes his clan.

Sa Ga Yeath Qua Pieth Tow, King of the Maquas

As it happened, Virginia's great men found it possible to exploit poor labor for profit in ways beyond the bounds of what was permissible in England. Plantation society became grounded in forced labor, a commitment that had consequences of the most profound sort. Englishmen, who prided themselves on being free and established the first European representative assembly in the Western Hemisphere, certainly had not expected to base their North American colony on slavery.

Other powerful and unforeseen developments took place as well, including changes in the very understanding of natural resources and their purposes. Many Native groups saw land as being valuable only for its uses and considered it a possession shared by clans or kin groups. By contrast, Europeans brought an idea of land as a commodity that might be owned, held, or sold through the market as a form of abstract wealth. Historian William Cronon has detailed the influence of such concepts of land on the natural environment and on Native lives in colonial New England. Transformations of the same order occurred, at different times, across the continent.[24]

Compared to the great gulf that separated European thinking and practice from that of Native peoples, the differences among various Euro-American conceptions of land were minor. That said, the societies that grew out of Jamestown, Québec, and Santa Fe developed distinct land systems. New Mexico's *encomienda* system was feudal. It entailed obligations on the landowner, who was bound to protect the laborers under his control and help bring them to Christianity. In return, he exacted tribute—payment in goods and labor—from the Natives. The bulk of ordinary Spanish colonists received no such holdings but rather worked as small farmers or as laborers on large ranches called *estancias*.

In Québec, French authorities awarded large tracts of land to minor nobles, army captains, prominent merchants, and others wealthy enough to recruit migrants to move from France to Canada. All farmers had to work under the feudal rules of the seigneurial system. Not only did these tenants have to pay rent in perpetuity for the land they received from a lord, or seigneur, but they also had to patronize the seigneur's gristmill, work on road

THE POOR UNHAPPY

Tranſported Felon's

SORROWFUL ACCOUNT

OF HIS

Fourteen Years Tranſportation

At *VIRGINIA*, in *AMERICA*.

IN SIX PARTS.

BEING

A remarkable and ſuccinct HISTORY of the LIFE
of JAMES REVEL, the unhappy Sufferer.

Who was put Apprentice by his Father to a Tinman, near
Moorfields, where he got into bad Company, and before
long ran away, and went a robbing with a Gang of Thieves;
but his Maſter ſoon got him back again: Yet would not he
be kept from his old companions, but went thieving with
them again; for which he was tranſported Fourteen Years.
With an Account of the Way the Transports Work, and
the Punishment they receive for committing any Fault.

CONCLUDING WITH

A WORD of ADVICE to all YOUNG MEN.

LONDON:

PRINTED AND SOLD BY J. EVANS, NO. 41, LONG-LANE,
WEST-SMITHFIELD.

Price One Penny.

1764

Land was divided along the St. Lawrence River into feudal domains, or seigneuries, which were generally long, narrow strips running perpendicular to the river. The church held valuable seigneuries close to Québec City and Montréal, but most went to men rewarded for military service. The seigneur, or lord, divided the land among his tenants (*censitaires* or *habitants*). Terms of tenancy were generous when the population was small and tenants were hard to attract, but tenants also had feudal obligations, such as road repair and use of the lord's gristmill.

construction within the domain (seigneurie), and pay fees on the sale of land leases. The seigneurial system shaped the landscape of the St. Lawrence Valley, with its narrow but deep farms running back from the river.

In Virginia, Governor Berkeley parceled out thousands of acres to promote a society dominated by great men, but powerful pressures also worked toward establishing a more egalitarian division of lands. To attract immigrants, in 1618 the Virginia Company established a "headright" system that awarded fifty acres to anyone who imported a settler to the colony. The system benefited the wealthy, who gathered headrights for each servant or slave they imported, but when servants completed their terms of indenture, they received fifty acres as well. In practice, roughly half of all English servants died before reaching freedom, and another quarter of the total spent their lives as tenants on the lands of the wealthy. Only a minority of those in Virginia actually became small landholders. As the elite

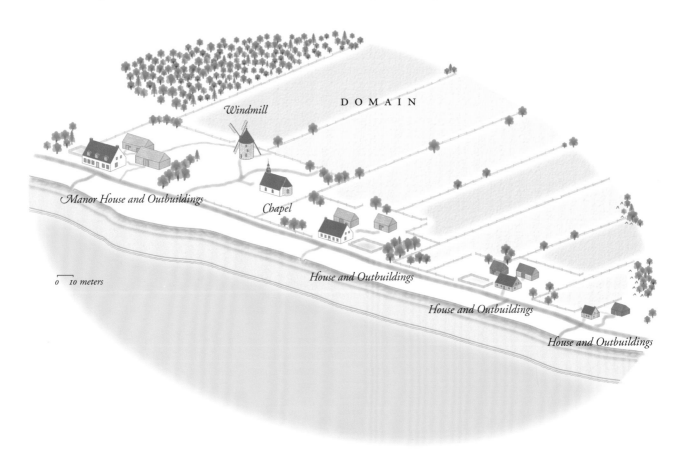

Windmill

D O M A I N

Manor House and Outbuildings

Chapel

0   10 meters

House and Outbuildings

House and Outbuildings

House and Outbuildings

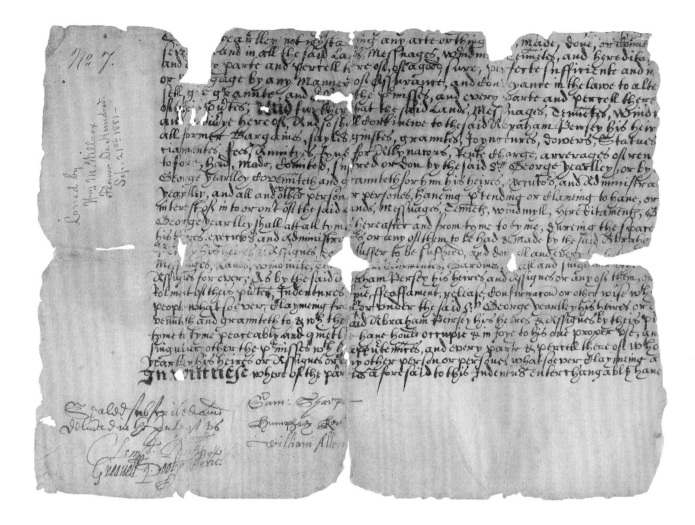

increasingly consolidated their landholdings and relied on slave labor, poorer Englishmen's opportunities for gaining land of their own grew slimmer.

In all these respects, the three colonies became hybrid societies rather than replicas of Europe. They were shaped by imperial desires and purposes, catering to the view held in mercantilist Europe that colonies existed solely to benefit the mother country. At the same time, the colonies were shaped by the presence and purposes of Native peoples and, especially in Virginia, Africans.

THIS LEADS to the intertwined topics of slavery and race. Seventeenth-century North America was a world that took unfree labor for granted. Native, African, and European societies all were familiar with various forms of

The Virginia Company allowed private ownership of land beginning in 1619. Flour de Hundred, or Flowerdew, was one of twenty-three "particular plantations" established beyond Jamestown to exploit the tobacco boom. First granted to Sir George Yeardley, the plantation was sold to Abraham Persey in 1624, according to this document. It may be the oldest surviving land deed in British North America.

This shackle from Jamestown could have been used during the imposition of martial law in the area or later in the slave trade.

unfreedom, and many men and women served masters to whom they were bound to one degree or another by law or by custom. To supply labor for the New World colonies, Europeans adopted a new form of servitude: service under indenture for a designated span of years. They also adopted a new form of slavery.

In the New World, many Native groups took captives in warfare who might become slaves in some sense of that term. Over time, such captives might become integrated into families within their new societies. Yet "chattel slavery"—an institution in which the slave held minimal legal rights, in which the slave could be sold, and in which the status of the slave was legally passed down through generations—was something quite different. This sort of slavery emerged from the imperial expansion of Europe in the New World, especially in the plantation societies of South America, Mexico, and the Caribbean.[25] When we speak about servitude and slavery, we need to keep in mind that such unfreedom came in various forms and degrees.

To help understand such a world, historian Ira Berlin offers a most valuable distinction. There were societies in which slavery was present, or "societies with slaves," on the one hand, and societies profoundly based on slavery, or "slave societies," on the other.[26] In the former, slavery was one among a number of forms in which people labored; it was neither a unique nor a central institution. In the latter, the relationship between master and slave became in many respects the fundamental commitment, one that shaped economic, social, legal, and cultural institutions in far-reaching ways. Slavery became the defining institution. Only the English colonies of the Chesapeake and Carolina—and French Louisiana—would become slave societies in this sense.[27]

In legal terms, chattel slavery scarcely existed in New Mexico. African slaves were rare, and the crown prohibited Native chattel slavery. Nonetheless, Apaches, Utes, and others were either captured in military forays or obtained through trade with neighboring tribes, and they commonly became slaves in fact if not by law. Their age and gender determined their fate. Colonists sent adult males south to work as de facto slaves in the

mines and fields of Mexico. Captive women and children remained in the colony, where they were put into household service and, depending on their master, might be granted freedom after they adapted to the new society.

New Mexico was certainly a "society with slaves," but the institution did not define the colony's economy or other institutions. Slavery was even less significant to the society that developed in Québec. Beginning in the 1670s, the fur trade linked the settlements on the St. Lawrence with the upcountry. Québec's Native allies and *coureurs des bois* frequently brought captives from that region to Québec and Montréal, where a modest trade in Native slaves existed by 1690. Early in the 1700s French authorities acknowledged the propriety of slaveholding and confirmed title to all previous slave purchases. Native slaves might provide useful labor in the colony, but authorities acted in large part out of two geopolitical considerations. First was imperial rivalry with Britain. If the French passed up the Great Lakes slave trade, the expanding plantations of English Carolina would benefit instead. Second, maintaining an alliance with the Huron, Illinois, and other Native groups required the French to purchase the captives they had taken from enemy tribes. Such slaves were symbols of friendship in the diplomatic world of Native America. Despite these factors, Native slaves never made up more than 5 percent of the population of New France, and African slavery hardly existed in the 1600s. The institution of slavery was part of French colonial life, but it was not critical to it.[28]

Decorated with porcupine quills, this Iroquois tumpline, or burden strap, could have been used to carry or drag loads or to bind prisoners of war. Captives were adopted by or married into the families of their captors, sold or offered as slaves or gifts to Europeans, or tortured and killed.

An Onondaga (Iroquois) warrior with a captive bound by a tumpline are the subject of this 1666 drawing attributed to Jesuit Joseph-Marie Chaumonot.

Opposite. The War of Spanish Succession spread from Europe to North America. On 29 February 1704 French and Native allies raided the English at Deerfield, Massachusetts, leaving 50 English colonists dead and 112 captured. Seven-year-old Eunice Williams was taken to New France, where she later chose to stay. She and Arosen, her Mohawk husband, lived at Kahnawake, near Montréal. The hide and porcupine quill bullet pouch, tobacco bag, wool and bead sash, and prehistoric red slate gorget were gifts to Eunice's brother, the Reverend Stephen Williams, during one of Arosen's four later visits to Massachusetts.

Color combinations and bead patternings signified the importance of a wampum belt. While the meaning of these figures is uncertain, the belt may have commem-orated the erection of the first European-style building in the Huron territories. Built by Jesuit missionaries in 1638, the timber chapel stood on the outskirts of Ossossané, a Huron village in southern Ontario.

Even in Virginia, Ira Berlin notes, the first generation of bound Africans lived and worked alongside people held in other forms of unfree labor. Natives and Europeans also labored in statuses that were not free. Only after several decades did the ruling men of Virginia choose African slavery. Purchasing slaves for life had advantages, as slowing demand in the lucrative sugar colonies of the Caribbean made slaves more affordable and as the colony's long-term commitment to tobacco culture became clear. Slaves would remain in bondage for life, and because their children would become slaves as well, they would add to the concentration of wealth in slaveholders' lands. Equally important, as historian Edmund S. Morgan points out, indentured workers eventually became free, and they tended to demand land of their own and even to expect a political voice in the colony. Enslaved workers would never be allowed such aspirations. Without outraging authorities in London, Virginia's governing planters could strip Africans of legal protections that were afforded to laboring English people by right. In a series of laws formulated in the 1660s and after, the General Assembly acted to do just that.[29]

What, then, of race? Although later writers would speak of North America as a meeting place for white, red, and black, the people who encountered one another in the seventeenth century did not think in such terms. They met as English, French, Spanish, Swedish, or Dutch; they knew themselves as Akan, Igbo, and Mande; they called themselves Kanye-ke'ronhq (Mohawk), Diné (Navajo), and Wendat (Huron). Quite possibly, each group thought of itself as superior to other groups in some sense—with truer beliefs and a more proper way of life. Certainly European settlers brought a clear sense that

theirs was civility and true religion. They believed their culture and their Christianity entitled them to dominion over Native peoples. In Mexico a century of colonization resulted in the development of new populations of mixed European, African, and indigenous background. There developed a caste system, a hierarchy that privileged Spanish identity and ancestry. Those who occupied the land of the Pueblo peoples brought with them the assumptions of that system, associating service with Native peoples and ruling with Hispanos.

In Québec, the French also expected the Natives to recognize that European ways were better than their own and to assimilate to the culture of the newcomers. Champlain's hopes for intermarriage between French men and Native women bespoke an openness toward mixing and a rough sense of equality, and a population of métis appeared. At the same time, contradictions arose in French attitudes toward Native peoples. A Native woman who married a French man gained status, while a French woman who married a Native man lost social standing. As plans for assimilation proved unsuccessful, moreover, some French thinkers expressed concern that marriage with Natives would debase French blood. In Louisiana, and in the Caribbean, the French demonstrated that they had few objections to slavery or to overlapping hierarchies of race and class.[30]

Substantial evidence indicates that, in Virginia, many Englishmen initially saw themselves as only somewhat different from Native peoples and Africans. Indentured English servants worked alongside African laborers, sometimes ran away with them to escape their masters, socialized with them, and had offspring together. Marriages occurred between African and English. No doubt, people recognized differences between individuals of diverse origins, but those differences took on vastly changed meanings with the shift to African slavery. Virginia lawmakers set about drawing invidious distinctions between white laborers and black, specifying greater punishments for the latter, for example, and cracking down on interracial cooperation and fraternizing. Laws defined the offspring of Natives and Africans as black, and Virginians increasingly came to see

themselves as divided into two racial groups. Over time, poorer whites gained the psychological and material support of racial advantage. They came to bolster the regime of the great planters, receiving in return the security of knowing that they and their children would never be at the bottom of society. Neither slavery nor race was ever entirely fixed. Their meanings depended on place, time, and circumstance, and Africans and African Americans contested their subordination in countless ways and unceasingly. Despite that, the seventeenth century laid the basis for a lasting tragedy of one major nation on the North American continent, which would become an empire long dedicated to liberty of a partial and racial kind.[31]

IN VIRGINIA, NEW ENGLAND, AND NEW MEXICO, there came moments when Native people made coordinated efforts to drive Europeans from their lands. Over time, it became clear that Europeans sought dominion and not merely trade. Confiscation of Native lands reached a point that threatened continued cultural existence, and economic (and in New Mexico, religious) demands became too great. The Powhatan leader Opechancanough led attacks in both 1622 and 1644 in Virginia. When the third Anglo-Powhatan War ended in 1646, the Powhatan polity dissolved.[32] Virginia's remaining Natives formally accepted status as tributaries of the king of England. Some thirty years later, in 1675, in New England, a Wampanoag political leader named Metacomet (called Philip by the English) united many Native nations against English settlements in the region. Suffering from growing competition for resources, a collapse in the area's fur trade, and pressure to sell more and more land to the English, many Natives united in King Philip's War, a last, unsuccessful effort to rout the newcomers.

No such revolt occurred in New France. Its relatively few settlers placed substantially less demand on the resources and peoples of the area. Although they sought to gain from advantageous exchange with Native fur hunters, their relationship with the societies around them was rooted in longstanding alliances. While French colonists pursued a substantially different policy toward

French officials sought to transform Louisiana into a profitable slave-based plantation economy on the model of the sugar islands of the Caribbean. This drawing is titled "Aboriginal people and African slaves in Louisiana, 1735."

The figure of the Indians fort or Palizado in NEW ENGLAND And the maner of the destroying It by Captayne Vnderhill And Captayne Mason

Hear enttera Captayne Vnderhill

The Indians houses

Their Streets

Hear enters Captayne Mason

RH

English victory in the Pequot War of 1637 opened the way for expansion of English settlements in southern New England. Captain John Underhill's engraving depicts an attack on the Pequot fort at Mystic, Connecticut, by the English and their Native allies. Six hundred Pequots were killed. The English enslaved the rest or sent them to other tribes.

Opposite. Native people used this bayonet of French manufacture during King Philip's War, an offensive against New England colonists in 1675 and 1676.

Native peoples in Louisiana, in Canada they faced attack only as allies of the Hurons in their region (and as enemies of the English). By contrast, Spanish authorities—both civil and religious—exploited Native labor and tried to suppress the Pueblos' sacred ceremonies. Drained of their surplus by the colonizers, the Pueblo peoples had little to trade with the Apaches and Utes. As a consequence, they suffered from raids by those groups, and in the 1660s and 1670s they were plagued by poor harvests as well. In this situation, the Pueblos organized around a leader named Popé to force the Franciscans and secular Spanish authorities from the area. The Pueblo Revolt of 1680 was the most successful of these efforts at ousting the invaders. Spanish settlers fled several hundred miles to the south, leaving the Natives in control of Santa Fe and the province of New Mexico for the next twelve years. In the words of historian Joe Sando, the revolt in New Mexico constituted the "first American Revolution."[33]

In Virginia, Bacon's Rebellion in 1676 was a different sort of conflict: it was a war against Native people, not by them. It arose from the English land-hungry tobacco system, in a world already populated by Native peoples, and by ambitious settlers' powerful demand for labor and for new forms of exploiting it. As indentured servants finished their terms of labor for others, they found it difficult to find land of their own. Their problems, as they saw it, came down to the presence of Natives, on the one hand, and the refusal of ruling men in Jamestown to make land affordable, on the other. Nathaniel Bacon was himself a member of the gentry class, but he led an uprising of poor whites, who targeted a variety of Native groups as well as the government of the colony itself. Native people, to some extent already marginalized from Virginia society, figured as scapegoats in this contest— or as the subjects of a disputed policy that set one class of Old World settlers against another.

A LAST COMPARISON notes the different avenues through which each European empire expanded its influence in North America. England developed numerous, well-populated colonies all along the Eastern seaboard. Rather

William Penn's motives for establishing a colony were both religious and economic. This weathervane stood atop his grist- and sawmill in Chester County, the first in Pennsylvania.

than being extensions of Virginia, however, these were separate ventures that originated in the Old World and were based in varied economic, religious, and imperial ambitions. Once English forces defeated the Dutch in New York and Anglo-American societies incorporated Swedish settlements in Delaware, British settlers laid claim to provinces between Canada to the north and Florida to the south.

Yet, in the hundred years it took the English to move as much as a hundred miles to the west, the French expanded their claims from the Gulf of St. Lawrence to the Gulf of Mexico. Indeed, while the English expanded by settlements, the French generally expanded by establishing strategic alliances and compact outposts. The heartland of New France was Québec City, along with the nearby settlements of Trois-Rivières and Montréal. From that base, explorers first probed the Great Lakes region and then, in the 1670s, came across the Mississippi River. Peace with the Iroquois and a fur trade boom in that decade allowed René-Robert Cavelier, Sieur de La Salle, to set up posts in the Illinois country. La Salle established Fort Saint-Louis on the Gulf coast of Texas; after his death there, other Frenchmen established Biloxi near the mouth of the Mississippi. To forestall English control of the Mississippi, France created Louisiana in 1699.

Left. Excavated near Philadelphia, this helmet is one of the few traces of the isolated forts and towns that the Swedes established on the Delaware River. New Sweden overlapped with the Dutch claim of New Netherland. Governor Peter Stuyvesant of New Netherland conquered the Swedish colony in 1655 and thus eliminated a competitor in the fur trade.

Below. Swedish immigration continued even after New Sweden ceased to exist. Broer Sinnexson of Sweden probably brought this chest (circa 1650–70) to the Delaware Valley in 1683.

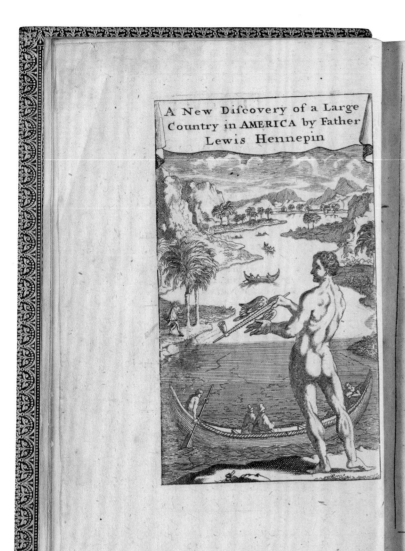

A New Discovery of a Large Country in AMERICA by Father Lewis Hennepin

A
New Difcovery
OF A
Vaſt Country in AMERICA,
Extending above Four Thouſand Miles,
BETWEEN
New France *and* New Mexico;
WITH A
Deſcription of the Great *Lakes, Cata-
racts, Rivers, Plants,* and *Animals.*
Alſo, the *Manners, Cuſtoms,* and *Languages* of the ſe-
veral Native *Indians* ; and the Advantage of Com-
merce with thoſe different Nations.

WITH A
CONTINUATION,
Giving an ACCOUNT of the
Attempts of the Sieur *De la* SALLE upon the
Mines of *St. Barbe,* &c. The Taking of
Quebec by the *Engliſh* ; With the Advantages
of a Shorter Cut to *China* and *Japan.*

Both Parts Illuſtrated with *Maps,* and *Figures,*
and Dedicated to His Majeſty K. *William.*

By *L. Hennepin,* now Reſident in *Holland.*

To which are added, Several *New Diſcoveries* in *North-
America,* not publiſh'd in the *French* Edition.

LONDON, Printed for *M. Bentley, J. Tonſon,
H. Bonwick, T. Goodwin,* and *S. Manſhip.* 1698.

Opposite. Louis Hennepin was a Récollet missionary who accompanied La Salle into the Great Lakes region in 1678, where he was captured by the Sioux and lived with them until 1681. Back in France the next year, Hennepin published the well-received *Description de la Louisiane*. A later book, published in English and shown here, destroyed his reputation when falsehoods were revealed, such as Hennepin's assertion that he traveled to the lower Mississippi River before La Salle's expedition in 1682.

Right. Franciscans who traveled to east Texas in 1689 created a story that Caddo people had told them of a "lady in blue" who had appeared in the sky to their grandparents, instructing them to seek salvation from the missionaries. The Spanish claimed she was Maria de Jésus de Agreda, a Franciscan nun living in Spain, who was said to have traveled in spirit to the New World to bring Christianity to the Native people.

A Spanish sword used in the late seventeenth or early eighteenth century was found near Oraibi, Hopi Third Mesa, Arizona.

For most of the 1600s, New Mexico consisted of Santa Fe and the pueblos and missions of the Rio Arriba region. El Paso del Norte, where Spanish settlers retreated from the Pueblo Revolt, was the second chartered town. Only when La Salle arrived along the gulf did Spain try to occupy the province of Texas. Neither France nor Spain could spare troops or send many settlers to the area, so they competed for alliances with the various tribes of the Hasinai confederacy. Franciscan priests from New Mexico also made efforts to convert the Native people of Texas. After an abortive attempt to build missions among the Hasinai in the 1690s, Spain succeeded in establishing an enduring presence in Texas in 1716. At the same time, Jesuits began to work among the Pimas in what is today southern Arizona. By the 1700s New Mexico was no longer alone on New Spain's far northern frontier.

WE BEGAN this project with the hope that bringing together the histories of Jamestown, Québec, and Santa Fe—settlements founded in the opening decade

of the seventeenth century—would reveal valuable contrasts and comparisons. We have hardly reached a full or final understanding of the era. We can catalog many aspects of cultural exchange. We can note of New Mexico, for example, that Pueblo peoples adopted sheep, horses, goats, pigs, chili, wheat, grapes, watermelons, and apples and that they developed new pottery forms based on Spanish ones. They learned a new language, Spanish, that paradoxically helped them communicate with one another to coordinate resistance and revolt. For their part, the Spaniards adopted Pueblo pottery, baskets, buckskins, herbs, dyes, and cuisine. Such lists of exchanges are informative but by themselves seem insufficient to capture the extraordinary transformations of the era.

Another approach is to view these events as they fit into a longer account of eventual Anglo-American dominance. In the eighteenth century, British North America would gain vastly in numbers and power. Repeated contests among British, French, and Native forces would end in the British annexation of New

France in 1763. The United States would annex New Mexico in 1848. Surely, seeds of that later Anglo-American dominance were visible by the close of the seventeenth century, not least in the sheer numbers of immigrants who moved from the Old World.[34] Yet in 1700 it was not entirely clear which European power, if any, would predominate, or how far Native peoples might still successfully resist.

Indeed, there is a problem in limiting ourselves to the perspective of empire. No doubt the British colonies "succeeded" in many terms. In New Mexico, Catholic institutions that Philip III sought to nurture did persist (although they were also transformed). Equally, the lasting alliances formed by the French and various Native groups might also qualify as being successful, as were the compromises reached by Pueblo peoples and Spanish colonists in the wake of the Pueblo Revolt. After reconquest, the Spanish in New Mexico abandoned the *encomienda* system and relaxed their vigilance toward traditional Native religious ceremonies. Pueblos and Hispanos came to ally themselves in the face of common enemies. And beyond the most visible and large-scale events, we want to mention the daring and resilience of many people of the seventeenth century, whose small and often unrecorded acts deserve our attention. We are thinking here of the individuals and groups—Native and immigrant, free and enslaved—who learned and adapted in the face of unforeseen circumstances, who survived both within and against the tide of empire, and who sometimes preserved alternatives to its logic. To step outside that logic, new narratives of history might begin not in a single landing point in the east but rather at points across the continent, where a myriad of nations met in the seventeenth century.[35]

Opposite. In 1697 the French crown issued orders to locate the mouth of the Mississippi River, build a fort, and prevent other nations from laying claim to the area. On 13 February 1699 Pierre Le Moyne, Sieur d'Iberville, and fourteen men landed on the mainland at Biloxi, which became the first French settlement in Louisiana and its capital from 1720 to 1723. This is a 1720 view of Biloxi.

Right. In his 1872 will, the museum donor of this chest claimed it to be "the Witch Bureau, from the middle drawer of which one of the Witches jumped out who was hung on Gallows Hill, in Salem."

LAC SUPERIE

PARTIE DU L. MICH

Vers ce lieu au rapport des Indiens
les Espagnols le passent a gué
sur leurs chevaux le Missouri allans
trater avec des Nations Situees
vers le Nord-Ouest d'ou ils
aportent du fer jaune
c'est ainsi qu'ils s'expriment

les Maha
Nation errante

les Tintons
errans

SIOUX DE L'EST
errans

SIOUX DE L'OUEST

Horketon
Mechemeton
Onghetgechaton

Isanti ton
Menestamenkton

Ouidaougeohunaton
Source du
Moingona

les Padoucas
10 Villages

40 Villages
des Panis

Ari-cara
prairies

Anaouez
Maha

les Anaouez ou
Village des
Paoutez

LES RENARDS

Padoucas prairies

les Panimaha
villages

Riv. des Panis

PAYS
DES
APACHES
ET DES
PADOUCAS

les Panis 10
12 Villages

les Cansez

Padoucas

les Quichaatcha
ou les Courtes jambes

Padoucas

Padoucas

Padoucas

Grande Riviere des Cansez

les Cansez
les Cansez

ILINOIS

Lac Pimitoui

les Pimitoui ou Peoria

les Misouris
Osages

PAYS DES OSAGES

les Grinaiches

les Paniassa
4 Villages

Pays plein
de Mines

LA   LOUISIA

Paniassa

NOUVEAU
MEXIQUE

Ste Fe

Quiohouhahan

Kanouhanan

Ionhouannez

LES
KANOATINOS

les Choumans

les Cannefy

les Chacakante

Quaineo

Chiakantesou   Ouatchitas

Nabili

Ouanahinan

les Menitous

Lac des
Mitchigamia

les Chicachas

Prairies et Coteaux
pleins de troupes de
Boeufs

LES
CADODAQUIOS

Caligoa

Nacanné

Nondaquo
errans

LES CENIS

Naouadiches   Ainais

Cenis

Cadodaquios

Natchitoches

Nassonis

Nacachez

Ouachita

les Chattas
ou Tetes Plates

les Akanfa

Alibamo

les Conchatez

les Taskegui

les
Abeikas

les Alibamous

Natchitoches
etabliSment François
fait en 1717 par Mr
de Bienville

Natchez

GOLFE   DU   MEXIQUE

Explication des Marques.
Habitations des Indiens.
Nations derangées.
Nations detruites.

Indiens errans et Antropophages

Embouchure du
Missisipi
ou Riviere S.Louis

Baye de la Ascension

A AMSTERDA
Chez JEAN COVENS et CORN
Geographes.

Echelle de cent lieues
10   20   30   40   50   60

Route de Soto et de Mocoso jusqu'au bas
du Mississipi ou ils furent poursuivis par les Indiens.

NOUVEAU ROYAUME DE LEON
Embouchure de Rio Bravo

BISCAYE

NOUVELLE

Parral

Guillaume de L'Isle was known as the
"first scientific cartographer." His circa
1700 view of North America was reissued
for many years afterwards and confines
English and Spanish colonies to small
strips on either side of the continent.
Everything else is French. While it is
considered a major cartographic achieve-
ment, the map reveals an underlying
political purpose.

Warren M. Billings

Jamestown

William Randolph, planter
and administrator in Virginia.

Opposite. James I of England granted a charter to the Virginia Company of London in 1606, but he revoked it eighteen years later due to mismanagement. His contempt for tobacco, which became the economic staple of Virginia, extended to his writing *A Counterblaste to Tobacco* in 1616, condemning tobacco's effects on the brain, kidneys, and lungs.

A musketeer carrying a matchlock musket decorates this tile from Jamestown. A Powhatan archer could fire ten arrows in the minute it took to reload a musket, but firearms had greater range and shooting them was easier to learn than becoming skilled at archery.

In December 1606 three ships cast off their moorings at Blackwall dock in London. Gathering headway, they glided down the river Thames toward the open sea bound for the Chesapeake Bay in North America. Londoners who paused at the sight of them saw nothing noteworthy because the port bustled with ships leaving for faraway places and returning with their holds gorged with cargoes from continental Europe, the Mediterranean, Africa, the Orient, and the Western Hemisphere. Trade, after all, sustained the realm, and London merchants of every stripe continually eyed ways to expand their commerce. To the seamen and passengers aboard this convoy, their departure was anything but mundane. They were embarked upon a great adventure, convinced they would succeed where earlier their countrymen had failed. They planned to establish a thriving English presence in the Americas, which they believed by right and by God's grace was theirs to have, and from which the king's good subjects would enjoy the fruits of a bountiful land. Five months later the fleet anchored off a spot of ground the voyagers named Jamestown in honor of their king, and for the next nine decades that settlement stood as the premier outpost in the first and largest of England's North American colonies.

The English way to Jamestown had been a long one, far longer indeed than the passage across the Atlantic, and it had been filled with twists, turns, and false starts. As far back as the 1430s, English seafarers had steered westward when Bristol merchants opened trade with Icelanders. Half a century later Bristolians and other West Country fishermen routinely plied the cod-laden waters off the Newfoundland coast and camped in semipermanent factories to cure their yearly catches. When Bartholomew Columbus importuned Henry VII to finance his brother Christopher's voyage of discovery, the tight-fisted king turned him aside. King Henry had a change of heart after Christopher Columbus landed in the West Indies under a Spanish flag, and he sent John Cabot to claim an English share of the Americas. Others followed, but Cabot's journey did not set off a rush to colonize the region. Newfoundland seemed too forbidding, and apart from codfish, there

In 1585 Sir Walter Ralegh established an outpost on Roanoke Island in what is today North Carolina. The English called their New World colony Virginia after their "virgin queen," Elizabeth I. The war of the Spanish Armada cut off supplies, and by the time a relief expedition finally arrived in 1590, the colony was mysteriously abandoned.

appeared little of value to lure the venturesome there. War with Scotland and France and the reformation of the English church turned energies elsewhere for much of the first half of the sixteenth century. Curiosity about "the new world" and its possibilities lay dormant until Elizabeth I (reigned 1558–1603) restored a measure of tranquility to her realm. Diverted from the discords that had set her subjects against one another, Elizabethans sought other outlets for their creative energies.[1]

Ideas for colonizing America captivated John Dee, Richard Eden, Thomas Frampton, and Richard Hakluyt the Younger, though among such learned men none was more smitten than Hakluyt. An Oxford-educated cleric,

Hakluyt edited or translated some two dozen travel books and devoted a lifetime to trumpeting the value of colonies. His chef d'oeuvre, *The Principall Navigations Voiages & Discoveries of the English Nation* (London, 1589; second edition, 1598–1600), numbers among the great works of Elizabethan literature. It still makes lively reading, especially because it vividly conveys that sense of wonder that inspired Hakluyt's contemporaries to sally forth in search of new worlds to master.[2]

At first only men with court connections jumped at the prodding of Hakluyt and the others. Martin Frobisher and Sir Humphrey Gilbert tried unsuccessfully to settle Newfoundland. Sir Walter Ralegh came next. Thrice he attempted, and thrice he failed, to plant a colony on the present-day North Carolina coast, which he called "Virginia" after Queen Elizabeth. His third try began just before the outbreak of the Anglo-Spanish War of 1588–1604, and for as long as that conflict continued, there was scant hope of retaining a foothold in Virginia. Even so, Hakluyt never lost faith, and throughout the war years he constantly pressed merchants to take up his cause. They generally kept clear of colonial ventures because they viewed such enterprises as the follies of courtiers, but the ever-persistent Hakluyt finally convinced them that permanent settlements in North America were inseparably joined to national interests and to their own economic well-being.

Soon after peace returned in 1604, a group of highly placed merchants and public men pressed Elizabeth's successor, James I (reigned 1603–25), for charter rights to colonize Virginia, and on 10 April 1606 the king granted the request. The charter authorized the petitioners to create two companies, one based in London and another in Plymouth. Defining Virginia as the territory between modern Maine and North Carolina and the Pacific Ocean, the document divided the tract between the two companies and instructed the Plymouth investors to settle the northern part while the Londoners would exploit the southern region. The charter also put the responsibility for governing each colony in the hands of resident councils, which it made answerable to royally appointed commissions that stayed in England.[3]

Sir Dudley Digges was one of the early investors, or "adventurers," in the Virginia Company of London. This joint-stock venture was intent on quick profit, which was never realized. In 1622 Digges and other investors were assigned land in the colony on the condition that they send "great multitudes of people and cattle to Virginia."

Sir George Percy, a poor relation of the Duke of Northumberland, was among the original hundred Jamestown "planters," or settlers. Fully 60 percent of the first colonists were gentlemen—men of high social status with registered coats-of-arms. Percy, a knight, headed the colony during the "starving time" in the winter of 1609–10.

Charter in hand, the newly formed Virginia Company of London prepared its expedition. Borrowing from their commercial experiences, the investors organized themselves as a joint stock corporation that pooled resources and the talents of experts as it spread the risks of the outlay of capital or labor among the shareholders. Following the advice of those who had soldiered in Europe or fought the Irish, company officials planned an initial settlement of men and boys who would live in palisaded villages akin to continental military encampments or fortified towns, such as those that had proved effective in the conquest of northern Ireland. They stockpiled supplies and recruited willing colonists; they hired ships and drafted detailed instructions to guide the settlers. When all was in readiness, the officials sent the expedition on its way under the command of the fleet's admiral, Christopher Newport, a veteran mariner who knew his way to the Chesapeake. Confident that they had prepared well, the officials predicted success in bringing Protestant Christianity to the local inhabitants, launching an English presence in America, and returning generous profits to the company.[4]

Onshore winds held the convoy in sight of England for weeks, but once the breezes shifted, Admiral Newport plotted a course that took his ships along the European coast to the Canary Islands, thence westward for Martinique, where the voyagers refreshed themselves, and finally north to the mouth of the Chesapeake Bay. Making landfall in April 1607, scouting parties searched for a suitable site to inhabit, and on 13 May the colonists alighted some sixty miles up a river they named the James.

Preparations that seemed suitable in London proved decidedly less so at Jamestown. No one could have known that in 1607 the worst drought in seven centuries gripped Virginia and made the sultry heat of summer all the more unbearable as it diminished the availability of foodstuffs the Native peoples might be willing to barter. The site of the encampment, while militarily defensible, lacked potable water, and its marshy terrain bred swarms of pests that fed greedily on warm-blooded creatures. That it was also the hunting ground of the local Paspahegh people added another unforeseen complication.

Admiral Newport sailed to England once his seamen finished offloading the colonists and gathering cargoes of lumber and what looked like gold ore. When he left in June, the colony appeared to be proceeding as planned, but looks proved to be deceiving. Stifling heat, disease, and skirmishes with the Native peoples consumed both supplies and colonists at rates faster than anyone in London calculated. Following the death of Bartholomew Gosnold, one of the colony's most promising leaders, his colleagues proved either inept or too sickly to govern. Only the determined John Smith, who rose to the council presidency in 1608, held the colony together until severe wounds from a gunpowder explosion forced him to return to England. With Smith out of the picture, the situation deteriorated, frightfully so during the winter of 1609 and 1610, when disease and famine reduced the colony from five hundred to about sixty people. The timely arrival of a new governor-general, Thomas West, third baron de la Warr (governed 1610–18) and more colonists in the spring of 1610 spared Jamestown from abandonment.

Within a week of landfall in North America, a group of Englishmen began seeking the Pacific Ocean. Among them was Robert Tindall, who drew this map in 1608. Jamestown was considered a base of operations, not an end in itself. Although the mapmaker placed south at the top, it is reproduced for clarity with north at the top.

THE PORTRAICTUER OF CAPTAYNE IOHN SMITH / ADMIRALL OF NEW ENGLAND.

Ætia 37.
Aᵒ 1616.

These are the Lines that shew thy Face; but those
That shew thy Grace and Glory, brighter bee:
Thy Faire-Discoueries and Fowle-Overthrowes
Of Salvages, much Civilliz'd by thee
Best shew thy Spirit; and to it Glory Wyn;
So, thou art Brasse without, but Golde within.

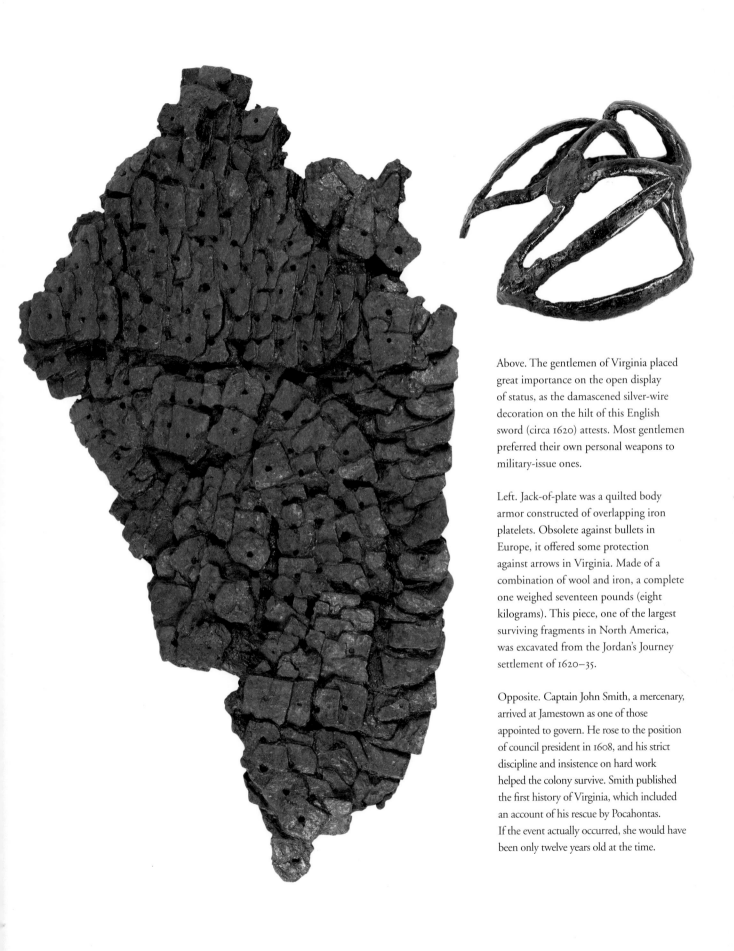

Above. The gentlemen of Virginia placed great importance on the open display of status, as the damascened silver-wire decoration on the hilt of this English sword (circa 1620) attests. Most gentlemen preferred their own personal weapons to military-issue ones.

Left. Jack-of-plate was a quilted body armor constructed of overlapping iron platelets. Obsolete against bullets in Europe, it offered some protection against arrows in Virginia. Made of a combination of wool and iron, a complete one weighed seventeen pounds (eight kilograms). This piece, one of the largest surviving fragments in North America, was excavated from the Jordan's Journey settlement of 1620–35.

Opposite. Captain John Smith, a mercenary, arrived at Jamestown as one of those appointed to govern. He rose to the position of council president in 1608, and his strict discipline and insistence on hard work helped the colony survive. Smith published the first history of Virginia, which included an account of his rescue by Pocahontas. If the event actually occurred, she would have been only twelve years old at the time.

Robert Cotton was a "tobacco-pipe-maker" who arrived at Jamestown in 1608. He used local red clay to form tobacco pipes, such as this one with an incised decoration. The undecorated pipe at the bottom is Powhatan.

Although the "starving time" marked the nadir of the colony's existence, basic structural difficulties remained, and the Virginia Company's inability to remedy those defects eventually led to its undoing. Colonists died almost faster than the company could recruit more, the costs of sustaining them beggared the imagination, and except for John Rolfe, none of them found anything that could return profits to the company. In 1612 Rolfe sought to cultivate a West Indian strain of tobacco in the hope that raising quantities of the weed in Virginia would satisfy an English rage for smoking. Two years later he marketed several hogsheads of his crop in London for a handsome return. Despite company officials' disdain for Rolfe's accomplishment, other colonists quickly followed his example, and plantation agriculture, grounded first in indentured servitude and then in chattel slavery, became the foundation of Virginia's economy.

That result was not immediately evident, so Virginia clung to life by the tiniest of threads as the colony's tenth anniversary approached. In yet one more effort to succeed, the company reorganized the colony in 1618. Gone was the military scheme of organization and governance that had prevailed since 1607. In its place were provisions for an agriculturally based colony that bore a resemblance to traditional English society. Legal arrangements were drawn from common law, and a corporate entity, the General Assembly, gave male colonists a collective voice in how they were governed. The company encouraged families to emigrate, and it even went so far as to recruit unmarried women as wives for the colonists.

It appeared for a time as though this effort had succeeded. It failed, however, in large part because of tense relations with the Native peoples, who disappointed the English. They were not the numerous, urbanized indigenous peoples the Spaniards encountered in Central and South America. Instead, they were a chiefdom of semisedentary tribes loosely held together by force of arms by their paramount leader, Powhatan.[5]

At first the Powhatans met the strangers in their midst warily, though willingly, because the number of colonists was small and the English died off almost

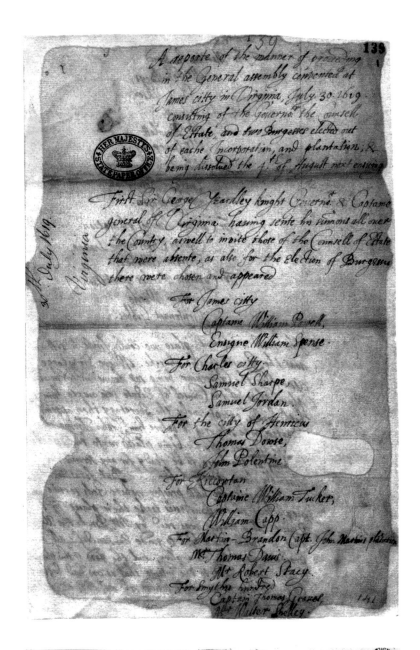

This is the first of a two-page list of the original members of Virginia's House of Burgesses, the first European representative body in the Western Hemisphere. The Governors' Council formed the upper house. Creation of a General Assembly in 1619 ended the military scheme of governance in Virginia.

The Virginia Company raised small sums of funds through lotteries, but in 1622 the king's withdrawal of its right to do so led to its collapse. This broadside of circa 1615 features an engraving of Eiakintamino, a Native person taken to London.

Left, top. Included on John Smith's 1612 map of Virginia is this image titled "Powhatan Held this state and fashion when Capt Smith was delivered to him [as a] prisoner."

Left, bottom. Besides adopting European metal goods, Native people in North America made ceramic wares, such as these fragments of shell-tempered pots found at Jamestown.

Opposite, top. Historians have described Pocahontas, daughter of Powhatan, as everything from the savior of English America to a traitor to her people. She served as a mediator and negotiator for the release of prisoners. Later she converted to Christianity and married John Rolfe, who made tobacco commercially successful in Virginia. The Virginia Company sent them to England as a celebrity couple— he to demonstrate the colony's potential for profit, she as living proof that Native people could be converted.

Opposite, bottom. Pocahontas has remained a celebrated figure long after her death in 1617. Simon van de Passe produced the only contemporary image of her, an engraving made in 1616 on her visit to London (opposite). In the familiar eighteenth-century "Booton Hall" portrait of her, of which this is a copy, the artist Europeanized her skin and hair.

Below. This gold button may be from the hat Pocahontas wore in the nearby portrait.

as quickly as they stepped ashore. The English offered trade goods, especially copper items, which were highly prized as badges of superior status. Other than food, however, the Natives proffered none of the gold or other desirable commodities the English expected to acquire. Wariness stiffened into hostility once the Powhatans realized that the English intended to stay, and mutual antagonisms bred the Anglo-Powhatan War of 1609–14, which lasted until Samuel Argall captured one of Powhatan's daughters, Pocahontas, as a hostage.[6]

Without doubt, Pocahontas was the most renowned individual associated with Jamestown in its early years. A curiosity while she lived, she became the protagonist for innumerable poems, novels, plays, and later, movies, all of which down the centuries after her death turned a mere young woman into a figure of mythic proportions. Her marriage to Rolfe and the threat of concerted attacks caused Powhatan to make peace, and until his death in 1618, his people and the English coexisted quietly.[7]

Native attitudes changed after Powhatan died and Opechancanough succeeded to the paramount chiefdom. By then all of the Native leaders grasped that the English intended to stay in Virginia. Colonial settlements ran along both sides of the James River, from its mouth to its falls, the number of settlers was growing, and some colonists were spreading northward toward the York River. Opechancanough assumed that if his people did not check this expansion, the day would come when they would be overwhelmed. Determined to prevent such an eventuality, he feigned amity with the settlers while he planned a massive attack. On 22 March 1622 his warriors struck without warning and killed a third of the colony's population. Had the Natives pressed their advantage along all fronts, they might have wiped out the entire colony. Instead, they fell back into their familiar tactics of hit and run, which gave the English breathing space to mount a counteroffensive that eventually wore down the Powhatans' ability to fight. Even so, the ensuing conflict dragged on for a decade before both sides wearied of fighting.

Matoaks als Rebecka daughter to the mighty Prince Powhatan Emperour of Attanoughkomouck als virginia converted and baptized in the Christian faith, and wife to the wor[th] M[r] Joh Rolff.

Si Pass sculp: Compton Holland excud:

Matoaks als Rebecka daughter to the mighty Prince Powhatan Emperour of Attanoughkomouck als virginia converted and baptized in the Christian faith, and wife to the wor[l] M[r] Tho: Rolff

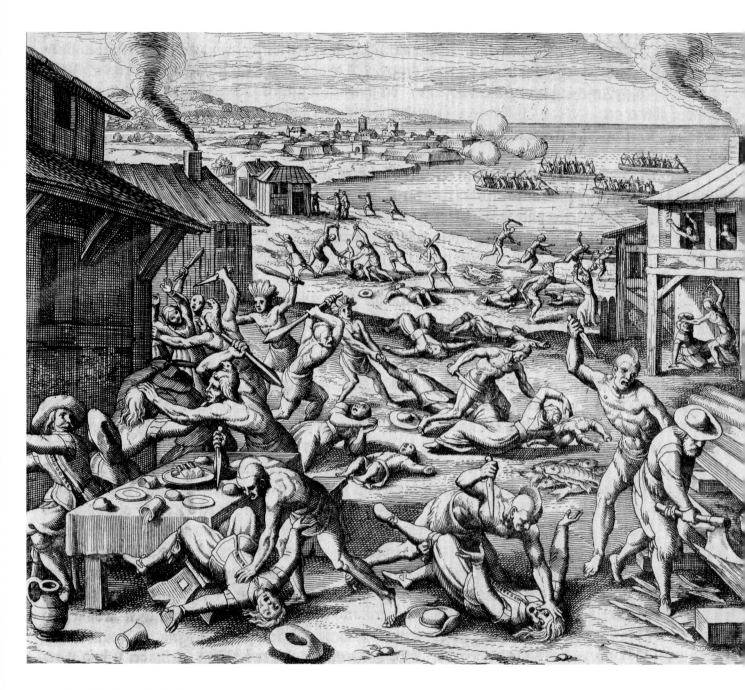

On 22 March 1622 the Powhatans made a
coordinated attack on dozens of English
settlements over a hundred-mile front.
The print is a purely European conjecture
of what happened.

The Anglo-Powhatan War of 1622–32 exacted an appalling toll in life and property, and the costs were not ones the Native peoples could easily recoup. Moreover, by launching the war, the Powhatans served notice that they rejected accommodation to the English world, whereas the colonists' response signaled a change in their way of thinking about the indigenous peoples. After 1622 the settlers were less inclined toward friendship with the Powhatans, and increasingly they regarded all Natives as savages with whom they would trade, but only if the trade was profitable. Otherwise, they were to be avoided or exterminated as the occasion demanded. That attitude drove colonial policy for the remainder of the century and beyond.[8]

Opechancanough's war intensified strains that led to the destruction of the Virginia Company. The reorganization of 1618 never met with the universal approval of all factions within the company, and those investors who opposed it kept up their criticisms, especially after news of the war reached London. Their clamor rose to such a pitch that James I intervened to restore quiet, but when he failed, he commanded his attorney general to go into court and sue to void the company's charter. The outcome of the suit was never in doubt, and the company was dissolved. James meant to reconstitute it under direct royal management, but he died before making good on his intention. In 1625 his son, Charles I (reigned 1625–49), proclaimed Virginia a royal dominion, and until 1776 it remained under crown control.[9]

Between the fall of the company and the outbreak of Bacon's Rebellion half a century later, Virginia turned into a place quite unlike anything its founders ever imagined. Jamestown itself outgrew the fort and took on attributes not only of an English village but also as the colony's capital. The transition began in the 1620s when William Claiborne laid out the New Town section, but the effort at urban development took a back seat to fighting the Natives. Once peace returned, Governor Sir John Harvey (governed 1628–35, 1637–39) encouraged various civic projects, most notably the raising of a brick church to replace a frame structure that since 1619 had also provided meeting space for the General Assembly.

The third Anglo-Powhatan War of 1644–46 ended in the dissolution of the Powhatan empire. Native survivors accepted the sovereignty of the English king and were confined to small areas. In 1662 Virginia officials issued silver and copper passport badges for Native leaders and warriors, without which they could not enter English settlements. This one is engraved "Ye King of" on one side and "Patomeck" [Potomac] on the other.

Virginia's God be Thanked,

OR

A SERMON OF THANKSGIVING

FOR THE HAPPIE

successe of the affayres in
Virginia this last
yeare.

Preached by PATRICK COPLAND at
Bow-Church in *Cheapside*, before the Honorable
VIRGINIA COMPANY, on Thursday, the 18.
of *Aprill* 1622. And now published by
*the Commandement of the said hono-
rable* COMPANY.

Hereunto are adjoyned some Epistles,
written first in Latine (and now Englished) in
the East Indies by *Peter Pope*, an Indian youth,
borne in the bay of Bengala, *who was first taught*
and converted by the said *P. C.* And after baptized by Master *Iohn Wood*, Dr in Divinitie,
*in a famous Assembly before the Right
Worshipfull, the East India Company,*
at S. *Denis* in Fan-Church streete
in *London*, December 22,
1 6 1 6.

LONDON
Printed by *I. D.* for *William Sheffard* and *Iohn Bellamie*,
and are to be sold at his shop at the two Grey-
hounds in Corne-hill, neere the *Royall*
Exchange. 1 6 2 2.

(The church tower is the only extant seventeenth-century structure at Jamestown.) After he left office, Harvey sold his residence to the assembly, which converted it into a statehouse. Additional improvements during the 1640s gave Jamestown the look and feel of a stable community, but town building ceased after Governor Sir William Berkeley surrendered Virginia to parliamentary rule in 1652. A decade later, Berkeley persuaded the General Assembly to approve his elaborate scheme for a proper capital city. The plan began with much fanfare, only to be killed off by England's wars with the Netherlands and the colonists' manifest lack of enthusiasm for city living or urban renewal. Despite those obstacles, Berkeley succeeded in erecting Virginia's first purpose-built capitol, which housed the General Assembly and other entities of provincial government until Nathaniel Bacon's rebels burned the town in 1676.[10]

In the best of times, Jamestown never numbered more than a few hundred permanent residents, although Jamestonians reflected characteristics of the colony's population as a whole. Their increase in numbers after 1624 bespoke a larger wave of immigrants that did not ebb until the 1660s. Of these, a few were Africans and a scattering were continental Europeans, but the greatest number were English. That ethnic dominance meant English cultural values would deeply tinge Virginia law, language, and customs. It also gave rise to the conceit that the English were the first Virginians and were of genteel origins. The reality was more prosaic.

In social terms, English immigrants invariably sprang from a class that Stuart Britons styled the middling sort, which is to say, collectively they ranked in wealth, stature, and influence just below greatness and just above poverty. All expected to find in Virginia better than what they abandoned in England. They were of two sorts: those with capital and connections, and those who had neither. The former, the smaller of the two groups numerically, plied their advantages and wedged their way to the head of Virginia society, while the second group, mostly young, single males, accounted for three-quarters of the colony's white population. Numbering in the thousands, they worked the fields of the great planters as bond

Opposite. At the request of the Virginia Company of London, the Reverend Patrick Copland delivered a sermon of thanksgiving on 18 April 1622. He assured his audience there was no danger of war or famine in the colony, where he personally was planning to settle. In reality, a quarter of the colonists had been killed in Powhatan attacks a few weeks earlier. When the news reached England, Copland and many others decided not to emigrate.

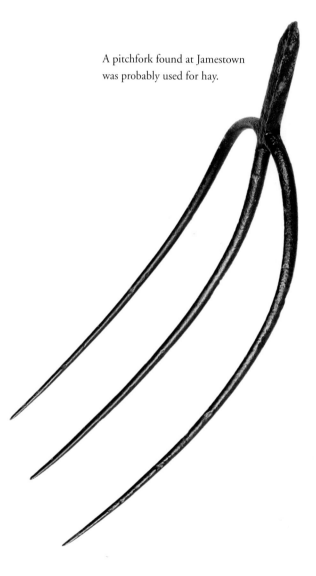

A pitchfork found at Jamestown was probably used for hay.

Opposite. In 1627 Richard Lowther of Bedfordshire, England, signed this contract, or indenture, to enter the service of Edward Lyurd, an ironmonger in Virginia. Lowther's motive was probably to pay for his passage and then become a small landowner, a status almost impossible for a poor man to achieve in England. Servants received room and board but were forbidden to marry or move without permission and were subject to harsh punishment by their masters.

Recovered from a well in Northampton County on Virginia's Eastern Shore, this rare toolbox once belonged to a working person. Since leather shoes and shoe parts were found in that and nearby wells, the box may have held shoemaker's tools.

servants. Cherished more for their labor than their humanity, they passed to the lowest rung of free society *if* they lived to complete their indentures.[11]

Poles and Germans were among the craftsmen that the Virginia Company sent to the colony in the early stages of settlement, and officials subsequently enlisted French vintners and sericulturalists. These skilled workers formed the vanguard of continental Europeans who occasionally wound up in Virginia after 1624. A few were French Huguenots or other Protestant exiles, but mainly the immigrants were Dutch merchants who insinuated themselves into the colonial social fabric through strategic marriages or political alliances.[12]

Africans were in Virginia by as much as a decade before a Dutch privateer famously landed twenty of them at Jamestown in 1619. Their arrival heralded neither the start of a massive black migration nor the beginning of chattel slavery. Slaves were there long before the institution received statutory definition, as it did from the 1660s onward, but an indeterminate number of African Virginians lived in freedom for much of the century. Actually, Africans of whatever status never accounted for a large portion of the total seventeenth-century population. A reckoning made in 1649 estimated that no more than three hundred Africans were in Virginia. Modern calculations fix the number at around six thousand by 1700.[13]

No matter their origins, immigrants altered Virginia in profound and enduring ways. More and more plantations spread across eastern Virginia, which worked against the ideal of a colony of compact settlements centered on towns. Scattered farm communities contributed to a decentralization of political authority between county and provincial government, thus enhancing the power of local magistrates. Tobacco farming caused irreparable environmental degradation as wildlife gave way to tobacco fields and streams silted up from agricultural runoff. Loss of habitat relentlessly eroded the Natives' traditional ways of livelihood. Staving off that destruction was among the reasons the aged Opechancanough launched the Anglo-Powhatan War of 1644–46. Once again he failed to dislodge his enemy, and

This writeing Indented made the Last day of July Anno Dm 1627 ... yeare of the raigne of our Soveraigne Lord Charles by the grace of God King of England Scotland and Ireland defendor of the faith &c Betweene Richard Lowther of Brooke in the ... of the County of Bedford Brewer of thone party and Edward Hurd Cittizen and ... of London of thother party witnesseth that the said Richard Lowther for the Consideratons here... bind himselfe to be remayne and Contynue this Covenant servant of him the said Edward h...

his heires and assignes to be by him or them sent and transported unto the Country of Virginia in the parts beyond the Seas & to be by him or them ymployed upon his plantacon ... and dureing the space of ffower yeares to beginn at the ffeast day of St Michaell tharch... next Comeing Dureing which said terme the said Richard Lowther shall and will truly and endeavour himselfe to the utmost of his power knowledge and skill to doe and ... and faithfull service unto the said Edward Hurd his heires and assignes in all such labours and busines as he or they their thinke good to use and ymploy him the said Lowther in, & he shall and wilbe treatable and obedient as agreed and a faithfull ser... to be in all such thinges as shalbe Comaunded him by the said Edward Hurd his heires in Virginia aforesaid or elsewhere Dureing the said terme In Consideracon ... said Edward Hurd for himselfe his executors administrators and assignes and for ... administrators and assignes by their prsts That he the said Edward Hurd his ... administrators or assignes shall and will att his and their owne charges not only transp... furnish out the said Richard Lowther to and for Virginia aforesaid and there ... and allowe unto him sufficient meate drinke apparrell and other necessaryes ... may not gruamt dureing the said terme But alsoe att thexpiracon of the said ... graunt assigne and allott unto him the said Richard Lowther the quantety of ... of Land in Virginia aforesaid to hold him his heires and assignes for ever as ... case shall without fraud or Co... witnes whereof the said prties to the ... wryteinge Indented Enterchange... sett their hands and seales yeoven and yeare first above written

Rich: Lowther

Sealed and delivered
in the presence of
John Barnes and
Andrew Ball
Servants to the
Thompson ...

The Sums totall of all ye Persons, Cattle,
Corne Armes houses, and Boats conteyned
in the generall Muster of Virginia taken
in the begininge of March. 1619

The number of all ye Persons men
Weomen and Children Enlish and
other Christians in Virginia ~~taken~~

Men	670
Weomen	119
Boyes serviceable	039
Younger Children	057
	005

Others not Christians in the
service of the English —

Indians in ye service of sevall plantacons	04
Negros in ye service of sevall plantacons	32
Negro men	15
Negro woomen	17
	921

Over and besydes all yose since ye Muster was taken
and summoned up their names home in ye Physiot
from tradinge for Corne att Dromatre Chrohanocke
who are now imployd hyer againe Thomas Davady
Interpreter, Aramnor Chatford, Thomas Tully, John
Maufran, Thomas Thornburrow, Edward watson
and Edward Chapman —

These yat are sent for Newfoundland in ye
Tempereure are not reckoned

Sum totall of all ye persons mayntyned
out of ye Collonny ————— 920

he died an English prisoner. Forever broken militarily, his people found themselves limited to small areas of land and forced to acknowledge English sovereignty.[14]

Opechancanough's second war claimed more lives than were lost in his previous attempt to destroy the colony, but the relative ease with which the English defeated him was indicative of just how swiftly Virginia had changed since 1624. Left to their own devices by a largely indifferent crown, the settlers in the space of two decades rapidly turned the colony from a tiny struggling outpost into a thriving place, whose changing features still roughly approximated its English origins. The Church of England remained the established religion, except for an eight-year hiatus during the time of parliamentary rule in the 1650s. Churches dotted the Virginia countryside well before 1624, but they always suffered from a shortage of priests and lack of direction from the ecclesiastical hierarchy in England. As a consequence, the governor, the General Assembly, local magistrates, and parish vestries assumed responsibilities that customarily fell within the purview of bishops or church courts.

Anglo-Virginians believed in an all-powerful, omnipresent God who habitually intervened in history. Worshiping him was central to their daily life and work. For them, the proper ways to honor God were set forth in the *Book of Common Prayer*, and those liturgies, rather than a set of crystal-clear theological premises, drew believers into communion with one another. Colonial church members read their Bibles, they prayed, and they turned to the prayer book for direction in their private or corporate devotions. Ultimately, they came to believe that the fundamental tenets of Christianity counted for more than theological correctness. Such an inference encouraged an ecumenical species of Anglicanism. It made a place for the uncertainties of faith and practice that inclined toward the Church of England without imposing a rigid version of Anglican ways upon the faithful akin to what Charles I sought to compel upon worshipers in Britain. By chance, then, the colonists shaped a church polity that allowed all to worship more or less in peace and in harmony.[15]

These hoes were employed at different stages of tobacco cultivation. The narrow, or hilling, hoe was used at Kingsmill to break up the ground and chop out roots. The broad, or Virginia, hoe kept the crop clear of weeds at Causey's Care plantation.

Opposite. This census of March 1619 (by modern reckoning, March 1620) divides the population of Virginia into Christians and non-Christians, which included 4 Indians and "32 negroes in the service of several planters."

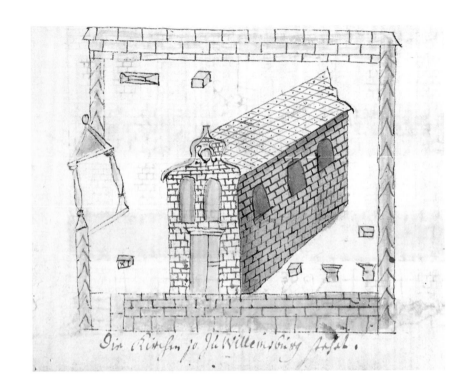

In response to Bacon's Rebellion, the gentry reinforced institutions that promoted social order, such as courts, churches, and a college. This 1702 watercolor depicts Bruton Parish Church in Williamsburg, which replaced Jamestown as the capital in 1699.

Mrs. Jacquelin Ambler presented this silver baptismal basin, made by Joseph Smith of London in 1733–34, "for use of the Church in James Citty" in memory of her son Edward. Jamestown ceased to be an active parish in the 1750s.

This Bible of 1639–40 has been used at Merchant's Hope Episcopal Church in Virginia since 1657. Theirs may be the longest continuous use of a Bible by any congregation in the United States.

John Rolfe introduced a West Indian strain of tobacco that grew well and was sweeter than the native Virginia plant. In 1614 he shipped a cargo to England that fetched a good price. By 1640 Virginians exported a million pounds annually, and the word Virginia became synonymous with tobacco. This printing block for a Virginia tobacco label dates to about 1700; the label printed from it is modern.

A few families, joined by ties of kinship, began to dominate a solidifying hierarchical social order made up of planters—great, middling, and small—and indentured servants and slaves. These families tightened their grip on the General Assembly and local government, especially after they ran off Sir John Harvey in 1635 in a dispute about their power to act independently of the governor-general. Commercially, the planters were tied to tobacco, which they marketed in ever-increasing quantities to England, though some colonists looked to outlets in Holland or strived to achieve a more diverse economy. Of the many individuals who gave shape, purpose, and direction to Virginia in the postwar years, none stamped a deeper impression on nearly every facet of colonial life than Sir William Berkeley.

Berkeley (governed 1641–52, 1660–77) came from an influential gentry family whose connections assured him a place at the court of Charles I. Serving a decade as one of the king's privy chamber men gained Berkeley a knighthood and social ties that stood him well for the rest of his life, but he achieved none of the offices and emoluments that drew him to Whitehall in the first place. Frustrated and disenchanted with royal policies that brought Britain to the brink of civil war, he looked for a fresh start in Virginia. In 1641 Berkeley purchased the office of governor-general from the incumbent, Sir Francis Wyatt (governed 1621–26, 1639–41). Thus began a transformation that mirrored those of other English colonists who immigrated to the Chesapeake area in search of personal gratification.[16]

Berkeley set about joining the ranks of the great planters soon after he arrived in Virginia. He built Green Spring House, located on land west of Jamestown, into the largest seventeenth-century residence in English North America and in the process created an architectural ideal that others emulated and brought to full flower in the next century. The fields about the mansion became his laboratory as he experimented with alternatives for tobacco. Within a matter of years he was marketing rice, spirits, fruits, silk, flax, and potash via a far-reaching network of commercial contacts around the Atlantic rim. Immersion in real estate development and trade with the Natives sharpened his concern for improving Jamestown and exploring the territory beyond the colony's frontiers. Collectively, these activities heightened Berkeley's affection for Virginia, and he became its chief promoter. To his way of thinking, prosperity depended upon freedom from London's direction. Self-reliance would allow Virginians to flourish in a deferential, closely knit community with a diversified economy that was geared to free trade. Such a province, he believed, would both benefit England and enrich himself.[17]

These views stemmed from Berkeley's more general approach to governing. He landed in Virginia intending to carry out the king's instructions to the fullest, even though he realized that he could expect little help from Charles I. Success depended upon his walking between

Sir William Berkeley was governor of Virginia from 1641 to 1652 and again from 1660 to 1677. He aligned with the great planters and recruited a ruling class of English gentry to emigrate. Berkeley tried to establish a diversified economy and free trade for the colony, but he was removed from office for his heavy-handed response to Bacon's Rebellion.

Sir WILLIAM BERKELEY *Brother* to IOHN *the first Lord* BERKELEY *of* STRATTON.

For the colony's ruling class, Governor Berkeley sought sons of royalist families that supported the crown during the English civil war. Among them was William Randolph of Warwickshire, a second son who stood to inherit nothing in England. Arriving in Virginia about 1670, he served as coroner, sheriff, speaker of the House of Burgesses, and member of the Governor's Council. An unknown British artist painted this portrait of Randolph circa 1695.

rival factions of leading colonists while he forged a following among them. Fundamental to that purpose was making common cause with the great planters. He showered them with lands and offices, he deferred to the sensibilities of his councilors, and he promoted the growth of the General Assembly into a bicameral legislature that became a little parliament. Sharing power in these ways not only won him allies, but it also furthered the dispersion of authority between province and county that all but guaranteed an unlimited right of local rule to an elite few. Even as Berkeley worked to achieve these ends,

he steadfastly affirmed Virginia's allegiance to the Stuarts, especially after the parliamentarians beheaded Charles I and abolished the monarchy. When a parliamentary army came to conquer the colony, he mounted a melodramatic show of force before he surrendered his government in 1652. His theatrics won terms that left Virginia's social and political arrangements whole and largely free of outside meddling.[18]

When a successor, Samuel Mathews, Jr. (governed 1656–60), died in January 1660, Berkeley returned to his old office. Governor once more, Sir William resurrected

In 1676 William Randolph married Mary Isham of nearby Bermuda Hundred, a Virginia plantation. Through inheritance from her father and brother, she became a woman of means. Known as the "Adam and Eve" of Virginia, this couple had nine children, whose numerous descendants included Thomas Jefferson, their great-grandson.

his dreams for diversifying Virginia's economy, but he realized they could not succeed without the support of Charles II (reigned 1649–85). Confident of his gifts for argument and the logic of his plans, Berkeley sailed to England in 1661 determined to win the king's blessings for his schemes. A place on the newly created Council for Foreign Plantations and friends in high places guaranteed him a ready hearing at court. He lobbied his case for a year, and to bolster his cause he drew up the *Discourse and View of Virginia*, which set forth his brief for the colony's improvement. Charles II

warmed to the possibilities of revitalizing Jamestown, increasing agricultural diversification, and reducing tobacco crops, but he volunteered no financial assistance, and he emphatically scorned Berkeley's appeal for free trade.[19]

Armed with new instructions, Berkeley returned to Virginia in September 1662, stoutly committed to executing Charles's instructions but in ways he thought best. That determination was one in a series of blunders and mishaps that at length undid him. Diversification flopped. Few Virginians could match Berkeley's wealth or his level of commitment, and he could not persuade the doubters to follow him. The planters' disbelief magnified as they paid the higher taxes that bankrolled the effort, and diversification was dead by the late 1660s. As for limiting the size of annual tobacco crops, Berkeley successfully negotiated a reduction, only to have the proprietor of Maryland veto the agreement and the crown retreat from its original support for the proposal.[20]

Berkeley neither accepted nor acceded to Stuart imperialism. His misreading of the crown's vision of empire flowed more from ignorance than arrogance. He never understood the predicates of Restoration colonial policy because his experiences differed from those of the architects of that system. Additionally, he lost influence at court as death or retirement thinned his allies, and by the 1670s he no longer had many advocates in Whitehall. Charles II and his younger advisers owed him nothing, but they made no move to sack him until Nathaniel Bacon gave them a reason. Berkeley never expected the loss of the Dutch trade that was a consequence of the Stuart trade laws. Nor did he anticipate war with Holland, the collapse of peace with the Natives, the revival of proprietary land grants, or being undercut by Charles II. Closure of foreign markets made tobacco less profitable, and the Second and Third Anglo-Dutch Wars threatened Virginia in ways Berkeley was powerless to prevent. He could brake, but not halt, the recurring frontier scuffles that flared into open warfare in 1675. The renewed grant of much of northern Virginia to Henry Bennet, first earl of Arlington, and Thomas Culpeper, second baron Culpeper of Thoresway, cast doubt on the validity of land titles in the region, which forced Berkeley into an expensive effort to buy out the proprietors.

Burdens of government, poor health, and the weight of years soured Berkeley and dulled his political antennae. As he aged, he came to depend upon a few intimates, none of whom he trusted more than his second wife, Frances Culpeper Stephens Berkeley, whom he married in 1670. His way of governing broke down because he was slow to correct the malfeasance of his favorites. Planters who did not enjoy his largess more and more doubted his capacity to lead. No one dared to defy him before disputes over policy toward the Natives drove his cousin Nathaniel Bacon to revolt.[21]

The route to Bacon's Rebellion started in July 1675 when a Native party attacked an outlying plantation. On its face, the incursion differed little from similar episodes that commonly occurred wherever Native peoples and settlers lived close to one another, but this one set off a series of murderous strokes and counterstrokes that quickly incited frontier colonists. Berkeley discounted the gravity of the trouble he faced, and by the spring of 1676 his leadership was gravely destabilized. A further challenge to his authority came in April, when Nathaniel Bacon accepted command of an unlawful band of volunteer Indian fighters.

Bacon paid no mind to Berkeley's stiff caution against leading the volunteers. Infuriated by Bacon's indifference, Berkeley assembled a troop of militia and tried to catch him. Bacon eluded capture, and Berkeley returned to Jamestown in a rage, but for the first time he understood the need to regain control or else his suddenly popular kinsman would eclipse him. He dissolved the General Assembly and declared Bacon a rebel. In a bid for popular support, he issued a remonstrance, wherein he defended his dealings with Bacon and promised to remedy whatever faults the voters found with his government. Privately, qualms about his capacity to control events vexed him, and just days before he convened a new General Assembly, he asked to be replaced.[22]

When the General Assembly began on 5 June 1676, an atmosphere of crisis pervaded the capital. Voters in Henrico County elected Bacon as one of their burgesses, but doubts circulated about his taking his seat. Those uncertainties abated after Bacon's capture, pardon, and subsequent return to his plantation at Curles Neck upriver from Jamestown. Bacon missed most of the session, during which the burgesses and councilors passed legislation to combat the Natives and remedied various voter grievances. As the Assembly concluded its business, Bacon unexpectedly trooped into town at the head of five

hundred armed men and extorted a general's commission from the terrified legislators before he marched off to attack the Natives.

From that moment, the duel between Berkeley and Bacon became a fight to the death over who would control the colony. Berkeley again proclaimed Bacon a rebel and tried to capture him. Few planters helped, and the governor fled to a stronghold on the Eastern Shore after Bacon doubled back on him. Now Bacon attempted to seize control of Virginia. To that end he bid for popular support by publicly condemning Berkeley and forcing councilors who were now his prisoners to swear allegiance to him. Bacon dispatched ships across the Chesapeake Bay to drive the governor from his sanctuary before he led his army on a hunt for Native people. The only ones he engaged were helpless tributaries, most of whom the troopers eagerly slaughtered. For his part, Sir William captured the forces Bacon sent to catch him.

This window casement came from a house built on Curles plantation, upriver from Jamestown, in 1674–75. The one-story house was sturdy and ornamental compared to the makeshift dwellings of the early 1600s, when families moved frequently.

Bacon's Rebellion in Virginia was a struggle between land-hungry settlers and the government at Jamestown. These exploded grenades, along with one still intact, perhaps were tossed at the statehouse in Jamestown by supporters of Nathaniel Bacon, who burned the town to the ground in 1676.

Opposite. *Bacon's Epitaph* laments the death of Nathaniel Bacon, leader of Bacon's Rebellion in 1676. He led tenants, laborers, servants, and other colonists who were frustrated with the rule of great proprietors and anxious to appropriate lands still occupied by Native peoples.

Right. In 1677 English authorities gave this silver badge, with the coat-of-arms of King Charles II, to Cockacoeske, who led the Pamunkey from 1656 to 1686. The English referred to her as queen of the Pamunkey to confirm her lands after Bacon's Rebellion. The Pamunkey lived about thirty-five miles from Jamestown.

Bacons Epitaph, made by his Man.

Death why soe crewill! what no other way
To manifest thy splleene, but thus to slay
Our hopes of safety; liberty, our all
which, through thy tyrany, with him must fall
To its sad caoss? Had thy riged force
Bin delt by retale, and not thus in gross
Griefe had bin silent: Now wee must complaine
Since thou, in him, hast more then thousand slane
whose lives and safetys did so much depend
On him there lif, with him there lives must end
    If't be a sin to thinke Death brib'd can bee
wee must be guilty; say twas bribery
Guided the fatall shaft. verginias foes
To whom, for secrit crimes, just vengance owes
Disarved plagues, dreding there just disart
Corrupted Death by Parasselsian art
Him to destroy; whose well tride curage such
There heartless harts, nor armes, nor strength could touch
    Who now must theire those wounds, or stop that blood
The Heathen made, and drew in to a flood?

31

Left. Marriageable English women had economic leverage in early Virginia, where most of the settlers were male. This gold wedding band of 1650–75 is engraved, "Time shall tell, I love thee well." Found at Poquoson, York County, it almost certainly was imported from England.

Opposite. The Morning Star bowl, made and marked in London in 1692, is one of two surviving pieces of seventeenth-century secular silver in Virginia. Reputedly named for a racehorse, the punch bowl descended in the family of Severn Eyre on the Eastern Shore.

He sailed across the bay and regained Jamestown. Fresh from his "triumph," Bacon besieged Jamestown, which he burned after Berkeley abandoned it and retreated to the Eastern Shore once more. With Berkeley on the run again, it seemed as though the rebel had won the day. Victory was fleeting, however, because Bacon died from the "Bloody Flux" and the "Lousey Disease." His sudden death all but ended the rebellion, although Berkeley did not stamp out its last vestiges until early 1677.[23]

Bacon's Rebellion forced the crown to intervene in Virginia affairs as it had not done since the demise of the Virginia Company. Responding to the news of the revolt with uncommon alacrity, Charles II and his advisers dispatched ships and soldiers to smash Bacon, and they established a commission to look into the reasons for the insurrection. Colonel Herbert Jeffreys, one of the commissioners, brought orders to replace Berkeley. The commission quarreled repeatedly with Berkeley before he sailed to England in May 1677. Sick and weakened by the voyage, he arrived in London wishing only to clear his name. Sir William never got the chance. He died six weeks after he landed, and his like as a colonial governor of Virginia was never seen again.[24]

Berkeley's passing marked a new day in Anglo-Virginia politics. His successors cared little for Virginia, its people, or its institutions. Staunch royalists, they merely mimicked their masters' visions of empire.

Governing mattered to them only in so far as it advanced the king's interest and benefited them personally. That turn of mind suited them well to the task of curbing the colony's independence of direction from London. Thus, the politics of confrontation became the order of the day, as the crown sought to minimize the powers of the General Assembly and colonial leaders tried to frustrate that ambition. By and large, postrebellion governors bested their adversaries, and by 1700 the Assembly was no longer an autonomous parliament in miniature.[25]

Virginia changed in other ways. Immigration from England slowed, and as it did, slavery replaced indentured servitude. The failure of Berkeley's diversification schemes left tobacco as the colony's financial mainstay. Plantations grew larger to offset lower prices caused by overproduction. Small operators found the challenge of competing for market share more daunting than in an earlier generation. Indeed, the distances between planters widened as prosperity increasingly created a stratified economy ever more dependent on African slaves.

Demographically, Virginia's population could sustain itself through natural increase as the ratio of women to men equalized. Great planter families tightened their hold on the top rungs of the social order. Their progeny regarded Virginia as belonging to an Atlantic imperial community whose center was London. Life in Virginia differed from life in Britain, but the colonial world was very much a part of an English world. The goal of making Virginia as much of a little England as conditions would allow had a long way to go, because by 1700 the colony amounted to little more than a series of widely disconnected settlements that lacked a town of any consequence.

Royal officials promoted town building throughout the postrebellion years, but their attempts to lure Virginians to urban living usually became victim to the foot dragging of colonial politicians. Jamestown itself met a similar fate as it recovered from the fire of 1676. Some colonists favored relocating the capital to land at Gloucester Point (across the York River from Yorktown), but the vocal opposition of Jamestonians effectively ended that attempt. Governor Thomas Culpeper, second baron Culpeper of Thoresway (governed 1677–83), showed no interest in rebuilding the town, preferring instead to live with his cousin, Dame Frances Berkeley, at Green Spring House. Residents took matters into their

own hands, and within a half-dozen years they had repaired or rebuilt their houses, and parishioners finished the reconstruction of the church by 1680. Even so, the statehouse remained a burnt-out hulk, forcing the General Assembly to meet in taverns. Governor Francis Howard, fifth baron Howard of Effingham (governed 1683–92), tried in vain to persuade the Assembly to fund the construction of a gubernatorial residence. He had somewhat better luck with starting the restoration of the statehouse. In 1684 he and the Assembly engaged Philip Ludwell to make the repairs. Ludwell had the house side of the building ready for occupancy within eighteen months, but then he and Governor Lord Effingham became embroiled in a political fight that led to his dismissal. Subsequently the Assembly hired Henry Hartwell to finish the job, which was finally done around 1695.

Two decades after the fire, Jamestown looked much as it had before Bacon's rebels set it ablaze. The restored capital met its end sooner than any of the colonists might

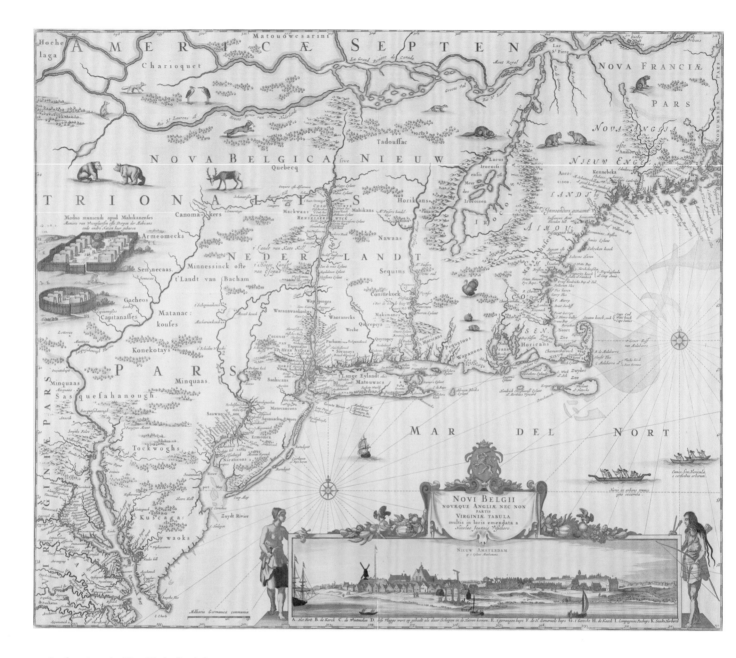

In the 1620s the New Netherland Company established New Amsterdam on "newly discovered lands situated in America between New France and Virginia." Since the English also claimed the area as part of Virginia, conflict was inevitable. The English conquered the disputed land in 1664 and gained it permanently by treaty ten years later. The Dutch capital of New Amsterdam (now New York) appears at the bottom.

Opposite. By the late 1600s, elite colonists could make ostentatious displays of their wealth and status. This Virginia court cupboard was intended for the display of silver, porcelain, and other showy valuables. Local yellow pine used in its construction dates this piece to about 1660.

James I distributed a thousand old bills, a type of weapon, from his armory in 1622. Nine bills, including this one, were excavated at Jamestown from that group.

have imagined. Fire broke out in the statehouse on 20 October 1698, and within hours the town lay in ashes once more. A year later Governor Francis Nicholson (governed 1690–92, 1698–1705) convinced the General Assembly to move the seat of government to a site at Middle Plantation that eventually flourished into Williamsburg.[26]

Some of the residents stayed in Jamestown. Their numbers dwindled, though they continued to elect a member to the legislature until after the American Revolution. Nearby colonists carted off bricks from ruined buildings and put them to good use. The church ceased to be an active parish in the 1750s. By the opening of the nineteenth century, vestiges of the town had all but disappeared. A few families consolidated the island into their ownership and farmed the arable land. Erosion ate away the narrow isthmus that joined the island to the mainland and portions of the shoreline as well. To save Jamestown as a historic place, the Association for the Preservation of Virginia Antiquities (APVA) in 1893 acquired more than twenty-two acres of land that embraced the church tower and the western section of the town site. The remainder of the island became part of the Colonial National Historic Park in the 1930s, and today what is now known as "Historic Jamestowne" is jointly administered by APVA and the National Park Service (NPS).

APVA and NPS archaeologists conducted extensive investigations over the past century. The most recent excavations, which the APVA Jamestown Rediscovery team began in 1994, solved a venerable mystery regarding the location of the original fort. Long thought to have washed into the James River, the footprint of the fort turned out to have survived largely intact. The ongoing dig at the fort site also yielded upward of a million artifacts that, in combination with earlier recoveries and extant documentary records, shed new light on Jamestown's importance to the beginning of the nation.[27]

In 1607 a band of colonists laid the first permanent English bridgehead in North America. The town that grew out of it bore witness to encounters between Native peoples, Africans, and Europeans, who opened a messy, often shrill, occasionally violent, but ceaseless conversation about what it means to be American.

This plaque with the arms of William III and Mary II of England decorated the pew of the governor of Pennsylvania at Christ Church, Philadelphia. The congregation enjoyed the patronage of the crown, but there was no established church in Pennsylvania.

Gilles Proulx

Québec

Marie-Charlotte Denys de la Ronde,
entrepreneur and wife of Governor
Claude de Ramezay.

Samuel de Champlain arrived in Canada in 1603 for an expedition up the St. Lawrence River. Further exploring the St. Lawrence in 1604, he noted sites for possible settlement as well as searched for minerals and a passage to Asia. On 3 July 1608 he chose a favorable site for a settlement and put his men to work building at Québec. Champlain played a central role in the consolidation of the French presence in Canada until his death in 1635.

Samuel de Champlain's *Geographic Map of New France* appeared in 1613. A gifted geographer and chronicler, Champlain published detailed descriptions of the land and contributed greatly to European geographical knowledge of the New World.

WHEN SAMUEL DE CHAMPLAIN stepped off his boat on 3 July 1608 to found a settlement at the narrowing of the St. Lawrence River, a place Native people called Québec, it was five years after he first passed by this tip of land, Cape Diamond. Perhaps Champlain had already set foot there in the summer of 1603 when, accompanying François Gravé DuPont, he sailed the St. Lawrence all the way up to the Lachine Rapids at the island of Montréal. Five years later Champlain's ship, the *Don de Dieu*, was anchored downstream at Tadoussac, at the mouth of the Saguenay River. The hazards of an uncharted St. Lawrence made that spot the terminus of French oceanic navigation for the next thirty years. To sail upstream from Tadoussac to Québec, sailors preferred the flexibility of smaller ships with one sail and a few oarsmen to the larger three-masted ships that crossed the Atlantic.[1]

During the days that followed, Champlain wrote,

I looked for the right site for our dwelling, but I could not find one more convenient or better located than the tip of Québec—so-called by the savages—a place full of walnut trees. Immediately, I used one group of our workers to knock them down in order to build our dwelling, another to saw the planks, another to dig the cellar and make the cesspools, and yet another to go by ship to Tadoussac to bring our provisions. With everyone's diligence and under my supervision, the warehouse for our supplies was quickly built.[2]

The deeds of the founder of Québec in July 1608 followed the fishermen and fur dealers who had frequented the North Atlantic coast ever since Jacques Cartier sailed up the St. Lawrence in 1535 on his 120-ton ship, the *Grande Hermine*, and spent the winter on the banks of the St. Charles River in the shade of the Cape Diamond promontory.

The earliest fur bartering in North America may go back to the Viking ventures about the year 1000. The Scandinavian sagas mention the trading of arms and fabrics for bundles of pelts among Inuits, Beothuks, and Vikings, but it is the arrival of Cartier that truly marked the beginning of the fur trade in the history of New France.[3] Cartier's first contacts with the Micmacs of the Baie des Chaleurs, for example, indicate that Native peoples were familiar with exchanging skins for European products. "And the moment they noticed us and started to flee, they gestured that they had come to trade with us; and they showed us skins of little value, which they themselves were wearing."[4] When Cartier left Québec with indigenous leader Donaconna in 1536, the Natives from Saguenay brought "three bundles of hare and stag skins from the Donaconna, and a big copper knife from the Saguenay."[5]

Cartier's discovery of Canada allowed Europeans for the first time to explore a route into North America, the only way known until the beginning of the seventeenth century. Extending all the way to Montréal, the St. Lawrence opened a vast and rich fur reservoir to European exploitation—and a thinly populated territory with an extensive network of waterways. The popularity of Canadian furs, such as otter, lynx, and marten, which were used to line garments, was

understandable because of the harsh European climate of the sixteenth century and the difficulties of reaching Siberian suppliers because of political conflicts.

The stories of voyages in the sixteenth and early seventeenth centuries mention numerous fleets of French ships on the banks of Newfoundland and the St. Lawrence River. Incidental at first, contacts between the French and Native peoples became more and more frequent throughout the sixteenth century. Two reasons explain this development. First, after 1550 competition on the banks of Newfoundland between English and French fishermen intensified, prompting the French to frequent the Gulf of St. Lawrence. Second, the need to increase the quantities of cod shipped to Europe led to the introduction of the cod-drying technique and, as a consequence, a search for ports at which to dry the fish. Dealings with the Natives increased, and from 1540 to 1580 a thousand Europeans worked and lived on the

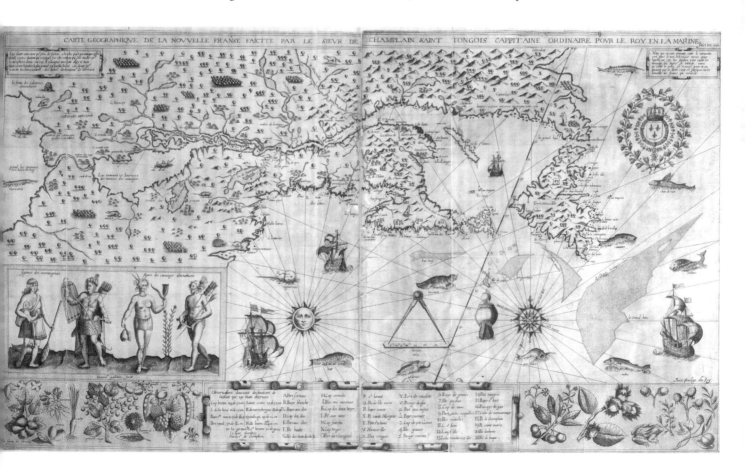

Henry IV of France, shown in an engraving of circa 1870, awarded a fur trade monopoly to a succession of private companies that had the authority and financial responsibility to found colonies and send settlers. Under his direction, Francois Gravé du Pont and Samuel de Champlain launched their first expedition up the St. Lawrence in 1603 and allied with the Montagnais and Algonquin nations.

shores of Labrador for six months of the year. The Basques—whale hunters—rendered the fat from these marine mammals, which was in high demand.

Trading activities on the St. Lawrence River did not extend beyond Tadoussac until the beginning of the seventeenth century. The hostility of the Iroquois in the St. Lawrence Valley toward Europeans, following the treatment some of their leaders received from Cartier and Jean-François de la Roque de Roberval, limited French trading to the Tadoussac. The Iroquois—an agricultural tribe living along the St. Lawrence River when Cartier arrived—had little to offer to the French, as opposed to the Algonquin and Montagnais nomadic hunters, who could better serve as intermediaries on the Saguenay with the inhabitants of the interior. The superior quality of the furs from Saguenay, navigational difficulties on the St. Lawrence River, and the need to stay close to the fishing territories also explain the importance of Tadoussac for the fur trade.

In an effort to restore the French economy, which had been devastated by religious wars, King Henry IV decided to promote the colonization of New France at the beginning of the seventeenth century. The creation of a monopoly of financially strong companies was desirable to manage business expenses over vast distances, to obtain supplies in large quantities, and to ensure a good start for Canadian production. Opposition to the colonial adventure of Henry IV's prime minister, Maximilien de Béthune, duc de Sully, forced France to entrust development of the future colony to private enterprise. For Sully, agriculture represented wealth for France, while the sites located north of the fortieth parallel, such as New France, were scarcely productive. Henry IV granted wealthy merchants the exclusive rights to conduct the fur trade, though the fisheries remained free.

In 1599 Pierre Chauvin and François Gravé DuPont obtained the first monopoly and tried to establish themselves at Tadoussac, but this early experience failed because of lack of financial resources and their difficulty in adapting to the harsh conditions. Aymar de Chaste replaced them in 1603 as a monopoly holder and dispatched Gravé DuPont and Champlain to Canada on

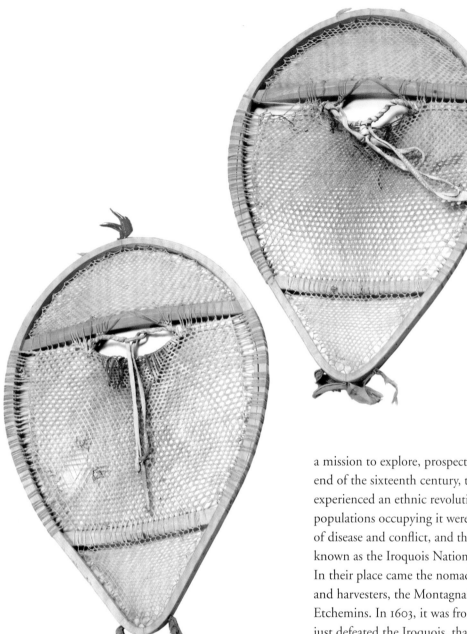

A Montagnais child wore these snow-shoes. They attest to the harsh climate of Québec, which discouraged French immigration. For the fur trade, the French adopted Native people's means of transportation, primarily canoes, snowshoes, and toboggans.

a mission to explore, prospect, and trade. At the end of the sixteenth century, the St. Lawrence Valley experienced an ethnic revolution. The sedentary populations occupying it were withdrawing, the victims of disease and conflict, and they essentially became known as the Iroquois Nations south of the Great Lakes. In their place came the nomadic populations of hunters and harvesters, the Montagnais, Algonquins, and Etchemins. In 1603, it was from these peoples, who had just defeated the Iroquois, that the envoys of Aymar de Chaste requested permission to settle. In return, the French offered to help them fight their enemies. The proposition was accepted, and thus began a century of Franco-Iroquois confrontation.

With the death of Aymar de Chaste later that year, Pierre DuGua des Monts took over a ten-year monopoly on the condition of bringing in one hundred colonists a year. In 1604 he and Jean de Biencourt, sieur de Poutrin-court, chose Acadia, with its more fertile land and milder climate, as a site to found a colony on the Bay of Fundy.

Champlain received this patterned belt of cylindrical shell beads, or wampum, in 1611 to conclude the first alliance between the French and the Huron. The warriors with shields represent the four constituent parts of the Huron confederation. Arranged in belts like this, wampum functioned as records of treaties or decisions and could be "read" by a trained wampum keeper. This belt became part of the French royal collection.

Opposite. A cotton and glass bead bag, probably Huron and dating from about 1721, came from the upper St. Lawrence or Great Lakes region of New France.

Champlain accompanied DuGua and explored the east coast of America in search of a possible route to the Pacific. In Acadia, strong rivalry with other merchants prevented DuGua from enforcing his monopoly and fulfilling his obligations. His privileges were revoked in 1607, but the next year he obtained the right to send Champlain to Québec in the hope he would find less aggressive competitors there.

As an observant cartographer at the service of a business enterprise, Champlain was fully aware of Québec's exceptional location as a permanent site for a trading post or a settlement. One was needed near Tadoussac, a stop for large sailing ships that could become a meeting place for the fur trade and where it would be possible to stock up on French products. While Tadoussac received all the furs from Saguenay, this small post could hardly become an adequate depot for fur resources from the St. Lawrence, the Mauricie, and Outaouais (Ottawa). Québec was the first place where ships could easily land beyond the mouth of the Saguenay, sheltered far from the rocks and cold winds of Tadoussac. Wild fruit, construction lumber, fertile soil, and drinking water from the St. Charles River were easily available. The narrowness of the river at Québec, though not yet protected by French cannon at the beginning of the seventeenth century, provided a good view of the comings and goings of friends and enemies alike. The Trois-Rivières and Montréal sites, which Champlain also knew, were undoubtedly too close to the Iroquois Nations for him to establish his first post there.

THROUGHOUT the first century of the French presence, the European population in New France grew from 28 in the summer of 1608 to 20,896 inhabitants in 1716. During this period, the city of Québec grew from 28 to 2,574 inhabitants. Québec counted 76 people in 1628, 547 during the 1666 census, and 1,407 in 1688.[6] Surprisingly, even though several nomadic populations had passed through the area, the St. Lawrence Valley was practically unoccupied. Large areas of fertile land were available for those emerging from a long civil war. The very slow demographic growth of the colony and its capital was understandable in light of the political and economic constraints. For half a century, New France and Québec belonged to private business enterprises that watched over their economic interests, even though the region was under the patronage of viceroys. For the Native peoples who provided the furs, the presence of a large European population was far from desirable. It was even counterproductive, because a growing sedentary population tended to reduce the number of fur-bearing animals. A few agents were enough to distribute European merchandise in exchange for furs.

From 1608 to 1628 Norman and Breton merchants from Caen, Rouen, and St. Malo controlled the business monopoly and managed the affairs of the colony. Approximately fifty employees, agents, and artisans exchanged merchandise for furs as well as built and repaired warehouses and stores in Québec. Champlain, who was not only their employer but also a representative of the French crown, worried less about business than about exploring the country and discovering the celebrated route to the Pacific. His sojourns in Québec rarely lasted two months, except when his young wife Hélène Boulé accompanied him from 1620 to 1624. Champlain became interested in the soil's fertility and its ability to support colonists. Members of the first colonist family, that of the apothecary Louis Hébert, established themselves on the Québec promontory after 1617. Five or six families were settled there by 1629. The firm banned Hébert from trading and only allowed him to cultivate the land during his free time. It pushed aside Champlain's proposal of 1618 to found the town of Ludovica on the St. Charles River, north of Cape Diamond, and instead moved three hundred families and three hundred soldiers there.

As a representative of the king, Champlain assumed responsibility for maintaining diplomatic relations with the Native inhabitants. In reply to invitations from the Montagnais and the Algonquins, he participated in raids against the Iroquois Nations. He also sought direct contact with other Native peoples allied with the nomads of the St. Lawrence Valley, such as the Crie and the Huron. These nations controlled fur reservoirs even

Opposite. The colonists, or *habitants*, reproduced French farming in the New World and imported familiar products, but they also adopted such local staples as corn, squash, and beans. A Native woman holding an ear of corn and a squash appeared as an illustration in Samuel de Champlain's *Geographical Map of New France* in 1612.

This imaginative illustration of beavers decorated a map titled *Carte tres curieuse* in an atlas of 1719.

richer than those of the St. Lawrence Valley, hence his interest in contacting them without intermediaries. Naturally, this caused friction with the Montagnais, who were already dissatisfied with the business monopolies that made all competition impossible for a long time, and they denied the French the right to sail the Saguenay. Several Frenchmen paid with their lives for attempting it. The Algonquins also tried to limit contacts between the French and the sedentary nations of the Hurons north of the Great Lakes. Champlain's stand against the Iroquois provoked hostility to the French presence in the St. Lawrence Valley. Courted by the Dutch and the English in New England, who were also in search of furs, the Iroquois began ferocious incursions, first against the

Native peoples who were allied with the French, and then against the French directly. These repeated attacks retarded the effort to populate New France.

Perhaps inspired by his wife's conversion to Catholicism, or influenced by the devout party surrounding the French regent, Champlain brought missionary monks of St. Francis of Assisi (Récollets) to Québec in 1615. Jesuits trained like soldiers followed them ten years later. Inspired by the effervescence of the Catholic Counter-Reformation in France, these newcomers wanted to minister to the spiritual well-being of their fellow countrymen, but above all, they planned to convert the Native peoples, "these savage beasts without religion."[7] To achieve this goal, a large number of the inhabitants had to be "Gallicized" and settled. The end of nomadism ensured superior control, while "Gallicization" made it easier to communicate Catholic values. Assimilation would hopefully result in an increase in the number of subjects of the French crown—at little expense. Thus, the monks wanted to hasten the arrival of Frenchmen in America to foster the spread of the French language and agricultural methods. Their proselytizing ignored the linguistic obstacle posed by the Indian tongues, and above all it denied the values of liberty, equality, and respect shared by the "sons of the forest."[8] Moreover, it completely overlooked Native American spirituality.

After becoming the king's chief minister in 1624, Armand Jean du Plessis, Cardinal Richelieu, attempted to increase the power of France by reviving its navy and colonies. This effort was set back for a time when David Kirke and his brothers, in the service of the English crown, captured Québec. The English remained until 1632 and practically ruined the Compagnie des Cent Associés, established in 1627 in order to transform Québec's trading post into a vast business colony. The Cent Associés, unlike preceding business enterprises, was supposed to populate New France by bringing in four thousand colonists within fifteen years and dividing the land into feudal estates and domains. With two thousand inhabitants in the whole of New France in 1653, of whom only four hundred were women, and with only six hundred people in the region of Québec, the company fell short of its objective. The

figure des sauuages a

initially disappointing financial results of the Cent Associés undoubtedly had a negative effect on demographic growth, both in Québec and in the entire colony. The Jesuits went back to their conversion work; female religious instructors and nurses followed them in 1639 to teach Indian children and to care for the sick.[9]

To get closer to the consignments of furs, the French spread out from Québec and established the posts of Trois-Rivières and Montréal in 1634 and 1642, respectively. Though seeking to ensure the safety of fur resources, the French paradoxically increased the insecurity of the colony by locating it on Iroquois trails. The results were particularly disastrous for the Huron Nation, which was decimated about 1648–50 by European diseases and attacks by Iroquois armed with

Anglo-Dutch weapons.[10] The survivors of that nation found refuge in the settlements of Sillery and Lorette in the second half of the seventeenth century. From approximately 1657 to 1660, they occupied an enclosure in the upper city of Québec, near the fort.[11] In 1660 rumors that twelve hundred Iroquois were about to attack Québec caused a panic. The attack did not materialize, but the rumor provoked France into sending one hundred workers and soldiers annually for each of the two following years.

The inability of the Compagnie des Cent Associés to fulfill its obligations led King Louis XIV to take charge of New France in 1663. These administrative changes, as well as the instability of the colony, led the crown to send soldiers and workers to fight the Iroquois and to work the land. In 1665 the regiment of Carignan-Salières and its twelve hundred men constituted the first major dispatch of troops to New France. Four hundred remained and settled in the country when the regiment went back to France three years later. From 1660 to 1688 nearly six thousand people—craftsmen, civil servants, unmarried women, and soldiers—settled in the region. These three decades undoubtedly constituted the most fruitful period of emigration to New France. The king wanted to ensure the safety of his subjects and promote development. Québec's population quadrupled between 1663 and 1700.[12] The 1666 census indicated that men constituted 65 percent of the population in Québec. In 1688 they made up 55 percent, a consequence of the immigration of unmarried women.

Opposite. In the spring of 1609 the Montagnais and their allies—the Micmacs, Algonquins, and Hurons—called on the French to join them in combating the Mohawks, one of the Iroquois Five Nations. The Mohawks fought in mass formation behind wooden shields. The firepower and surprise of three Frenchmen with muskets turned the tide of battle. From that time forward, the Iroquois were enemies of the French.

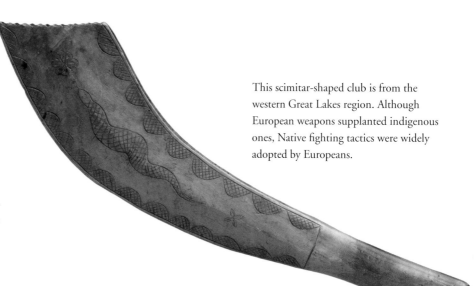

This scimitar-shaped club is from the western Great Lakes region. Although European weapons supplanted indigenous ones, Native fighting tactics were widely adopted by Europeans.

Above. Designed for Native converts, this religious medal was discovered at the King's Stores site in Québec City. Such devotional medals made of copper alloy illustrated missionary teaching and served as recompense for pious converts.

Right. Native people called Jesuits "Black Robes" because of the color of their cassocks. Jesuits immersed themselves in Native societies, whether sedentary or nomadic, and learned indigenous languages.

du 9e Octobre 1703. Engagement marie francoise Sauveau a antôine Sortin;

Pardevant Le Notaire Royal en la prevosté de quebec Soussigné y Residant et Témoins cy bas nommez, fut present René Sauveau dit deslorriers habitant demeurant en la Seigneurie de beaumont veuf de deffuncte Elisabeth boissonneau lequel estant reduit a une extresme pauvretté et hors detat de pouvoir faire subsister et soigner quatre enfans en bas age desquels il est demeuré chargé apres la mort de sa femme, a pour prouvoir l'avancement de Marie francoise Sauveau agée de quatre ans et demy et luy assurer ce qui est necessaire a la vie et a l'entretien de son corps, a Engagé lad. fille pour dés a present Jusques a l'age de vingt ans accomplis En qualité de Servante domestique à Anthoine Sortin Maistre de bouquet demeurant en l'isle et paroisse Saint Laurent a ce present et acceptant qui a pris et Retenu lad. Sauveau en lad. qualité pour luy Servir durant, pendant lequel temps elle sera tenue de servir luy Sortin et sadite femme Selon son pouvoir et sa qualité avec toute la fidelité requise, Et Engagement ainsy fait a la charge par led. Sortin de la nourir humainement et de la nourir, loger blanchir, et entretenir d'habits et linge a son usage Selon sa qualité, de l'instruire et faire instruire des choses principallement necessaires a salut; Et outre ce de luy payer pour tous gages, Salaires et recompenses pour tout led. temps Jusques aux age de vingt ans accomplis la somme de cent Cinquante livres outre tous les habits qu'elle aura alors a son usage, estant neant moins convenu que Sy lad. fille trouve lieu de se pouvoir par mariage avant leur age de vingt ans accomplis, que luy Sortin sera en ce cas Seulement tenu sy elle meurt ou Semarie depuis quinze Jusques a dix sept ans accomplis de payer avec ou aves huitieme soixante quinze livres et ses habits, Sy c'est depuis dix sept Jusques a dix neuf ans accomplis Cent vingt livres et ses habits, Et sy c'est apres les vingt ans accomplis la somme de cent cinquante livres et ses habits; Car ainsy &c ont obligé &c Renoncant &c fait et passé aud. quebec en l'estude dud. notaire avant midy le Neufiesme Jour d'octobre mil Sept cens trois En presence de messieurs Jaques grouard Serrurier Et Estienne Chiburge tonnellier Témoins demeurans aud. quebec qui ont aves luy Sortin et notaire Signé, laq. Sauveau ayant declaré ne sçavoir signer dece enquise;

Grouard   Antoine Sortier   St Thiberge

Chambalon

While in its first half century the population of Québec consisted mainly of single males employed by monopoly companies engaged in the fur trade; demographics underwent a significant change after 1660. Québec's society became more diverse: governor, *intendant,* bishop, councilors, civil servants, merchants, seamen, soldiers, artisans, clergy, servants, and even slaves rubbed shoulders. The censuses from 1666 and 1681 cited thirty-five to forty-five professions grouped as follows: services (civil servants, the military, surgeons, members of religious orders); business (merchants, transportation, food); processing (artisans in all trades, such as wood, stone, iron, leather, and textiles); and nonspecialized (servants and day laborers). Since they were all of French origin, religion, and language, the Québecois of the seventeenth century formed a coherent group in spite of their diverse occupations. The French feudal castes, which were based on aristocracy by birth or wealth, were not generally transplanted to New France. Certain social classes existed, but it was possible for the people of Québec to move from one to another, depending on their degree of initiative.[13] Québec had a large number of men and women in religious orders—one in every eight inhabitants, according to the census of 1666. The orders were responsible for education and hospital care, as well as for alleviating poverty.

As a civil and military administrative center, Québec attracted both aristocrats and gentlemen. In the seventeenth century, seven Québec inhabitants even obtained titles of nobility. The state conferred its public office titles and ranks on the nobility, while military staff posts were open to local gentlemen. Often entrusted to the nobility were civil administration and justice posts and the posts of treasurer, controller of the navy, surveyor, and police marshal. Many members of the Sovereign Council, the court of appeals in New France with head offices in Québec, were gentlemen. The king's officers, high officers of finance, and police were part of the urban middle class. Given privileges that exempted them from performing forced labor or housing soldiers, they aspired to become part of the nobility. Civil servants, court clerks, and agents who wished to increase their income served as notaries, surveyors, or prosecutors.

Opposite. This agreement for hiring a four-year-old servant in Québec in 1703 reads in part, "Reduced to extreme poverty and the father of four young children, René Favreau, a resident of the domain of Beaumont, engages his four year old daughter, Marie Francoise, for her advancement, as a servant to Antoine Fornier . . . Fornier undertakes to treat her humanely, to see to her bed, board, and laundry, to instruct her, and to provide her with all things necessary for her salvation." Fornier agreed to pay her 150 *livres* at her marriage at age twenty, or 75 *livres* if married at seventeen, or 120 *livres* if married at eighteen.

A chest was an essential furnishing in any household, rich or poor. The carving on this one of circa 1650 suggests both that the owner was wealthy and the chest was imported from France. Since most immigrants brought few possessions with them, many *habitants,* or colonists, built their own furniture.

Being the only port of entry and exit for the St. Lawrence Valley, Québec was a place of fierce business competition. City merchants had to compromise with businessmen from metropolitan France as well as with ship owners who controlled supplies and maritime commerce. They also had to deal with itinerant merchants passing through Québec during the summer. These peddlers sold their cargo to the inhabitants at retail prices and often went into the fur business.

Finally, artisans and professionals represented one-third of the working people in Québec in 1681. The lack of masterships and guilds facilitated the growth of trades. Most workers started as apprentices or employees, while some supplemented their income by being innkeepers, quite often with the help of a spouse. Day laborers, soldiers, employees, servants, and some slaves—black, but mostly Native peoples—made up the poorer classes.[14] Scorned by the ruling classes, they were sometimes the victims of poverty, subjected to working conditions of near slavery. The idle ones and the soldiers were more often the troublemakers than were the working members of society. As for the slaves, they were considered assets that, after the death of their masters, were treated in the same manner as domestic animals.

Claude de Ramezay came to Canada in 1685 as a lieutenant. He later became governor of Trois-Rivières, then a longtime governor of Montréal, and finally the acting governor of New France in 1715 and 1716. He was famous for building projects, including his mansion in Montréal, and entrepreneurial activity in lumbering. Created in 1635, the post of governor was responsible for the military and foreign affairs of the colony, such as relations with Native peoples and the English.

THE PERIOD from 1608 to 1645 witnessed the foundation of the three main cities in New France and marked the beginnings of a colony in which the economy was not entirely sustained by fisheries. Québec, at first a trading post between the French and the Native peoples, slowly developed into an important business and commercial center because of its port and maritime activity. After the treaty of Saint-Germain-en-Laye of 1632, when French authorities regained control over New France, Québec replaced Tadoussac as a terminal for oceanic crossings. Ships stopped there to drop off travelers, immigrants, and products needed for colonial life. The Montréal and Trois-Rivières traders went to Québec to do business with local vendors and representatives of the metropolitan ship owners. It became necessary to build warehouses to store merchandise arriving in Québec that belonged to merchants and religious communities. Later, warehouses were added for the king and the Compagnie d'Occident. The well-protected port of Québec harbored many sailing ships, though they could make only one transatlantic round-trip crossing per year because the port was blocked with ice for nearly six months each winter. The crossing from France to Québec lasted an average of eight to ten weeks, with six or seven weeks to return. During the summer months—June through October— life in Québec had an intense, active rhythm, one connected with the unloading and loading of ships and the mail exchange. Within a relatively brief time, Québec turned into a thriving import-export center.

The fur trade constituted the main economic activity in New France and made up most of the exports leaving the port of Québec in the seventeenth century. Native peoples trapped the furs, and French businessmen monopolized their export. Even so, international Anglo-Dutch competition restrained the activities of the French companies. Faced with failure, the monopolies changed hands, and in 1645 members of the Cent Associés leased their monopoly to the Communauté des Habitants, comprised of Canadian lords and merchants. This group perpetuated the same monopolistic practices, but profits from the sale of fur in France now went to Canadian interests. After they defeated the Hurons in 1649, the Iroquois forced Canadians to collect the furs that the Hurons used to bring to them. Pierre-Esprit Radisson and Jean-Baptiste Chouart Des Groseilliers, among others, then became freelance, unregulated fur traders, the *coureurs de bois*. The arrival of furs in the St. Lawrence Valley remained highly sporadic, and New France was nearly ruined by the time Louis XIV decided to take control in 1663.

As a royal colony, New France was handed over to the Compagnie des Indes for a period of ten years. The Compagnie, responsible for population and governmental duties, received certain rights to the fur business, which, for the first time since the sixteenth century, was completely free. The arrival of the Carignan-Salières regiment of twelve hundred men and the military campaigns of the marquis de Tracy pacified the Iroquois threat and opened a route to the Great Lakes. In order to control the Iroquois, the colonial authorities established military posts along Lake Ontario.

Marie-Charlotte Denys de la Ronde was a member of one of New France's leading families. On 8 November 1690 she married Claude de Ramezay in Québec, and she became actively involved in his commercial pursuits in addition to bearing him nine children. She continued to operate her husband's sawmill, considered a male occupation, after his death in 1724.

Above. Early French farmers in the St. Lawrence Valley tilled the soil with hoes. After 1650 plows, such as this one from the late eighteenth century, were used in New France to work fields of wheat, oats, barley, and corn. Vegetables, orchards, and livestock also contributed to the colonial diet.

Below. Members of the Attikamek Nation, who live north of the St. Maurice River in Québec, built this modern canoe in the traditional manner. Rapids, waterfalls, and ice made navigation on the St. Lawrence River and its tributaries difficult. Canoes were remarkably adapted to such conditions. Light and narrow, they could go farther upriver than other kinds of boats, and men could carry them on their backs around most obstacles.

Right. Found in a cave on an island in the St. Lawrence River, this French axe could have been used to cut firewood, a major cash crop at Québec. European-manufactured axes also served as trade items in North America.

Opposite. Enslaved people of African descent were purchased through elaborate European networks. This 1744 deed of emancipation for a black slave in New France reads in part, "I have granted his freedom to Jean Francois Dominique Mentor, my negro, immediately upon my death in recompense for the good services he has rendered me and for the devotion and loyalty he has always shown in my service. . . . He may take with him all he may require for his service."

4 mars 1745 Deposé par un notre chou

no 2376

Aujourdhuy ~~au~~ par devant les
notaires royaux de la jurisdictio[n] Royalle
de Montreal y residents soussignez, est
Comparu sieur Dominique nafrechou
Demeurant ordinairement a la longue
pointe tant ce jour en cette ville, lequel
a apporté et deposé a nou Dauré Lunde,
& notaires soussignez un papier cacheté
de deux cachets de cire rouge avec
empreinte d'un aigle dont la suscription
porte liberté a condée au mentor, après en
un amour, pour etre mis rang au ~~o~~ en ses
minuttes luy en delivrer toutes Expeditions
necessaires traques il y appartiendra &c
dont acte celuy et roy quy fu fait le
passé au d Montreal l'onze de du dit
Dauré l'an mil sept cens quarante cinq
le quatre mars de relevée en signe
L'un ne faille Deux mots Barez nuls
tau
& Declarant au surplus led sr nafre chou
qu il veut et entend que le dev en terroir au
sa liberté qu a sa dittio qu il le servir a
fidellement en jurques il jnstans de son
deceds en effets or qu il ait obmis ce dans sa
Declaration voulant en outre qu il L'emporte
avec luy son lit en hardes a son usage

Nafrechou

Themas   Dauré Lunde

When the allied Native peoples gathered around these forts and no longer went east, they deprived those in Montréal of important fur resources. With the end of the Iroquois raids, Canadians went farther into the forests to trap the furs that the Hurons had formerly collected. Various means of transportation borrowed from the original inhabitants—canoes, snowshoes, and sleighs—served the trappers well. Forest excursions quickly became more frequent, especially with the explorations of Louis Joliet, Jacques Marquette, and Robert La Salle on the Mississippi. This development allowed more European goods to reach Native peoples, thus creating greater demand and growth in the fur business.

Louis XIV retained control over New France in 1674 and granted farmers in the western domain a monopoly on the sale of Canadian furs, along with a commitment to buy all of the Canadian fur in exchange for certain fees. This assured market and uncontrolled trapping led to overproduction, with more furs being sent to France than were needed. The authorities then tried to do away with trapping while still maintaining military posts around the Great Lakes. Through the spread of trapping and missionary evangelism, the borders of the colony expanded and the cost of business grew. The need to provide ever-increasing amounts of equipment and provisions to face longer voyages forced merchants to consolidate. Unable to eliminate trapping completely, colonial authorities tried to control it by introducing trading permits in 1681. The authorized number of seventy-five boats was quickly exceeded as a result of political pressure exerted by friends of those in power.

Overproduction continued. While France's annual consumption of furs stayed at approximately forty-five thousand pounds, Canadian production was around one hundred fifty thousand pounds from 1675 to 1685. The accumulation of furs, combined with a change of fashion in the hat industry, limited the demand for Canadian beaver pelts. This created a real crisis in the fur trade and led to the elimination of trading permits in 1696.

Thanks to two French trappers, Radisson and Des Groseilliers, the English settled in Hudson Bay in 1668. In addition to providing a new way into North America, this region possessed the most beautiful specimens of fur-bearing animals. These two trappers generated plans for commercial development in the area, but their efforts did not raise the necessary funds when they were initially proposed to Canadian authorities. English merchants, however, listened attentively to the Radisson-Des Groseilliers proposals, and this led to the foundation of the Compagnie des Aventuriers de la Baie Hudson (Hudson Bay Adventurers) in 1670. The arrival of the English in Hudson Bay served as a warning for the Canadian colonial merchant class and ultimately threatened the richest source of supply for the Canadian fur industry. In response, importers in Québec founded the Compagnie du Nord in 1682 to counter the English experiment in Hudson Bay. To confront English competition, Canadian authorities also pursued a policy of military aggression. The expeditions of Pierre Lemoyne d'Iberville drove the English out of Hudson Bay, but with the Treaty of Utrecht in 1713 they returned.

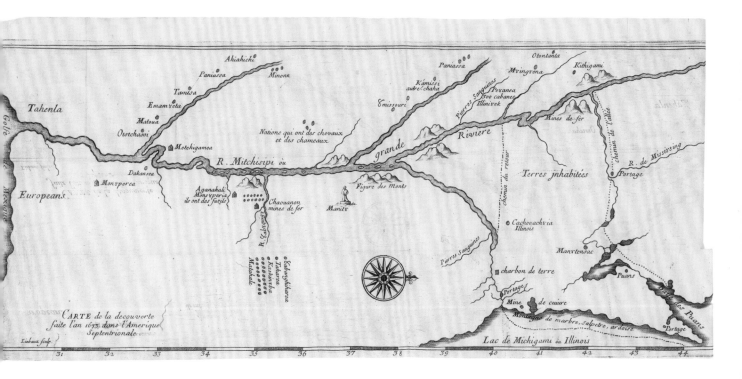

CANADIAN ATTEMPTS to establish a monopoly in fur trading led to a ruinous oversupply of beaver pelts as well as futile efforts to limit competition. All of these surpluses and restrictions encouraged smuggling, a practice that had already been established during previous attempts to suppress trapping and the subsequent abolition of permits. Contraband trade with the English colonies permitted the free flow of goods and payments of duties on the furs. Smugglers also received immediate rewards for their furs. (Those who legally exported furs to France often had to wait a year to receive payment.) Some sources estimate that contraband amounted to two-thirds of Canadian production.

Québec was greatly affected by fluctuations in the fur trade. For its merchants, the ups and downs in furs could mean riches or ruin. After 1650 Native peoples stopped coming to Québec to trade their furs; trading took place mostly in Montréal instead. Although the spread of trappers around the Great Lakes contributed to Québec's decreasing importance in the trade, the city remained the post where all furs that were to leave the territory legally were gathered, stored, and packed. In the same manner, merchandise traded for fur had to pass through Québec.

A drawing by Father Jacques Marquette, a Jesuit missionary, served as the basis for this 1681 *Map of the Discovery Made in the year 1673 in North America,* which shows the upper Mississippi River. Marquette arrived at Québec City in 1666 and spent a year at Trois-Rivières learning Indian languages. In 1669 he founded a mission at the western extremity of Lake Superior, where he made contact with the Illinois. Four years later he and Louis Joliet located the Mississippi River and explored it to near the modern border of Arkansas and Louisiana.

Opposite. About 1700 a *voyageur* or *coureur des bois* used this wooden cup designed to be hung from a belt. The nomadic lifestyle of a fur trapper and trader appealed to young Frenchmen eager to avoid agricultural labor on a large estate, or seigneurie. Until the western trade was legalized in 1681, French officials in Canada often considered them outlaws.

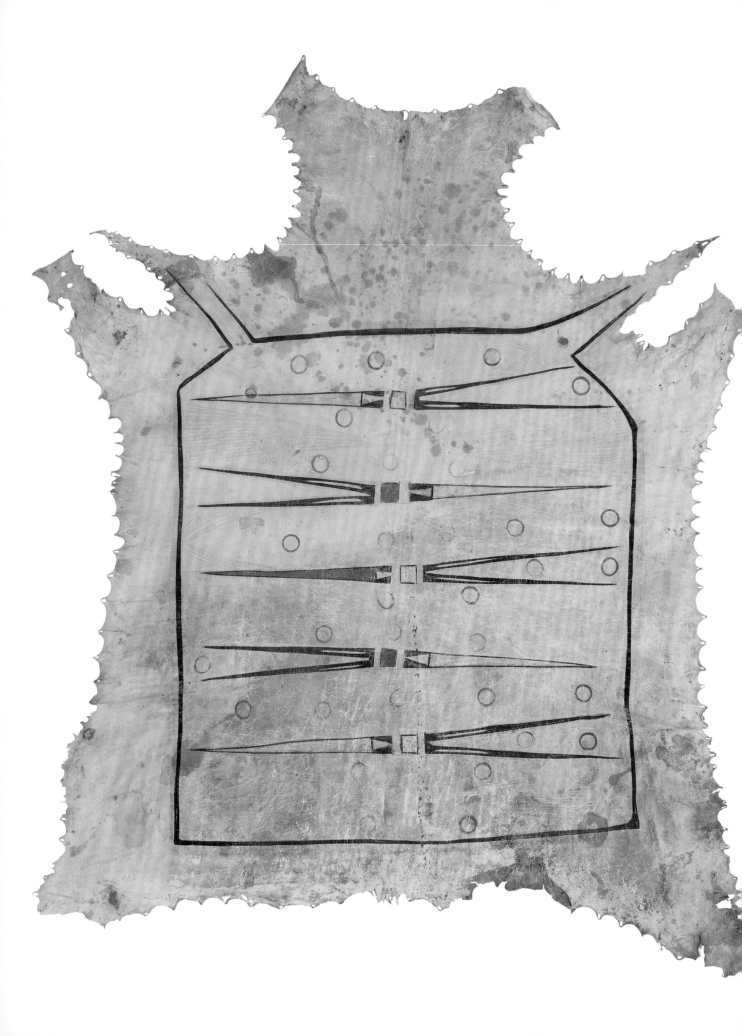

The trading company was the only vendor until 1648, and Canadians did not engage in any commercial activities on an individual basis. Permits granted to Jacques Boisdon to own a hostelry and a pastry shop in the upper city of Québec and to operate a pub for three years represented the first breach in commercial monopolies. In 1654–55 Simon Denys de la Trinité obtained a bakery concession at Rue Sous le Fort. Pierre Denys de la Ronde took over the brewery on the same street.[15] The trading company's progressive retreat from commerce other than fur also led to private individuals engaging in commercial activities, such as fishing for sea perch in the gulf and fishing in the river for salmon, carp, and eels.

Jean Bourdon, Jean-Paul Godefroy, and Louis d'Ailleboust, three Québec residents, founded a company in 1653 to establish a triangular trade among Québec, the West Indies, and France. Jean Talon, *intendant* of Canada from 1665 to 1672, promoted this type of trade. Serving as his mentor was Alexandre Prouville de Tracy, lieutenant general of the French colonies in America, who had spent a year in the West Indies and had come to Canada to subdue the Iroquois. Talon, who wanted to undertake a rational and systematic exploitation of New France while executing Jean-Baptiste Colbert's economic policies, attempted to make Canada self-sufficient and able to supply the kingdom with its own production. He therefore promoted Canadian agriculture, commerce, and industry with a view to revitalize the West Indies in the event France fell short there.[16] About sixty ships participated in this triangular commerce in the thirty years from 1669 to 1699. In the seventeenth century, intercolonial commerce involved New France with the Hudson Bay, because Québec merchants had formed the Compagnie du Nord to collect furs from there under the leadership of Aubert de la Chesnaye, with Plaisance in Newfoundland furnishing wood and lime.[17] This commerce, like the triangular trade, developed even further in the eighteenth century.

In spite of the mercantilism advocated by French authorities, who made the colonies their providers of raw materials and prohibited them from competing with the metropolis, Québec bustled with activity from 1665 to

North American furs appeared in European markets as early as 1570. When large-brim hats made of beaver felt grew into the latest fashion, the Canadian fur trade became highly profitable. French hat makers often sought pelts that had been worn by Native people for two years, which made the animal skins more supple and easy to work. Hunters sometimes used hooks to drag beavers from their lodges. These are from Mingan, a trading post in the province of Québec from 1661 to 1922.

Opposite. The Illinois may have given this painted buffalo or bison hide, used as a garment or mat, to Father Jacques Marquette in 1673 or 1674.

Cardinal Richelieu created the position of *intendant* in France in the 1630s to reinforce royal authority in the provinces. Jean Talon, the first *intendant* of New France, was responsible for virtually all civil administration. Talon sought to diversify the economy and increase the colony's population. Indeed, the population of Québec soon doubled, growing from 3,200 in 1666 to 6,700 by 1672.

1672. Not only were there preparations for military expeditions and the upkeep of troops, but small industries were also established by the new *intendant*, Talon. In the summer of 1665, 152 flatboats were built in the St. Charles basin to transport the troops of the Carignan-Salières regiment. At the initiative of Talon, a 120-ton ship was built in 1667, and five years later work was started on two ships, of five hundred and eight hundred tons, respectively. The rigging, ironwork, and pulleys came from France. In spite of the sawmill installed by Talon, the lumber trade remained limited because of the shortage of ships. The manufacture of beer never really flourished because the Canadians preferred wine and strong spirits. Talon's brewery, capable of producing four thousand barrels a year, closed its doors shortly after the departure of the *intendant.* More successfully, Talon established tanneries in order to manufacture shoes. An effort to produce potash began under Talon's administration, as did the manufacture of soap and bleaching products. Local inhabitants were reluctant to contribute cinders from their fireplaces, however, which prevented the industry from becoming profitable. The production of bricks, tiles, and slate in the two brickyards built under Talon's orders was somewhat successful in the seventeenth century, providing materials for homes, powder magazines, and kitchens.[18]

Talon's departure caused a marked slowdown in the development of Canadian production beyond fur. The naval industry was limited to small troop transports until the eighteenth century. After 1672, war with Holland caused economic stagnation that resulted in the departure of merchants from Québec, and with them a flight of their meager capital. The fire that destroyed a large part of the lower city in 1682 reduced the capital available for commerce. Processing wheat to make bread and crackers was then one of the most important food industries in Québec. In 1685 four mills inside or near the town produced flour to sell in Québec or to supply the crews of merchant sailing ships and fishing boats.

Starting in 1670 and until the end of the century, nearly twenty-five hundred soldiers debarked at Québec. At first, their keep and lodging were guaranteed in town, even though the cost of fortifications and military expeditions was considerable. Day laborers and port workers, navigators, craftsmen and civil servants, carriage drivers, officers of the western domain who regulated the rights to enter and leave, and military personnel all made Québec a burgeoning city. [19] Several inns and taverns, along with some small stores, sprang up as a result of commercial and maritime activity. Over the years the excessive exploitation of furs certainly caused a saturation of the European markets, and the beaver trade fell into ruin. Maritime warfare closed commercial outlets, French protection was inadequate, and French businessmen turned to the West Indies. Privateering itself became a commercial enterprise for Québec merchants such as Riverin, Prat, and Gaillard, who sailed the Gulf of St. Lawrence and the Newfoundland banks.

UNDER CHAMPLAIN, Québec's rudimentary government consisted of an administrative system comprised of a lieutenant, an ensign, a king's prosecutor, a lieutenant of the military police, and a clerk. Champlain, who was offended if anyone questioned his authority, had no means to assert himself with the companies during his short stays in Québec. He held command as lieutenant general of the viceroy until his death in December 1635. All authority, military and civilian, then passed into the hands of Charles Jacques Huault de Montmagny, first official governor of New France. A representative of the king and the Compagnie des Cent Associés, he was the only person to make decisions for the entire region and administer justice. Only his lieutenant could substitute for him. A clerk serving as secretary to the governor drew up official documents and also acted as a notary. An engineer and a surveyor completed the administrative structure.[20] The other administrative agents, assistants, and interpreters were employed by the commercial company.

After 1663 the St. Lawrence Valley was divided into three administrative districts, or governments, all placed under the authority of the governor of New France. The latter was also governor of Québec. Although equal in title, the governors of Trois-Rivières and Montréal,

Fashionable in the first half of the eighteenth century, the *justaucorps* was worn over a waistcoat and breeches. With cloth buttons, it was appropriate for civilian everyday use or as formal wear, depending on the quality of the fabric and the amount of trimmings. With brass buttons, it could be part of military dress. Diplomatic meetings with Native people usually involved exchanges of gifts, often clothing, and *justaucorps* were occasionally offered to Native leaders.

as well as later those of Plaisance, Louisiana, and the Isle-Royale, all derived their authority from the governor of Québec.[21] In terms of authority, the situation was similar for the *intendant* and the ordinance officers in the various local governments. Québec was the capital of New France—but a capital that was somewhat itinerant. It was always the official political headquarters of the colony, but from June to September the governor and the *intendant* governed from Montréal, essentially "in connection with the affairs of the savages."[22] They stayed there in order to receive ambassadors of the Native peoples.

Representing the king, the governor held absolute power within the colony. In addition to relations with the original inhabitants, he was responsible for all military questions, both of war and peace, from troops to fortifications. The administration of money to pay troops, fund military operations, and build defensive works was not his responsibility but that of the *intendant*, with whom he drew up the budget for the colony. In collaboration with the bishop, he had to promote religion and protect missionaries. Jealous of the bishop's authority, the governor refused the Church the right to intervene with its sanctions in matters such as the liquor trade. With his authority to issue passports and permits, the governor had an important role in the fur trade. He also appointed the post commanders and granted them the right to bring in merchandise in order to defray their set-up costs. The governor left the police under the authority of the Sovereign Council, of which he was also the president.

The *intendant* was directly responsible for justice, the police, and finances. He exercised total control over finances and could influence the military by authorizing salaries and payment for defense works. He could inquire into all crimes and render final judgments. A late creation, the *intendant* only appeared in New France in 1665. Previously, the governor, assisted by the Trade Council and the company agent, was sufficient for the civil administration of the colony. The *intendant* sat on the Sovereign Council and presided over it in the absence of the governor. With these powers, governors and *intendants* played a major role in urban administration. Town planning, the course and width of roads, the

alignment of buildings, maintenance and cleanliness, animal control, and fire prevention were the objects of their constant attention in Quebec. Setting the price of food and drink, dividing lands, and controlling the port police also fell under their jurisdiction.

The Sovereign Council was essentially a court of justice created in 1663 to hear all civil and criminal cases. Its judgments were final. Although in the beginning the council appointed judges and court officials, it later transferred that responsibility to the *intendant*. Composed of the governor, the *intendant*, the bishop, and five to seven councilors who were appointed by the king upon the recommendation of the governor and the bishop, the Sovereign Council recorded royal edicts, the acts of faith and homage of the nobility, and diverse police regulations. Its ordinance of 11 May 1676 constituted a veritable municipal code for the towns of New France. Through its edicts, the Council took particular interest in the regulation of trade associations, commerce, fire protection, standards of behavior, refuse collection, and hygiene—in other words, issues that greatly affected urban life. It oversaw the weights and measures of the millers, bakers, and butchers, set the hours for the opening and closing of taverns, expelled prostitutes, and forbade vagrancy and begging. To combat poverty, the Sovereign Council instituted the Bureau of the Poor in 1688, which identified the indigent people of Québec, looked for work for those who were able, and organized special collections to subsidize those who were not.[23]

Until 1650 the judicial apparatus consisted of the governor, who directed and judged alone. The seneschal's court, a tribunal created in 1651, constituted a lower court for minor legal issues. At the time of the formation of administrative districts, lower courts appeared with the Court of the Provostship of Québec or of the Bailiwick of Montréal. Their officers, lieutenant general, prosecutors, clerks, and bailiffs conducted investigations for the proceedings. They also ensured compliance with ordinances and regulations by paying unexpected visits to construction sites, bakeries, butcher shops, and taverns. The accused argued their innocence before the courts, while the litigants, whether plaintiff or defendant, established the facts of their cases principally by applying the Custom of Paris to all private law.[24] The civil, criminal, and maritime codes promulgated by Louis XIV from 1670 to 1681 applied to the colony as well. No attorney argued in Québec or in all of New France. The only persons with legal training were the king's prosecutors, who had to establish the guilt of the accused. The other court officials, such as the clerks, bailiffs, notaries, and prosecutors, had no special training, although the judges, the lieutenant general, and the bailiff were generally familiar with the law.

As a police department, the constabulary force, established in the 1670s with its provost and its four or five bowmen, pursued and arrested criminals. If need be, soldiers sought fugitives. In the world of the Native peoples, justice was above all collective, seeking to make amends and provide compensation, while French justice was individual and punitive.[25] Imprisonment existed only while awaiting the proceedings. To make the accused confess to a crime, French authorities used ordinary or extraordinary methods. For example, in order to gain a confession, they sometimes placed the feet or hands of an accused person in the fire or wedged his legs between two planks until his bones were broken. According to the gravity of the offense, the sentence was banishment, being pilloried, whipped, branded with a hot iron, or sent on a galley ship in the Mediterranean. Hanging or quartering, with strangling preceding this final torture, awaited thieves and murderers. An executioner, held in contempt by society, carried out the sentences in public. After the execution in the public square, he displayed the corpse in the market or the lower city of Québec before tossing it in the river or the garbage.

WHO DOES NOT MARVEL, when walking the streets of the old city of Québec, at the beauty of its setting? Erected on a spit of land protruding into the river at the promontory of Cape Diamond, which runs along the majestic St. Lawrence River, Québec is enclosed by two mountain chains, the Laurentians to the north and the Appalachians to the south. The countryside of the île d'Orleans protected its harbor installations to the east, and the stone ramparts on the west are unique in North America. Still fortified, its architectural structure, mainly inherited from the nineteenth century, rises along a network of roads shaped during the previous two centuries by adapting to the uneven topography. Champlain chose this location in 1608 to build his headquarters, since it could be protected by moats and fences that were somewhat reminiscent of medieval castles. These modest beginnings were plagued by difficulties. The rapid construction of lodgings and warehouses using undried wood made repairs necessary

This copper kettle, excavated at the Place Royale in Québec City, would have made an important diplomatic gift or valuable trade item. Such vessels were also used as raw material for making copper tools and jewelry.

two years later, followed by their demolition and rebuilding in 1620.[26] These early structures disappeared during the Great Fire of 1682. After 1615, some employees built other houses and workshops, while the Franciscans set themselves up on the St. Charles, and Louis Hébert established himself on the top of the cliff in 1618. The Jesuits joined the Franciscans after 1625. In 1620 military defense of the site was strengthened by the construction of Fort St. Louis on top of the cliff, a building that also had to be replaced six years later.

AFTER HAVING SERVED as a place to dry eels during the occupation by the Kirke brothers, the fort resumed its role as a fortress with the return of Champlain. Although some buildings were erected at the port, Champlain had the first church, Notre Dame de la Recouvrance, built in Québec near the fort. He distributed large tracts of land on the promontory for agriculture. If Québec, during the administration of Champlain, was only known as a settlement, the arrival of Montmagny changed the prospects. Charged by the Compagnie des Cent Associés to create a city, the governor delineated building regulations according to an extensive plan, rebuilt and enlarged the fort, opened the first roads on the plateau, and made an effort to recover territory already granted to some colonists and to the Jesuits.[27] The male and female religious communities, which were established nearby to take advantage of the security offered by the fort, also received vast tracts of land, a move that affected the entire urban landscape. Though colonists arrived regularly, and numbered two hundred to three hundred people annually after 1632, very few settled in Québec. They preferred instead to live in the surrounding countryside. In November 1650 the Jesuit Paul Ragueneau noted, "Québec is called a city; it would be more accurate to say that, apart from the fort, our house and the two convents, there is nothing to give the appearance of a city, only of a humble village. You can see thirty homes of Frenchmen, dispersed here and there in no particular order."[28]

The assumption of the monopoly of the Compagnie des Cent Associés by the Community of Habitants, the appearance of a trade council and a mayor, the liberal-

ization of wholesale and retail commerce, the creation of a sensechal's court—all these events strengthened Québec's urban foundations. The construction work completed at the fort, the buildings of the religious communities, and the reconstruction of the parish church that burned in 1640 attracted workers to the city. In the middle of the 1650s, the entire lower city was divided into lots with about a hundred construction sites, twice as many as in the upper city. "Nothing has appeared to me to be so fine and magnificent as the situation of the town of Quebec," wrote Governor Frontenac, who took office in 1672, "which could not be better located were it to become the capital of a great empire. One day, but I find, or rather it seems to me, that a very grave error has been committed in allowing private individuals to build houses to suit themselves, and Without any order, because in settlements such as this, which one day may grow to a great size, I believe that one should Consider not only the present situation, but also the future state of things."[29] Impressed by the site of Québec, the new leader was nevertheless shocked by its eccentric layout. In addition, instability caused by the Iroquois menace doubtlessly worked against the full implementation of Montmagny's urban planning.

By 1663 the town trading post of the Champlain years, with its several warehouses and few houses, was no more. Québec now had about a hundred houses, three-quarters of them located in the lower city. The remaining quarter, including the religious and administrative buildings, were situated in the upper part. By the end of the century the number of buildings had doubled. Charles de Monseignat, the governor's secretary, declared in 1690 that "Québec is located across and a little bit above the headland of Levy. It is divided into the upper and lower city, connected only by a single rather steep road. The churches and all the communities are in the upper city. The fort is on the top of the mountain towering over the lower city, where the most beautiful houses are, and where all the merchants live."[30] He also confirmed the commercial character of the lower city and the tremendous importance of its buildings. The increase in construction in this sector made expansion necessary,

Excavation of Champlain's second residence, or *habitation,* in Québec uncovered artifacts, including this tobacco pipe, testifying to the early life of the colonists. The first *habitation* was located on the same site, but a fire in 1682 destroyed whatever remained of either *habitation.*

even on the banks of the river, and above all the development of another quarter on the northeast periphery of the plateau of Québec on lands belonging to the general hospital. This location, where Talon installed his brewery during his tenure, became the site of the palace of the *intendant* after a fire broke out in the lower city in 1682. Following that conflagration, which destroyed approximately fifty buildings, more three- or four-story stone structures were built. Changes were less pronounced in the upper city until the eighteenth century. Although some large stone houses were constructed in the lower city, the most imposing buildings were on the promontory and belonged to the religious communities. Even though built of stone, most of them unfortunately were victims of fire several times.

In 1644 Marie de l'Incarnation, an Ursuline nun, was one of the first to describe in detail the materials used in the buildings in Québec: "There are buildings of stone, wood and of bark. Ours is completely made of stone. . . .

That of the Reverend Father, of Madame our founder, of the Mothers Hospitallers, and of the settled savages, are made of stone. Those of the habitants are half-timbered with stones, and two or three of them also are all made of stone."[31] In the seventeenth century, stone predominated in private homes and large architectural developments, such as convents, churches, and military buildings. Wooden houses, usually warmer than those made of stone, were equally popular. Many of the structures in Québec were half-timbered with stone. This construction technique was brought over from France and consisted of a frame building with stones placed between the wooden posts. Private homes were small, of one-story height in the upper city on rather large lots and of two stories in the lower city, where they occupied the entire front of their narrow properties. The roofs were most commonly made of boards and shingles.[32] The plots of land in both the lower and upper cities often encompassed sheds and small stables for the domestic

A.Redoute du Cap au Diamant.
B.La Catedrale.
C.Les Recolets.
D.Les Iesuites.
E.L'hotel Dieu.
F.Les Vrselines.

Veüe de la Ville de Quebec en Canada N̄
Septentrionale, auec Eueché dependent du S.̄ Siege. veue du cot̄

animals that many Québec residents kept. In the upper city the larger plots of land allowed people to keep gardens and sometimes grow fruit trees.

After the 1650s a network of roads was put in place in the entire town with the concession for plots of land. The steep road to which Monseignat alluded represented one of the two first roadworks in Québec, for in 1621–23 Champlain constructed a road to link the lower city to the fort built on the cape. Another project was the road joining the city to the settlement of Franciscan monks on the St. Charles. The streets in the lower city were often narrow, from twelve to sixteen feet wide, with some alleys and dead ends. In the upper city, the streets ranged from twenty to thirty-six feet wide and often had to skirt large properties, but above all, they had to conform to the declivity of the terrain. At the end of the century, new streets were opened on the seminary and other institutional properties. In both the upper and lower cities, and in spite of the wishes of the people, none of the roads was paved. A small canal snaked in the middle of the streets for sewage. With the rains and the melting snow, the streets of beaten earth were often muddy and full of potholes. Debris from construction, firewood stacked outside houses, the steps, and the large staircases of the multistory houses of the lower city often encroached upon the public roadway. Animals roamed freely in the streets and hindered traffic. Hygiene in Québec, without the services of garbage collectors, left much to be desired as the city grew. [33] The small plots of land often caused rubbish and animal dung to end up in the street, despite the prohibitions of the Sovereign Council. Not all of the residents had carts to get rid of their waste; those who did usually dumped it in the river. Some residents, especially in the lower city, had no latrines, and chamber pots were sometimes emptied in the streets once night fell. Besides the foul smells, all of this detritus harmfully affected public health.

Defense, whether facing Europe or the interior of North America, was an important concern for Québec's inhabitants throughout the seventeenth century. Even before Champlain confronted the Native peoples, his ships were attacked by Basque pirates along the Tadoussac

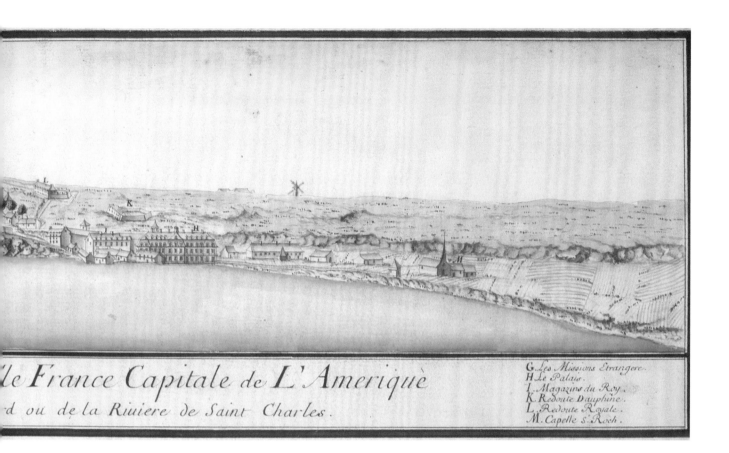

le France Capitale de L'Ameriquè
d ou de la Riuiere de Saint Charles.

G. *Les Missions Etrangere.*
H. *Le Palais.*
I. *Magazins du Roy.*
K. *Redoute Dauphine.*
L. *Redoute Royale.*
M. *Capelle S.t Roch.*

in June 1608.[34] By surrounding his dwelling with moats and stockades and by strengthening it with cannons, Champlain tried to protect the city and himself against the possible hostility of Native peoples. When he erected his fort on the promontory, thus commanding "the settlement and the course of the river," Champlain was aware of Sir Samuel Argall's attacks on Acadia and of the Franco-English rivalries on the Atlantic. [35] Unfortunately, that was not enough to convince the commercial companies to populate and better fortify Québec, which fell into the hands of the Kirke brothers in 1629. The first skirmishes on the St. Lawrence River date back to 1628. With the establishment of outposts in Trois-Rivières and above all in Montréal in 1634 and 1642, Québec was less vulnerable to the Iroquois. The destruction of the Huron country and an increase in Iroquois incursions into the St. Lawrence Valley brought that vulnerability to the forefront. The fort of Québec, with its double wall of earth and wood on the west side and its batteries of cannons as protection against a river attack, was then enlarged. A stockade encircled a Huron encampment next

As seen in this "View of the City of Québec in Canada, New France, Capital of America," which dates from about 1721, Québec City resembled Brest and other French port cities. The lower town adjoined a large harbor to shelter ships, but the port was bound by ice half the year. Religious and government buildings were located in the upper town. The fortifying wall, begun in 1690, served as protection against English invasion.

An example of a high-status object used in early New France, this armchair in the style of Louis XIII (reigned 1610–43) was made later in the seventeenth century. It is typical of the colonial furniture of Jamestown, Québec, and Santa Fe in that it would have been considered old-fashioned in Europe at the time of its creation in New France.

to the fort. The convent of the Ursulines, the college of the Jesuits, the mill of Simon de la Trinité on the cape—all of these buildings with their stone walls were transformed into defensive redoubts with sentinels.

The prospect of European-style attacks with pitched battles and sieges of fortified towns, brought on by English rivalries with Holland and France, forced a change in strategy concerning Québec. It was necessary to fortify the city, which was open to the countryside on the west, the only sector not protected by the cliffs of Cape Diamond and well-installed batteries. In 1664 the engineer Jean Bourdon proposed constructing a wall bastioned in the arc of a circle to enclose the city. The treaties of Bréda and Aix-la-Chapelle in 1667 and 1668 brought peace to Europe and made the proposed fortification less urgent. Louis de Buade, comte de Frontenac, tried to start again on his planned walls, but the Anglo-Dutch Wars of 1672–78 placed too great a financial burden on France for it to invest in defensive fortifications in Québec. The pacification of the Iroquois after the arrival of the Carignan-Salières regiment proved temporary. Rather than building defensive fortifications, France sent two contingents of soldiers to Canada by way of the port of Québec during the 1680s. Military reinforcements did not stop the Iroquois from killing several Canadian families in the village of Lachine, on the isle of Montréal, in early August 1689.

War began again in Europe in 1689, pitting France against Holland and England. Wanting to neutralize the Iroquois, the French launched several frontier raids against English colonists who bought furs from the Iroquois. In the face of Iroquois threats and the American danger, Frontenac ordered Major François Provost to build in six weeks in the spring of 1690 the first wall closing off Québec on the west.[36] It consisted of a wooden palisade and several stone redoubts. Other construction in Québec stopped, and all citizens were conscripted to perform this work. Still, that same year an English expedition under the command of William Phips of Massachusetts captured Acadia and tried to take Québec. Phips had to return empty-handed because of insufficient time to lay siege to the city before the arrival of winter.

Stockades erected in Canada lasted only three or four years. The engineers Boisberthelot de Beaucour and Levasseur de Néré proposed a new fortification with bastions and terrepleins. After the defeat of the French navy at the Battle of La Hougue and with the circulation of new rumors about attacks against Québec in 1692, and without waiting for royal permission, Frontenac and *Intendant* Champigny launched a fortification project that continued for the next five years. These works imposed different constraints by restricting the available space in the interior of the city, by requisitioning manpower, or by drying up the aqueduct that provided the local hospital with running water. The new fortification constricted the town too tightly, forcing engineers to develop new projects. Not until the middle of the eighteenth century, with a wall built a little further west to allow more space and to prevent the heights from dominating the city, did the people of Québec definitively enclose their city with the ramparts that are still visible today.

SICKNESS was a major concern from the founding of Québec in 1608. That winter, for example, disease nearly eliminated all the French from the area. Only eight of the twenty-eight residents survived scurvy. For sailors and travelers, the confined world of a ship during the weeks that it took to cross the Atlantic was not favorable for hygiene. Conserving drinking water on board was difficult; eating fresh meats and fruits, sources of needed vitamins, was rare. Storms often prevented stoves from being lit for cooking. Travelers had to wear wet clothes for prolonged periods of time. All of these conditions fostered illness.[37] And when a sailing ship docked at Québec, there was no quarantine service to receive the crews and isolate those suffering from fevers. The sicknesses transported on board, combined with the poor hygienic conditions that prevailed in Québec, sometimes ravaged the town and colony. Within a period of three months in 1703, approximately 350 people out of 2,000 died from smallpox in Québec.

Seventeenth-century medicine was an art practiced by physicians and surgeons who were often ignorant of the causes of disease and who sometimes administered

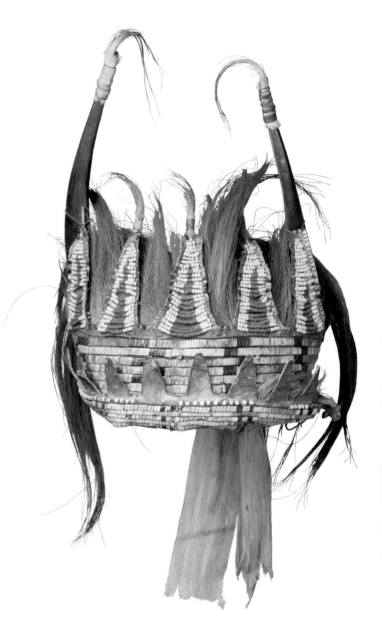

This Native ceremonial headdress of horsehair, horn, beads, and porcupine quills originated in the Great Lakes region of New France.

Above. Jacques Le Ber, a merchant and noble seigneur, or lord, journeyed to Canada in 1657. As a member of the Militia of the Holy Family, created to defend Montréal against the Iroquois, he risked his life several times to protect the city. In keeping with the veneration of relics of saints, martyrs, or sacred persons, this frame contains a fragment of Le Ber's remains.

Right. Those operating fur monopolies worried that immigration would introduce competitors and expanding settlements would drive away fur-bearing animals. Under royal rule, however, officials recruited hundreds of *filles du Roy* (king's girls) to become wives for workers in New France. This child's commode chair serves as a reminder that complete families resided in early New France.

inappropriate medication. While physicians had a university education, surgeons were primarily barbers who had received rudimentary practical training from their colleagues. Surgeons who arrived in Canada with contingents of soldiers frequently made extensive use of bleeding and purging. As physicians of the king, only three or four doctors ventured to New France before 1760 to supervise the surgeons and hospitals in the colony. The first one, the brilliant Michel Sarrasin, arrived in Québec in 1683. A correspondent of the Academy of Science in Paris, he conducted research in anatomy, botany, and zoology, as did his accomplished successor Jean-François Gaultier. Sarrasin performed complex operations and amputations. In 1700 he completed the first excision of a breast cancer in New France, and until his death in 1734 people came from everywhere in the colony to be treated by him at the Québec hospital.[38]

Nursing at that time in France and in the colonies was practiced by male or female members of religious communities. In 1639 three nurse nuns landed in Québec to take care of all the sick, both French and Native peoples. They were installed originally in a building of the Cent Associés company, and between 1640 and 1644 they moved to Sillery, three miles outside town, to care for Native peoples with smallpox.[39] Threats of an Iroquois attack drove the nurses back to Québec, where they welcomed other nuns from France and a first Canadian member in 1648. They built their hospital in the upper city in 1654 and enlarged it twenty years later. Two rooms with a maximum capacity of fifty beds separated the men from the women. Hospital stays were free of charge at that time, with the king paying for sick officers and soldiers.

Nursing the sick included caring for old people, people without families, the poor, and the physically and mentally handicapped. To provide for their needs, the second bishop of Québec, Monsignor de St.-Vallier, established his general hospital in 1691 on the rue St. Charles in a monastery building bought from the Franciscans. The hospital replaced housing created several years earlier for the poor. The Church gave them

a shelter where they could, if they worked, enjoy the fruits of their labor. In France, poverty was managed by the state, and if a poor man was jailed, his work profited the directors.[40] The Poor House, created in 1688 to combat public begging, was the first in North America. In 1655 surgeon Etienne Bouchard in Montréal initiated a private insurance system for some thirty families.[41] For a payment of five francs annually, he promised to treat, bandage, and medicate them, but he would not treat infectious diseases, such as the plague or smallpox.

When Champlain appealed to the Franciscan order in 1615 and to the Jesuits ten years later, he acted according to the faith of his time, which sought to save unbelievers and non-Catholics. The point of converting Native peoples by assimilating them into French culture was to populate the colony without draining metropolitan France of its own citizens. These conversions could not occur without the teaching of French values. In France, education was the responsibility of the religious orders. Their passage to Canada was thus aimed at transmitting the values of French society to nations that shared neither its faith nor its law. Just as Champlain sent young Frenchmen to the Native peoples to learn their languages, the missionaries went into the woods with the same goal. They could profit from the expertise acquired by Brûlé, Marsolet, and other interpreters who worked for Champlain. The Franciscans and the Jesuits first wanted to open seminaries for Native peoples. At their monastery near Québec, the Franciscans taught at most ten young men between 1617 and 1629.[42] They chose to separate the young people from their elders to avoid parental influence. The seminaries did not teach any practical subjects to the Native peoples, who rebelled against the discipline and fled the institutions. Unlike the Franciscans, the Jesuits did not want to assimilate the indigenous peoples into French culture in order to convert them. Instead, they tended to settle them in an effort to teach them more easily and to isolate them both from Native practices that clashed with Roman Catholicism and from European immorality.

Although specialized in advanced education, in 1635 the Jesuits opened a primary school for boys in Québec to satisfy the demands of parents and to prepare candidates for secondary school. Primary instruction was centered first of all on religious instruction, reading, writing, and arithmetic.[43] Even though they adapted their disciplinary methods and used Native languages to communicate, the Jesuits did not convince their students. Native youths were not as malleable as had been expected, and they were extremely attached to their lifestyle. It was easier for a Frenchman to become a "savage" than for a "savage" to become a Frenchman, wrote Marie de l'Incarnation to explain the difficulty of assimilating Native peoples. The destruction of the Hurons and the incursions of the Iroquois forced the Jesuits to retreat to Québec and dedicate themselves to educating whites. Although some missionaries returned to France, most of them settled in Québec. Their school offered first a commercial course and then a course in the humanities. By 1670 some sixty students, whites only, attended the school.[44]

When New France became a royal colony, Minister Colbert again insisted that the Native peoples be assimilated into French culture. In response, Monsignor de Laval opened a small seminary in Québec for Native and French boarders. The results were no better than what the Jesuits and the Franciscans had previously achieved, and for the same reasons. The young whites studying for the priesthood boarded at the seminary and studied at the Jesuit school. The secular priests of French origin, whom the bishop employed in his parishes, found it difficult to adapt to the country. Pastors had to be found locally for the Canadian church, and so the idea arose of a great seminary to provide their training. The first native-born priest in Québec was ordained in 1665, and twenty years later the Church had eleven Canadians in its ranks. Several men who were registered at the seminary left because of lack of talent or an incompatible disposition for the clerical life and instead turned to other fields of study. One of these men from Québec who abandoned an ecclesiastical career was Louis Joliet, the future explorer of the Mississippi.[45]

In 1667 he defended a thesis in philosophy before Bishop Laval, Governor Courcelles, and Administrator Talon. To train craftsmen Monsignor de Laval opened a school of arts and trade under the direction of the seminary. In their school, the Jesuits taught courses in navigation, mathematics, and hydrography to prepare future pilots and ship captains.

Education for girls was left to female religious communities. Hélène Boulé, the first female educator in Québec, taught catechism from 1620 to 1624 to a few Native girls. Only upon the arrival of the Ursulines in 1639 was there a sustained effort to teach Native and French girls. Before instructing them in reading and counting, however, the nuns taught home economics to the Native peoples and the whites to make them pious women and good mothers. The Ursulines studied Native dialects using lexicons and dictionaries prepared by the Franciscan and Jesuit orders. In general, the girls seemed more receptive to instruction than the boys. Between sixty and eighty Native girls attended the Ursuline convent school in 1663 in separate classes. Mixing Europeans and indigenous peoples in classes was a failure. The presence of Native peoples in the convent declined after 1680 to no more than ten young women.

With the religious communities and the secular priests involved in education, a whole cultural universe opened to the people in Québec. Beginning early in the seventeenth century, music was part of all the religious rites. Accounts of the time most often mention flutes, violins, and especially trumpets.[46] The Ursulines attracted Native girls with instruction in violin, and musical instruments were used during Mass. Starting in 1657, a musician played the organ in the church of Notre Dame. The Jesuit school taught singing and in 1666 hired François du Moussart, a nineteen-year-old drummer of the Carignan-Salières regiment, as a music professor. In the school of arts and crafts opened by the seminary, painters, wood sculptors, and goldsmiths were trained to work mainly in religious art. Books and reading were also part of the life of the people of Québec. Religious orders and schools used them to meet their cultural and

Showing the blending of European design
with a traditional Native medium, this
hide robe was decorated in the Louis XIV
style by a Native person in New France.

educational needs, but books circulated in other environments as well. In the last decade of the seventeenth century, for example, books appeared in 35 percent of the inventories of wills drawn up by residents.[47] The quantities of books were limited, with two or three volumes per household, but the contents were diverse, led by theology, with science and art books approximately equal. History, literature, and law were also represented.

In addition to schools, the people of Québec discovered the theater. Students produced plays by Corneille and Racine and presented them to the governor. Martial Piraube, Montmagny's secretary, produced a play in 1640 to celebrate the birth of Louis XIV. At the end of the century, Frontenac had the work of Molière presented in the theater. This provoked the anger of Bishop St.-Vallier, who considered comedy as reprehensible as dance.[48] The quarrel between the governor and the bishop over theatrical performances lasted until the conquest of New France. No doubt other less intellectual distractions were offered to the Québec public. Each summer the arrival of ships bringing important persons were occasions for celebration. For instance, Chartier de Lotbinière gave a reception in 1667 to celebrate his appointment as lieutenant general of the district. The erection of a "maypole" in front of Fort St.-Louis each year was the cause for bonfires.[49] In winter, Christmas after the abstinence of Advent and the days of Carnival just before Lent were times to eat well and dance. The clergy had difficulty trying to keep people from celebrating too much. Craftsmen, sailors, and soldiers played cards, threw dice, and bowled in the streets; merchants and officials preferred chess, backgammon, and card games.

As a port city and the capital of New France, Québec had a large number of hotels.[50] The signs that marked inn and tavern entrances, such as the Ville de la Rochelle of Jean Maheu or the Signe de la Croix of Laurent Normandin, attracted civilians, sailors, and the military. The 1716 census listed one such establishment for every hundred people, or approximately twenty-five of them. When hotel operations took place in private homes,

Originally designed to instruct young Louis XIV, this playing card published in Paris in 1644 or 1645 shows a Native person of Virginia. The text explains that Virginia is located next to New France.

Opposite. This is the oldest known bell in Canada, dated 1666. That year, surgeon Robert Giffard, first physician of the hospital (*Hôtel-Dieu*) of Québec as well as a local seigneur, or lord, paid for a bell for the first parish church, built around 1662. It was cast in France and sent to the Beauport Chapel. The bell bears the letter *L* for King Louis XIV as well as the royal emblem, the fleur-de-lis.

Copper was a valued commodity among the Native allies of New France. This French coin of 1722, called a *sou,* reads "Colonies Françaises" and may have been used as a gift or trade item.

Opposite. One of the stallions that King Louis XIV of France sent to Canada between 1665 and 1670 is illustrated in this watercolor. Some of the first horses brought to Canada were from the Perche region and are known as Percherons.

every family member was required to adapt. As fellow workers and managers, women were a key presence in the hotel business. For many families, operating an inn provided an important additional source of income. Unlike employment that took place outside the home, in a workshop, or sometimes in a store, the hotel business was a real family enterprise.

SELECTED for its eminently defensible location and its proximity to furs, the site of Québec was urbanized slowly amid concern over its safety. The port was locked by ice for six months a year, and this inhibited aggressive inclinations by any competitors who did not want to be trapped by the river. The location also greatly slowed down migrations and remunerative commercial exchanges. Québec's economy, which was based solely on the fur trade, made it sensitive to the whims of the market as well. It was a commercial town and the political capital of a vast colony with frontiers that expanded as quickly as canoes could advance along the waterways. That expansion thus drained it of a part of its energy, but throughout the colonial period, Québec was the largest population center in New France.

From 1608 to 1760, tens of thousands of Frenchmen followed the steps of Champlain. More than six thousand landed at the port of Québec in the seventeenth century, coming from all the regions of France and mostly from modest circumstances. Like Champlain, they yearned for discovery and adventure, but they were sometimes too inclined to impose their values on their new environment. In their attempt to build a better world for themselves, they brought the political-economic rivalries of Europe to North America. The political unity of New France, governed by Québec, had the power to confront the English colonies at the turn of the eighteenth century. By mid-century, however, New France, with a population of sixty thousand spread from Acadia to Louisiana, faced 1.2 million English-speaking people to the south along the Atlantic Coast. Demographics were pushing the English westward, and they were poised to enter into conflict with New France. The shock was unavoidable and its conclusion was inevitable.

Vu des Etalons que Louis Le
grand fit Envoyer avec soisante belles jumens dans
La Nouvelle france jl y a plus de trente ans dou
son sortis de stras debses beau chevaux comme
nous Lauons vu —

David J. Weber

Santa Fe

Detail of *The Assumption of the Virgin,*
c. 1700, attributed to Juan Correa.

From 1540 to 1542 Francisco Vázquez de Coronado sought in vain for the nonexistent city of Cíbola, shown on this 1556 map. He was disappointed to find neither gold nor silver, only agriculturally based Native pueblos.

Opposite. This eighteenth-century family tree of Martínez de Montoya, notarized by Spanish officials, suggests Santa Fe was settled earlier than 1610, the year many textbooks have stated it was established.

SANTA FE has remained continuously occupied since its founding in 1608, serving as New Mexico's capital under Spain, Mexico, and the United States. Only two European communities have had a longer history of continuous occupation: St. Augustine, founded in 1565 by the Spanish, and Jamestown, established by the English in 1607. French Québec had its beginnings in the same year as Santa Fe.

The origins of Santa Fe are the most obscure of these earliest European settlements. It is known that in 1608 a few Spanish colonists led by Captain Juan Martínez de Montoya established a tiny settlement at the foot of the Sangre de Cristo Mountains at a place they named Santa Fe, after their holy faith. The next year the viceroy of New Spain, Luis de Velasco, referred to that fledgling village by name when he sent a new governor and captain general, Pedro de Peralta, to New Mexico with a small military retinue and a few priests. Peralta carried instructions to found a chartered town, or *villa,* at the site where settlers in New Mexico had already begun to build the new community at Santa Fe, some fifteen hundred miles north of Mexico City, the viceregal capital.[1]

Spaniards had scoured New Mexico long before Peralta's appointment, but Santa Fe was the first town in the province that they built from the ground up. As early as 1540 Francisco Vázquez de Coronado had come north from Mexico and forcibly lodged himself among Native people whom Spaniards would come to call "Pueblos." Spaniards named New Mexico's sedentary inhabitants for the towns, or *pueblos*, in which they lived, in sharp contrast to the hunters and gatherers whose lands Spaniards had passed through to get there. Coronado had burst into the Pueblos' world with high hopes of finding treasure and wealthy inhabitants. Finding neither, he withdrew his forces in 1542.

The permanent European occupation of New Mexico got under way a half century later, in 1598, when a small army—about 130 men of fighting age—took possession of New Mexico for the Spanish crown. These Spaniards (that is, Hispanicized people, whatever their ethnicity or race, who considered themselves subjects of the Spanish crown) traveled north from Mexico with their wives,

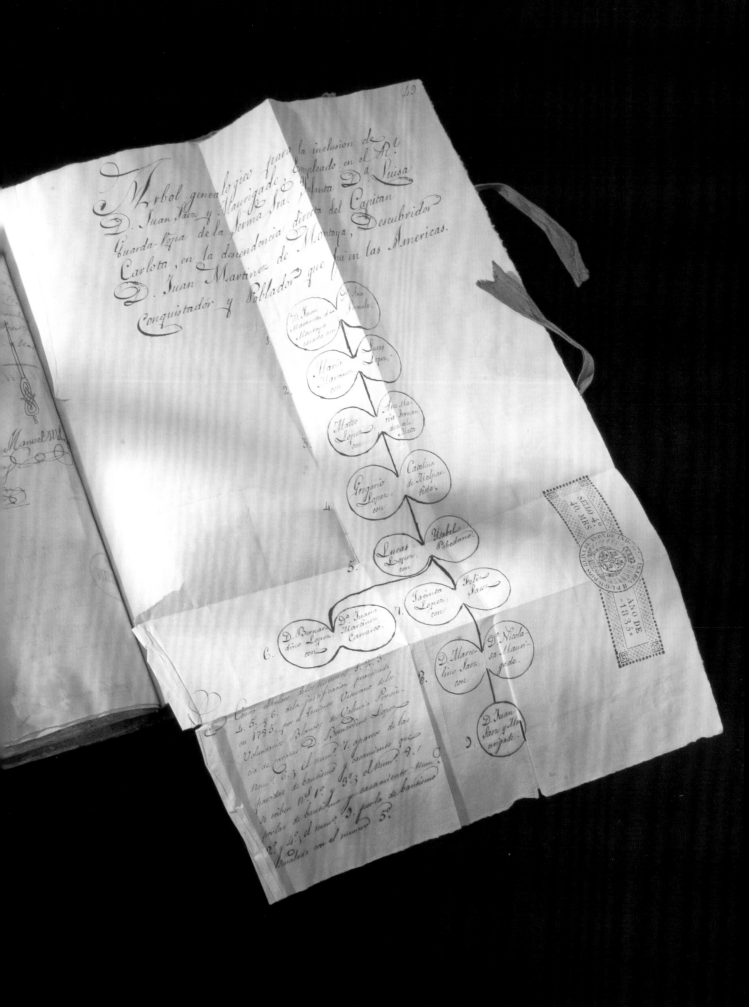

Philip III of Spain considered abandoning the New Mexico colony in 1608, but Franciscan missionaries persuaded him that the souls of converted Natives might be lost if he did so. The colony cost ninety pesos of expenses for each one of income it provided.

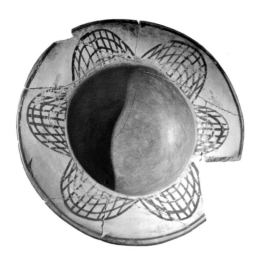

Although the soup-bowl form was unknown in New Mexico before Spanish settlement, it was adopted by the local Native peoples, as seen with this Tewa polychrome ceramic bowl from the pueblo of Cuyamungue.

Opposite. John K. Hillers photographed Taos Pueblo in 1880.

children, Native servants, and ten priests—over five hundred in all—to a place so remote that it stood eight hundred miles beyond the nearest Spanish settlement, the mining town of Santa Bárbara. King Felipe II had authorized the group's leader, the *adelantado* Juan de Oñate, heir to a mining fortune, to enter the Native-controlled territory of New Mexico.

Although he made his *entrada* into New Mexico under the color of Spanish law, Oñate broke that law by settling his colonists in Native towns—towns of Tewa-speaking Pueblos. Oñate made his first headquarters at Ohke, on a rich alluvial flood plain on the east side of the Rio Grande about twenty miles north of present-day Santa Fe. With steel and gunpowder, Spaniards occupied the Pueblos' dwellings, renamed the town San Juan de los Caballeros, and forced its residents to feed, shelter, and clothe them. Two years later Ohke became crowded with new Spanish arrivals and with indigenous people whom Spaniards had seized from other pueblos. Oñate moved his colonists out of the village and across the Rio Grande to Yúngé, another Tewa pueblo. This time he evicted most of the residents. Yúngé, which Spaniards renamed San Gabriel, served as New Mexico's capital until Governor Pedro de Peralta arrived and completed the move to Santa Fe that Captain Juan Martínez de Montoya had begun in 1608.

Oñate and his followers had invested their fortunes and risked their lives to invade the lands of the Pueblos. The Spaniards expected to find a new Mexico on the Rio Grande—a place of wealthy Natives, precious minerals, and a waterway through North America that would give them ports on the Pacific and the Atlantic. Like Coronado before him, Oñate failed to understand how the North American continent grew wider from east to west as one traveled north. Oñate's generation knew of the recently established English colony at Roanoke, and he supposed that he could readily reach Roanoke from New Mexico. In 1601 he journeyed out to the buffalo plains, getting at least as far as what is today north-central Oklahoma before he reluctantly turned back. If the mules and oxen that pulled his wooden carts had not become exhausted and his men restive, Oñate believed they could have continued to the Atlantic, "which cannot be very far away."[2]

New Mexico disappointed Oñate as it had Coronado. After losing a half-million pesos of his family's fortune on the enterprise, Oñate hoped to shift the costs from his own purse to the Spanish treasury. Toward that end, he continued to send glowing reports of New Mexico's potential back to the viceroy in Mexico City, but disaffected colonists fled southward with grimmer news. They reported that colonists had quarreled with one another as well as with the Pueblos and that the colony had disintegrated. In 1605 Viceroy Montesclaros recommended removing Oñate as governor, and the next year the king's advisers, the Council of the Indies, agreed. Word traveled slowly back to Mexico, but in August 1607, before the news reached him in New Mexico, Oñate resigned. His colony had come under attack from Apaches and Navajos, and it seemed unlikely that the crown would send reinforcements.

On 27 February 1608 Luis de Velasco, who had replaced Viceroy Montesclaros, accepted Oñate's resignation. The crown would have to decide whether to abandon the province or to maintain what would surely become a money-losing enterprise. Meanwhile, Viceroy Velasco sent word to New Mexico that Captain Juan Martínez de Montoya, who founded Santa Fe later that year, was to replace Oñate as governor.[3] The viceroy's wishes notwithstanding, Martínez never took office. In August 1608 members of the town council, or *cabildo*, at San Gabriel voted to reject him. Oñate's supporters,

who made up the *cabildo,* questioned Martínez's military service and hinted at darker reasons for denying him office. In his place they designated Oñate's son Cristóbal, an eighteen year old who had some experience fighting Apaches but could barely read and write. Unimpressed with his qualifications, the viceroy vetoed the appointment. That same month Martínez left New Mexico in apparent disgust.

Before he ran afoul of the *cabildo* of San Gabriel, Captain Martínez had begun to establish Santa Fe, laying the foundations of what Viceroy Velasco would see as a future *villa.* It is not certain if Martínez began the new settlement under the orders of Oñate, as Oñate's

biographer suggests, or if Martínez started it on his own as head of a faction opposed to Oñate.[4] It does seem clear, however, that Martínez returned to Mexico City in December 1608 with news of the "*villa*" in New Mexico "that was being attempted," thus prompting Viceroy Velasco to instruct the new governor, Pedro de Peralta, to complete the task and found an official *villa* at the site.[5]

Peralta's arrival in New Mexico, some time in late 1609 or early 1610, marked a dramatic change in New Mexico's status. What had been a colony funded and administered by a licensed private entrepreneur, or *adelantado,* with a lifetime appointment (what the English would call a proprietor) became a royal colony

headed by governors on the king's payroll with limited terms in office. The crown knew that remote New Mexico would be a nightmare to maintain. In contrast to its revenue-producing colonies in Peru and in central New Spain, New Mexico would drain the king's coffers as it had the Oñate family's fortune. Nonetheless, royal officials concluded that Spain could not afford to abandon New Mexico. Franciscan missionaries who had accompanied Oñate convinced the viceroy that they had baptized some seven thousand Pueblo peoples.[6] If Spaniards left, the Native peoples would fall into apostasy and their souls would be lost to perdition. As Viceroy Velasco told the king, "We could not abandon the land without great offense to God and great risk of losing what had been gained."[7] Rather than offend God, the crown invested ninety pesos for every peso New Mexico produced in revenue in the decades that followed.[8]

Governor Peralta thus arrived in New Mexico as the head of a colony that existed to promote Christianity. Viceroy Velasco instructed him to see that

the Indians of those provinces [of New Mexico] who are settled peacefully and reduced to our holy Catholic faith be maintained and protected in justice and be properly instructed. In other matters in these provinces you will govern in such a way as to better serve God and me, preventing individual expeditions against the Indians who are not at peace, allowing entradas [incursions into Indian territory] only by friars who may wish to go on apostolic missions to plant our holy faith.

In contrast to Englishmen, who preferred to turn Native peoples into Europeans before converting them to Christianity, Spaniards sought to turn them into Spaniards and Christians simultaneously.[9]

Before all else, however, the viceroy instructed Peralta "to settle or found the *villa* [of Santa Fe] . . . in the shortest possible time in order that the settlers may begin to live in an orderly manner."[10] In contrast to the haphazard growth of towns on the Anglo-American frontier, Spanish towns were, in theory, to rise from the ground in an orderly grid pattern with straight streets, laid out to the points of the compass, and with a full-fledged government. As historian John W. Reps has

This wooden cross from New Mexico, probably dating from the eighteenth century, features a fusion of Hispanic and Native motifs.

Opposite. The Spanish in New Mexico used this comb helmet and breastplate, both of Italian manufacture. Found in a cave, the helmet is engraved on one side with Christ on the cross and a kneeling figure. Our Lady with the Christ child, with a full nimbus of light rays, appears on the opposite side. The breastplate also is engraved with an image of the Virgin and Child.

Juan Correa was a Mexican painter of mixed African and indigenous ancestry, who worked in the European baroque tradition. His paintings, such as *The Assumption of the Virgin* of circa 1700, were exported to New Mexico missions, including one at Pecos Pueblo.

Opposite. Santa Fe appears in the lower right of this circa 1760 map of the New Mexico region. Created as a presentation piece for the viceroy of New Spain in Mexico City, the map of oil on canvas probably was painted there. Bernardo Miera y Pacheco, who made the drawing on which the painted version was based, was a native of Spain who came to New Mexico in 1754.

explained: "To a far greater degree than any of the other colonizing powers in the New World the Spanish followed a system of land settlement and town planning formalized in written rules and regulations."[11]

No description of the founding of New Mexico's new *villa* and capital remains, but Governor Peralta surely would have traveled to Santa Fe to execute the viceroy's orders. There, he would have found that Captain Martínez had sited his village well. Its commanding height allowed early detection of approaching enemies. The grazing lands and dry climate, with its cold winters, mild springs, hot summers, and cool autumns, would have made Spaniards from Castile feel at home.[12] Spanish farmers could also thrive there. "Though cold, the spot is the most fertile in all New Mexico," one enthusiastic friar exclaimed.[13] Indeed, the fertile area in and around Santa Fe had attracted generations of Pueblo people and their predecessors, but happily for Peralta no Native settlement remained on the site.[14] Since royal orders forbade Spaniards from building towns that displaced indigenous people, Peralta could proceed with a clear conscience.

Captain Martínez had selected an uninhabited spot but one with plentiful wood and water as the crown also required. In that land of little rain, he had placed his village hard by a marshland, created by perennial springs and seeps, and next to a mountain-fed stream.[15] Santa Fe sits at the southern tip of the Rockies, at the foot of the Sangre de Cristo Mountains that rise rapidly to twelve thousand feet and often have a snowpack well into June. With spring thaws, the trout-filled Río de Santa Fe rushes down from the Sangre de Cristos through a forest of aspen, spruce, and ponderosa pines before emerging onto the piñón- and juniper-covered tableland where Santa Fe sits at seven thousand feet. From there, the river continues westerly into the Río Grande, nearly two thousand feet below.

In ordering the establishment of a *villa* at Santa Fe, the viceroy envisioned an officially chartered town—a settlement larger than a hamlet or village (*plaza* or *lugar*) but smaller than a city (*ciudad*). The founding and operation of *villas* in Spanish America were to follow the

Ordinances of 1573, a set of detailed regulations that Spaniards adapted to local circumstances by following their spirit rather than their letter.[16]

Viceroy Velasco's orders to Peralta distilled the Ordinances of 1573. He instructed Peralta to establish a town council, or *cabildo,* made up of four *regidores,* or councilmen. Two of the four would serve as *alcaldes ordinarios,* or judges, empowered to hear civil and criminal cases within the *villa* and for five leagues around it. Their

jurisdiction, the viceroy explained, did not extend to Native peoples, who fell directly under the governor or his lieutenant. The *cabildo* was empowered to mark out the physical space that the town would occupy—six "*vecindades,*" or districts, and a rectangular town square for the public buildings. The *cabildo* could also grant land to every citizen of the town—lots for their houses, gardens, vineyards, and olive trees, as well as grazing land and farmland. Individuals who received grants of land

The Pubelo chamber pot was a pottery form introduced by the Spanish.

in Santa Fe had to live in the town for ten continuous years or else lose the rights to their property.[17] Along with the power to allot farmland, the new *cabildo* had the right to distribute water to irrigate it. Without water, land in New Mexico had little value. To water their fields, Santa Fe's earliest residents apparently coerced Native laborers to dig two main ditches, or *acequias madres*, along each side of the Santa Fe River. From those main ditches, smaller *acequias* fed water into individual fields.[18]

Peralta or his designee marked off the *villa's* rectangular town square, or *plaza mayor*, to the north of the Río de Santa Fe and its tributary, the Río Chiquito (today's Water Street), and southwest of the springs and marshland in the area where a smaller version of the plaza still stands today.[19] He may have regarded the wetlands as contributing to the *villa's* defense, but more likely he hoped to situate the community between two sources of water, with the perennial springs being more dependable than the seasonal river. Then, too, it appears that those families who had begun to settle along the Santa Fe River before Peralta's arrival had constructed their homes on the south side of the river, and Peralta did not wish to disturb them.[20]

Santa Fe took shape as Spaniards abandoned Oñate's settlement at San Gabriel and resettled there. It served as New Mexico's new capital and only formally organized Spanish town until 1680. That year, Pueblo people expelled all Spaniards and their Native allies from northern New Mexico and sent them fleeing three hundred miles down the Río Grande. The refugees established their seat of government at El Paso del Norte, at the site of a Franciscan mission on what is today the Mexican side of the river at Ciudad Juárez. Considered part of New Mexico, El Paso became the province's second officially constituted town, after Spaniards returned to reoccupy Santa Fe in 1693.[21]

During the Spaniards' thirteen-year absence from Santa Fe, Pueblo rebels occupied the town. They destroyed the church, government buildings, and other symbols of Spanish power and burned the archives.[22] Scholars seeking to understand seventeenth-century New Mexico must now rely on the work of archaeologists

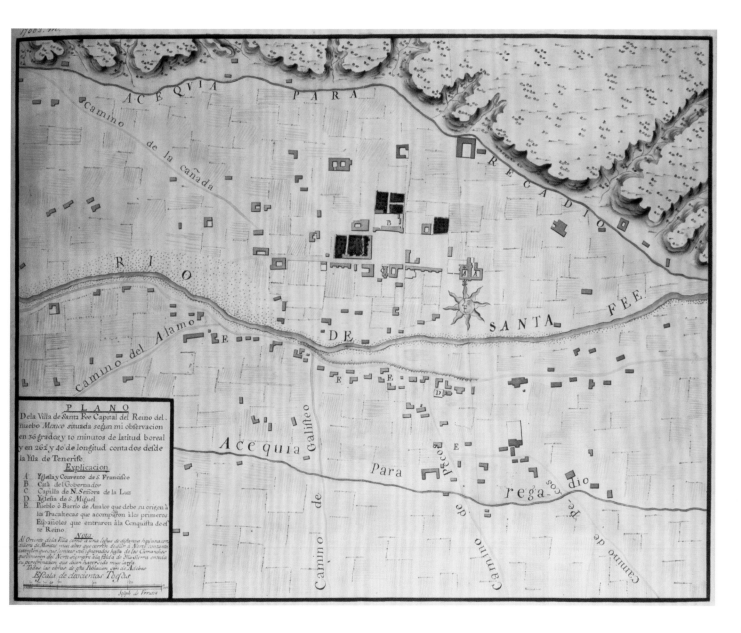

and on scanty documentation, largely official correspondence sent out of New Mexico in the years before the Pueblo Revolt.

Much about Santa Fe's beginnings remain shrouded in mystery, including the size and exact location of the *plaza mayor* that Peralta laid out in 1610. Some evidence suggests that the plaza extended farther eastward than it does today. If so, its north-south dimension should also have been larger, because the royal ordinance of 1573 specified that a plaza should be a rectangle half as wide as

it is long. If anyone produced a sketch of the early plaza in the 1600s, however, it apparently has disappeared. The seventeenth-century boundaries of the plaza remain the subject of dispute.[23]

The earliest known drawing of Santa Fe dates to 1766, a century and a half after its founding. It is the work of Lieutenant Joseph de Urrutia, a skilled draftsman who visited Santa Fe on the first leg of a two-year military reconnaissance of northern New Spain.[24] Lieutenant Urrutia called attention to five of the town's special

Above. Governor Peralta marked off a rectangular town square, or *plaza mayor,* much larger than what remains today. The Palace of the Governors, begun in 1609, was built on the north side of the plaza, and it remains the oldest public building in continuous use within the United States. Nicholas Brown's photograph of the palace dates to 1868.

Left. In this photograph taken around 1865, San Francisco Street in Santa Fe looks east toward La Parroquia.

Opposite. This Tewa polychrome ceramic bowl was excavated at the site of the Palace of the Governors in Santa Fe.

features. Four of the five date back to Santa Fe's earliest years, and in much altered states they remain landmarks of the city yet today: the church of San Francisco, the Palace of the Governors, the *barrio* of Analco, and the church of San Miguel.

On Urrutia's map, the parish church of San Francisco (A) occupies a point just beyond the southeast corner of the plaza. Governor Peralta oversaw the construction of a church on or near that spot during the *villa*'s first years. In later years, when Franciscans excommunicated Peralta in a nasty quarrel in 1613, they ordered his chair tossed out of the church and into the street.[25] That first church, however, was a "poor hut," according to Fray Alonso de Benavides, who arrived in New Mexico in 1625 to take charge of local Franciscan operations. His fellow friars, he said, had devoted all of their attention to building churches among the Pueblos, whom they were converting, and had neglected Santa Fe.[26] Benavides then "built a very fine church" with the aid of the townsfolk.[27] That church served Santa Fe until the Pueblos destroyed it during the Revolt of 1680, setting fire to it even before they forced Spaniards to evacuate the *villa*.[28] Once back in power, Spaniards rebuilt the parish church in 1714, on or close to its earlier location. In various permutations, that adobe parish church lasted into the 1880s, when it gave way to the much larger Romanesque stone cathedral that occupies the site today.[29]

The governor's house—the *Casa del Gobernador* (B)—appears on the north side of the plaza on Urrutia's map. Documents of the era also refer to it as the royal houses or royal palace (*casas reales* or *palacio real*), for it housed government offices as well as served as the governor's residence. (Today called the Palace of the Governors, it functions principally as a museum.) Construction of the palace apparently got under way in 1610, with its first walls taking the form of a defensive stockade made of mud-chinked upright timbers. Those walls soon gave way to adobe, and the *casas reales* grew to encompass an area much larger than it does today, with an interior courtyard perhaps four times the size of the current one. During the Pueblo Revolt of 1680, it held some thousand Spaniards who took refuge behind its commodious walls, along with a reported five thousand sheep and goats, more than four hundred horses and mules, and three hundred head of cattle! It is little wonder that Spaniards fled the *palacio* when the Pueblo besiegers cut off their water supply. Archaeologists assert that the mid-eighteenth-century *palacio* that Urrutia saw actually bore little resemblance to its seventeenth-century predecessor. Although the size of the seventeenth-century palace is known, its appearance remains a mystery.[30]

Along the south (left) bank of the Santa Fe River, Urrutia depicted the "town or neighborhood" (*pueblo o barrio*) of Analco (E). By the 1640s, if not before, the

No Spanish furniture survives from before the Pueblo Revolt of 1680. This pine "priest's chair," from a church in northern New Mexico, dates to the late 1700s but is likely consistent with earlier forms based on sixteenth-century Spanish prototypes. The stiles slanted back above the seat are typical of New Mexican style, while the deeply grooved rails, along with the 𝒞M cut-outs and differently shaped splats on the upper and lower parts of the chair, are characteristic of much Spanish colonial furniture.

left bank of the river had become the neighborhood of a servant class of Natives from central Mexico, including Tlaxcalans. From those Nahua-speakers, the *barrio* took the name Analco, meaning "the other side of the river."[31] In Urrutia's time, the neighborhood's Nahua beginnings were still remembered. According to Urrutia's map, Analco "owes its origin to the Tlascaltecans who accompanied the first Spaniards who embarked on the conquest of this region." Today, the neighborhood still carries the name Analco.

The church of San Miguel (D), which served the *barrio* of Analco, dated back to the 1620s. It was destroyed in the 1640s and rebuilt, only to be destroyed again in the Pueblo Revolt. In 1710 Spaniards rebuilt it from the ground up in the configuration that it retains yet today. Claims that it is the oldest non-Native place of worship in what is now the United States have not withstood archaeological scrutiny. Although it occupies a seventeenth-century site, its walls and wood date from 1710. Several of New Mexico's mission churches are older, including those at the pueblos of Isleta and Ácoma. The church of San Miguel is, however, the oldest church in Santa Fe.[32]

Urrutia's map also features the Chapel of Nuestra Señora de la Luz (C) on the south side of the plaza. Built in 1760 as a subsidiary of the parish church, it fell from ecclesiastical use in the mid-1850s.[33]

Although attention is not called to it, Urrutia's map of 1766 reveals one other prominent feature—an urban grid much modified from the orderly geometry prescribed by the Ordinances of 1573. A priest who visited Santa Fe in 1776, a decade after Urrutia made his map, put it vividly: "The Villa of Santa Fe (for the most part) consists of many small ranchos at various distances from one another, with no plan as to their location, for each owner built as he was able, wished to, or found convenient."[34] The same judgment might have been rendered a century earlier.

The urban center, or *civitas,* was the locus of civilization for Spaniards. There, and only there, could law, order, and morality flourish.[35] Nonetheless, most Spaniards in New Mexico lived in scattered homesteads.

Some resided just outside of town, as Urrutia's map records. Others built homes well beyond the towns, in river valleys to the north of Santa Fe or along the Rio Grande flood plain that broadens to the southwest of the city at Santo Domingo Pueblo and runs southward through present-day Albuquerque and Belén. Spanish officials expressed their disquiet with this tendency of the settlers to live in remote places where they could not readily band together for defense, but Spanish settlers chose to live near their flocks, herds, and fields and close to Pueblo peoples, the chief source of their labor and revenue, particularly in the 1600s.[36]

From New Mexico's founding in 1598 to the Pueblo Revolt of 1680, Spaniards depended on Pueblo peoples for their very existence. Although the crown had decided to maintain New Mexico as a center for converting Native peoples, it recognized the need to populate the province with Spanish settlers who could protect missionaries. Rather than pay armed men to defend the region, the crown shifted the cost of this maintenance to the local citizens and the Pueblo peoples, using a time-tested but highly imperfect feudal institution called the *encomienda*. Spaniards who supported Oñate or Peralta at their own expense for five years could petition for an *encomienda*— a grant of Native peoples that in theory made the recipient, or *encomendero*, the Natives' trustee. Depending on the individual Spaniard's status and the extent of his service, his *encomienda* gave him the right to collect tribute, or taxes, from a specified number of Native households. In turn, *encomenderos* had responsibilities. They and their lieutenants were obliged to provide military service for the colony and to defend the Native peoples with whom they had been entrusted and see to their conversion and spiritual welfare. The crown granted *encomiendas* for a lifetime, and often beyond. For services in campaigning against Apaches, for example, Juan de Oñate rewarded Captain Juan Martínez de Montoya an *encomienda* at the pueblo of Jémez, not just for himself but for his heirs for the next two generations.[37]

Some *encomenderos* also received gubernatorial appointments as local magistrates, or *alcaldes mayores*. These administrators made their headquarters at pueblos,

This silver crucifix, made in Mexico or Spain in the late seventeenth or early eighteenth century, is similar to those used in New Mexico.

from which they dispensed Spanish justice, took charge of local affairs, and allotted Native laborers for public and private works through a special levy called the *repartimiento*. These administrative positions carried no salary, but Spaniards coveted them because they provided additional opportunities to profit from Native labor, legally and illegally.[38]

In New Mexico, Pueblo peoples who converted to Christianity were to pay tribute to their *encomenderos* in a set amount of corn, cotton cloth, deerskins, or buffalo hides. *Encomenderos* were not to require labor from their Native wards without paying them. In practice, *encomenderos* abused the system, requiring labor as well as tribute and demanding higher tributes than laws allowed. As early as 1609 reports reached Mexico City that "the taxes [tribute] imposed and collected from those natives [in New Mexico] are excessive, causing them great vexation," and the viceroy ordered Governor Peralta to halt the abuses.[39] They continued nonetheless. A decade later another set of viceregal instructions ordered a new governor to stop *encomenderos* from allowing their stock to feed in the Native Americans' fields, to halt the illegal practice of using Pueblos as burden bearers, to cut down percentages of Natives enlisted in the *repartimiento* system, and to pay them for that work. Native women sent to Santa Fe under the *repartimiento* had suffered, as the viceroy delicately put it, from "offenses to God" committed by Spanish men. The governor was to stop sending Pueblo women to Santa Fe unless they went voluntarily and with their husbands.[40]

Although burdensome to the Pueblos, the *encomienda* and the *repartimiento* yielded profits for Spaniards. Governors, *encomenderos,* and their lieutenants extracted sufficient labor and tribute to produce a surplus that they then exported over the fifteen hundred miles of the *camino real,* New Mexico's sole link with the outside world. A wagon train, subsidized by the crown, plied the trail every three years, more or less, to bring supplies to the missions and to haul some of the missions' produce back to central Mexico. The mission supply caravan also carried merchandise back and forth for the settlers. On the southbound leg its wagons groaned with products made by the Pueblos for their *encomenderos:* painted buffalo hides, antelope skins, candles, pine nuts, salt, wool, and locally woven cloth and blankets.[41]

Two other exports from New Mexico accompanied the caravans on foot—sheep and indigenous slaves. Spaniards introduced sheep (along with horses, cattle, and goats) to New Mexico, where they flourished. As early as the 1630s New Mexicans began to ship them southward, on the hoof, to provide meat and wool for mining camps being established around Parral.[42] Native slaves were also in demand in the mining regions. The crown forbade the enslavement of indigenous peoples, but even officials charged with enforcing the law engaged in this lucrative business. Raiding parties of Spaniards and Pueblos took Apache and Navajo prisoners, keeping women and children as household servants and shipping male captives south to labor in the silver mines of northern Mexico.[43] Although New Mexico itself lacked mines, Spaniards in New Mexico turned a profit by exporting slaves to work in distant locations. In so doing, they sowed the seeds of a bitter, long-lasting enmity with Native neighbors.

With profits from their exports, Spanish New Mexicans imported manufactured goods. Much of this merchandise was utilitarian, such as iron and copper utensils, firearms, swords, daggers, chain mail, armor, and horse gear. Some must have seemed luxurious, ranging from silk and satin fabrics, shoes from Córdova, Chinese porcelain, and Mexican majolica to religious medals, gold and silver jewelry, books (including *Don Quixote*), and furniture. Francisco Gómez Robledo owned a desk with nine drawers and a lock and key, which does not seem likely to have been made locally.[44] To maintain a familiar way of life, Spaniards needed things from Spain. Their identity and honor depended on it. Spaniards did utilize some local manufactures. They relied heavily on Pueblos for ceramics, for example, and on their own smiths for ironware. Yet, even to trade successfully with neighboring tribes, Spaniards required items they could not obtain locally, such as combs, knives, glass beads, flutes, and mirrors.[45]

Above. Sheep, goats, cattle, and other livestock were important components of New Mexico's economy.

Left. Three types of wooden boxes were used to measure grain and other dry goods in New Mexico. The *almud* was the middle size.

The Aztec people of Mexico introduced the Spanish to their bitter drink, chocolate, which was used as currency, a beverage, and in ceremonies. The Spanish may have been the first to add sugar to it. In the colonial era, chocolate sets were brought to New Mexico along the royal road, or *camino real.* This set, utilized for making and serving hot chocolate, consists of a copper pitcher that was placed on the metal firedog to heat the liquid and then was lifted off with tongs. The strainer filters the chocolate as it is poured into the cup. A *molinillo,* or stirring stick, whips the chocolate into a smooth froth.

The earliest New Mexico tables were made for churches, although many were later used in homes. Centuries of Moorish influence in Spain are evident in the chip carved skirts of this table. Instead of a drawer, a small door with an iron lock gives access to the interior.

Opposite. When the Acoma Pueblo resisted the power of Juan Oñate in 1598, a small Spanish force destroyed the town and enslaved the population. Edward Curtis took this photograph of Acoma centuries later.

Force and fear underlay the Spaniards' economic relations with the Pueblos. From the outset, Spaniards made it clear that they would visit terrible reprisals on Native Americans who resisted their demands. In 1598 the pueblo of Ácoma turned on a group of Spanish soldiers who had come to collect food and blankets, killing eleven of them. Juan de Oñate responded brutally. He authorized a war with no quarter against the pueblo, which occupied a seemingly unassailable mesa top. In three days a small Spanish force destroyed Ácoma, killed over half the population, and took the remainder captive—some eighty men and five hundred women and children. Children under twelve were taken from their parents and put under the care of Franciscan priests.

Those over age twelve were distributed among the colonists, condemned to twenty years of personal servitude. Before their new masters claimed them, Ácoma men over twenty-five years old were sentenced to have one foot cut off. Intended to send a powerful message, the mutilations were to be carried out publicly at Native pueblos near Santa Fe. Historian John Kessell has noted, however, that there is little evidence that this last horrible command was carried out. Spaniards, he suggests, may have commuted the sentence at the last minute to demonstrate their magnanimity. Oñate's order to sever the feet of Ácomas, whether executed or merely a bit of theater, was not unique to Spaniards in America. At the fledgling English colony of Jamestown, Thomas Gates

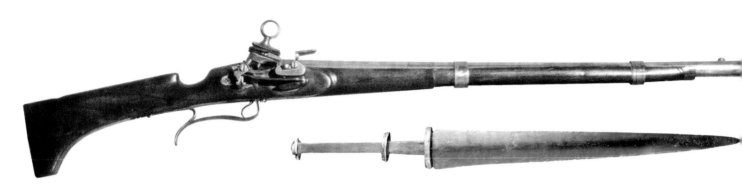

had the hand of a Native cut off as a warning against spies. Another Jamestown colonist, eager to force the Potomac peoples to trade with him, cut off two of their heads "and other extremetyse."[46]

Well-armed Spanish *encomenderos* continued the tradition of instilling fear. As one missionary, Alonso de Benavides, put it, "To keep up this fear, when it is in order to punish some rebellious pueblo, they use great rigors with them."[47] If they did not, Benavides observed, "The barbarians and those who have not yet been converted would have eaten us alive and also the Christian Indians."[48]

Benavides's metaphor was pure hyperbole. Spaniards were not on the menu; there is no evidence of cannibalism among Native peoples in New Mexico in that era. His larger point, however, rings true. Pueblos alone, with or without the aid of neighboring Native nations, could have extinguished the Spanish colony because they had overwhelming numbers on their side. Spanish males capable of bearing arms probably numbered fewer than two hundred fifty through the 1640s, with the total Spanish population never surpassing a thousand. (In 1640, even after their numbers had declined precipitously, the Pueblos outnumbered Spaniards in New Mexico by fifteen to one.) By the time of the Pueblo Revolt forty years later, the Spanish population—that is, of persons culturally Spanish—may have stood at some twenty-three hundred.[49]

Spanish *encomenderos* maintained a climate of fear that helped sustain the work of missionaries even as they sustained themselves by exploiting Native labor. The *encomenderos'* demands on Pueblo peoples, however,

brought them into conflict with the very missionary enterprise that the crown had ordered them to support. Missionaries, no less than *encomenderos*, depended on Native labor.

Ten Franciscan missionaries traveled with Oñate, and although most of them left in the colony's first difficult years, other friars traveled north from Mexico to replace them. In 1629 the arrival of thirty new Franciscans brought their number to fifty. By that year, Fray Alonso de Benavides claimed, the Franciscans had baptized more than eighty-six thousand Native peoples, most of them Pueblos, and built fifty churches with accompanying residences for priests. Pueblos themselves did the construction work, with women building the adobe or stone walls, as they did with their own homes, and men doing the carpentry.[50] Along with construction projects, the friars pushed Pueblo peoples to produce an agricultural surplus for export to southern markets with the triennial trade caravan.[51]

If Pueblo workers followed the missionaries' directions out of fear, they did so for other reasons as well. First, they had few places to which they could flee and reconstruct their agricultural economies in that dry country.[52] Second, they had something to gain. Franciscans offered spiritual power and solace, as well as animals, crops, and tools that Pueblos had never known. Third, Franciscans, who often demanded that hunters and gatherers make profound changes in their daily lives by settling in permanent communities and taking up agriculture, made no such demands on the Pueblos who already lived in towns and farmed nearby fields. Initially, missionaries who had little success with neighboring

Opposite, top. Called an *escopeta*, this Spanish carbine or light musket is of a type the Spanish used when fighting alongside Pueblo allies against Comanches, Navajos, Apaches, Utes, and Frenchmen in the 1700s.

Opposite, bottom. This late seventeenth-century Spanish dagger was found among the Apache people of northern Mexico.

Left. Mission priests who proselytized among the Native peoples of New Mexico frequently instructed local craftsmen to render likenesses of St. Anthony of Padua. Imported canvases were prohibitively expensive and hard to obtain. Consequently, images were frequently rendered on animal skins for local use or for export to mining towns in northern Mexico.

Cats played a role in European households and mythology, but they were new to Pueblo peoples. Indigenous potters added ceramic cats and mice to their repertoire of animal forms in order to appeal to the Spanish consumer, as in this example made at Pecos in the seventeenth or eighteenth century.

Decorated with a cross, this ceramic bowl was excavated at the archaeological site of Kuaua, New Mexico.

Apaches made inroads among the Pueblos. In part, they did not demand radical changes in Pueblo daily life, except in the religious sphere, and even there Franciscans appear to have proceeded gingerly in the first decades of evangelization.[53]

Missionaries and settlers vied for the lives and labor of Pueblos as they did throughout the Spanish empire, but in remote New Mexico, which lacked powerful mediators and had no other source of wealth, the competition was especially intense. From the founding of Santa Fe to the Pueblo Revolt, struggles between Church and State played themselves out as high drama—and sometimes low comedy. Starring roles went to the leaders of the two groups: the civil governor and captain general of New Mexico, who made Santa Fe his capital, and the Franciscan prelate of New Mexico, who established his initial ecclesiastical headquarters at Santo Domingo Pueblo, twenty miles away.[54] The physical separation of these representatives of Church and State was more than symbolic.

Conflict began during the term of Governor Pedro de Peralta, when an irascible and unscrupulous new prelate, Fray Isidro de Ordóñez, arrived in Santa Fe in 1611. Ordóñez brought a viceregal order that permitted *encomenderos* and other settlers in New Mexico to leave the beleaguered province. The order stunned Peralta, whose own instructions from the viceroy required him to build up New Mexico and make it more defensible. Several years went by before authorities discovered that Ordóñez had forged the viceroy's orders, apparently hoping to rid New Mexico of all Spaniards except missionaries. By then, however, the damage was done. Ordóñez twice excommunicated Peralta, and Peralta and his lieutenants came to blows with Ordóñez and his churchmen. Peralta's governorship ended in 1613 when Ordóñez arrested him and held him prisoner for months in a remote pueblo before a new governor arrived the next year to set him free. In Mexico City, authorities vindicated Peralta and reprimanded Ordóñez, but similar conflicts between strong-willed representatives of Church and State continued to rock New Mexico in the seventeenth century.[55]

As *encomenderos* and friars competed for the labor of Christianized Natives, the numbers of the indigenous people declined. The most recent study of Pueblo population suggests that in the forty years following Oñate's arrival, the number of Pueblo peoples fell from about 60,000 in 1598 to 15,500 in 1641, a three-fourths decline. The Pueblo population recovered in the next few decades, but by the 1670s it had fallen back to 17,000. As their population shrank, Pueblos abandoned some of their towns to move into others, and that consolidation resulted in a decline in the number of Pueblo towns. The number of towns dropped by over half, from eighty-one in 1598 to

thirty-seven in 1641; by 1680 it had declined further to thirty-one.[56] These figures are based on sketchy documentary and archaeological sources, and the margin of error is high, but there is no mistaking the downward trend of the Pueblo population or that the biggest decline in numbers occurred from 1636 to 1641. The causes are clearer than the numbers. A smallpox epidemic that swept through the Pueblo world at that time was the primary killer. Other traumas, however, also weakened the Pueblos economically and psychologically, perhaps leaving them more susceptible to epidemic disease. In addition, demands for labor by *encomenderos* and missionaries,

Chests, such as this eighteenth-century colored leather chest from New Mexico, were the most common item listed in colonial inventories.

Left. The Pueblo Revolt of 1680 involved
communities separated by hundreds of
miles and speaking six different languages.
One of the coordinators of the revolt
was Pópé of San Juan. This statue by
Jemez Pueblo Clifford Fragua stands in
the United States Capitol.

Opposite. This painted lintel or corbel
is from a ceiling at the Pecos mission,
one of those destroyed in the Pueblo
Revolt. Ruins of the Pecos mission are
seen in the photograph.

Spanish disruption of traditional Pueblo trade with Apaches and other Plains people, and intensifying Apache raids as they acquired horses and became more powerful enemies were other probable causes.[57]

Over the years revolts broke out in individual pueblos, but Spanish overlords handily quelled these isolated outbreaks of resistance. In the 1660s and 1670s, however, pressures built on the Pueblos until they erupted in a large-scale revolt that involved multiple pueblos, separated by hundreds of miles and speaking at least six different languages. Years of drought, which began in the mid-1660s, shrank the resources on which Pueblos and Spaniards depended. The remaining crops, flocks, and herds drew the attention of nomads, who intensified their raids. Although missionaries ameliorated the effects of the drought by releasing surpluses from their granaries, hunger stalked the land, and Pueblos abandoned their most vulnerable communities on the edge of the Great Plains. In this time of crisis, many Pueblos seemed to lose their faith in Franciscans and their religion. They returned to the traditional leaders and religious ceremonies that had sustained them in the past. As Pueblo religious revivals escalated, Franciscans tried to stop them by taking harsh measures against Native American priests. Pueblos now had one more compelling reason to be rid of Spaniards.[58]

In 1680 the Pueblos struck a blow for religious freedom. United under Popé, a religious leader from San Juan, most of the Pueblo communities aimed to rid themselves of Spaniards. When the revolt began on 10 August, those Spaniards who lived in isolated farms and

ranches were caught off guard and became easy prey. So, too, were priests at isolated missions. Pueblos killed twenty-one of the province's thirty-three missionaries and desecrated the mission churches and their sacred objects. As word of the revolt spread, Spaniards from the countryside took refuge at Isleta, one of the few pueblos that did not revolt, and at Santa Fe. In the *villa*, Governor Antonio de Otermín soon found himself besieged by some two thousand Pueblos, many armed with guns, lances, swords, and armor seized from Spanish victims. Of the thousand Spaniards in the *villa*, Otermín would later report, only a hundred bore arms. The Pueblos forced the defenders into the *casas reales*, cut off the water flow to the capital, and sacked and burned homes. With no prospect of victory and the likelihood of defeat and death, Otermín led the defenders out of the charred remains of Santa Fe on 21 August to begin the retreat that would eventually take them and their Pueblo allies to El Paso.[59] Santa Fe, founded as the headquarters for a costly spiritual conquest, seemed lost forever.

For the next thirteen years, Popé made Santa Fe the capital of his operations, turning the Spanish *villa* into a fortified town. The Pueblos built multistory houses in, around, and atop the former government buildings, replaced the parish church with kivas, added defensive walls and towers, and erected a structure in the center of the large plaza that divided it into two smaller squares.[60] Their destruction of all things Spanish was nearly complete. Traces of Spanish material culture that archaeologists have unearthed from this era tend to be durable religious medals, jewelry, and pieces of ceramic or metal, rather than more perishable objects of wood, cloth, paper, or hides.[61] One of the rare wooden objects to survive was a statue of the Virgin Mary, popularly known as Our Lady of the Conquest (*Nuestra Señora de la Conquista*), renamed in 1990 as Our Lady of Peace. Spaniards had taken the statue with them when they fled Santa Fe. When they returned they proudly restored it to its place as "patron saint and protectress" of the *villa*.[62]

Diego de Vargas, who led the reconquest of New Mexico, hoped that diplomacy would return the Pueblos to the Spanish sphere. A foray into the province in 1692 convinced him that would be possible. When he returned the next year, however, Pueblo insurgents refused to surrender Santa Fe. Vargas's force, made up of Pueblo allies as well as Spaniards, retook the *villa* by force and executed seventy Pueblo leaders who survived the battle. That did not end Pueblo resistance, which continued into 1694 and erupted again in 1696 in another major revolt that took the lives of five Franciscans and left more churches and friars' quarters in embers.[63]

Spaniards, however, had returned to stay, and the Pueblo Revolt of 1680 marked a turning point in their relations with Pueblos. Rather than risk another rebellion, Spaniards in eighteenth-century New Mexico made fewer demands on the Pueblos. They did not reestablish the *encomienda*, and they did not forcibly suppress Pueblo religious ceremonies. Although Pueblos had not won permanent independence in 1680, they nevertheless gained a measure of freedom. In the eighteenth century, new common enemies—Comanches and Apaches—further encouraged peaceful coexistence

Left. In 1692 Diego de Vargas peacefully forged alliances with various Pueblo peoples to allow a safe Spanish return to Santa Fe. The next year, when Vargas led returning settlers into the area, the group met with resistance but not united opposition from some Pueblos. To avoid continued conflict, Vargas promised to protect Pueblo peoples' legal rights, and religious authorities tacitly allowed some traditional practices. This modern copy follows an original portrait of Vargas that was painted in the 1660s and is now in a private chapel in Madrid.

Opposite. Josefa Sambrano de Grijalva carried this three-foot-tall wooden statue of the Virgin from Santa Fe to El Paso at the onset of the Pueblo Revolt. Spanish troops brought it back to Santa Fe during the reconquest of 1692–93. Our Lady of the Rosary became known as *La Conquistadora*, but the seventeenth-century statue was renamed Our Lady of Peace in 1990.

between Pueblos and Spaniards. In the face of perceived threats from indigenous raiders, and from Frenchmen who provided them with arms, the military gradually supplanted the missions as New Mexico's most important institution.

In the 1700s New Mexico no longer stood alone as the only Spanish province in what is now southwestern United States. Spain extended its reach into today's Arizona, as Jesuits built missions among the Pimas; into Texas, founded as a bastion against French expansion; and into California, in an attempt to halt Russian and British expansion. Until the Spanish colonial era ended in 1821, New Mexico, with Santa Fe as its capital, remained the most vital and self-sufficient province on New Spain's far northern frontier. In sharp contrast to the present day, when the vast majority of residents of the Southwest live in California or Texas, New Mexico had the largest population of *gente de razón*—people of reason—as Hispanicized people termed themselves.

In 1821 Spaniards in New Mexico numbered close to thirty thousand (not counting ten thousand Hispanicized Pueblo peoples), with some five thousand living in Santa Fe and another eight thousand residing in El Paso, then considered part of New Mexico. New Mexico's Spanish population far exceeded that of Texas (twenty-five hundred), or California (thirty-two hundred), or southern Arizona (a thousand).[64]

Mexican independence from Spain in 1821 and the opening of the Santa Fe Trail that same year introduced new American products to Santa Fe and new markets for New Mexican goods. It also brought Anglo Americans who found much to dislike about houses made of mud, as they described adobe, and about the dark-skinned Catholic people who lived in those structures. Anglo Americans' disdain for Mexicans and for things Mexican intensified as relations between Mexico and the United States deteriorated into war in 1846–47 and lingered long after that war converted Mexico's Far North to the

American Southwest. Beginning in the mid-1800s, Anglo American newcomers remade Santa Fe into an American city, disguising many of its old adobe buildings with the veneer of a local variant of Greek Revival.

In the late nineteenth century, the movement to Americanize Santa Fe shifted into reverse, supplanted by a countermovement to re-invoke its indigenous architecture (or what architects and others imagined to be its indigenous architecture), romanticize its Hispanic residents, and celebrate its Spanish roots. Greek Revival facades of wood trim and brick were stripped away. Old buildings were restored and new adobe or faux-adobe buildings rose in styles known by various names— Pueblo, Spanish-Pueblo, New Mexico Mission, and Santa Fe. Reconstructed in a nostalgic and distinctively regional mode, Santa Fe continues today to remind its numerous visitors in myriad ways of its origins as one of America's oldest non-Native towns—the oldest west of the Mississippi.[65]

Pedro de Villasur led a party of Spaniards and Pueblos, who found common foes in the French-armed Plains Indians. Twelve Pueblos and thirty-two Spaniards died in a surprise attack in Nebraska in 1720. This hide painting shows the last stand of Villasur's expedition.

Contributors

JAMES C. KELLY is Director of Museums at the Virginia Historical Society in Richmond. Among his previous books are *Bound Away: Virginia and the Westward Movement* (with David Hackett Fischer) and *The Virginia Landscape: A Cultural History* (with William M. S. Rasmussen).

BARBARA CLARK SMITH has curated major exhibitions at the National Museum of American History and published both scholarly and popular essays on early America. She is completing a book on the American Revolution titled *The Freedoms We Lost*. She is Curator in the Division of Politics and Reform, National Museum of American History, Smithsonian Institution.

WARREN M. BILLINGS, author of many books on early Virginia history, including *Sir William Berkeley and the Forging of Colonial Virginia*, is Distinguished Professor and Historian of the Supreme Court of Louisiana and Director of Graduate Studies at the University of New Orleans.

GILLES PROULX was a historian for the National Historic Sites of Canada at the Fortress of Louisbourg and in Québec City. He wrote *Between France and New France* and *Fighting at Ristigouche*. He has also contributed historical papers to the French journals *Neptunia* and the *Revue d'histoire de l'Amérique Française*.

DAVID J. WEBER, author of many books on the American Southwest, is the Robert and Nancy Dedman Professor of History at Southern Methodist University, Dallas, Texas, where he also directs the William P. Clements Center for Southwest Studies.

Detail of native-painted hide robe, New France.

Acknowledgments

This exhibition reflects the extraordinary efforts of many scholars and museum professionals, to whom we express deep appreciation. First, we acknowledge our debt to our respective chief executive officers, Dr. Charles F. Bryan, Jr., President and CEO of the Virginia Historical Society, and Brent Glass, Director of the Smithsonian National Museum of American History, for their support.

Next, we are proud to be associated with the three distinguished scholars who contributed essays to this book: Warren Billings of the University of New Orleans, Gilles Proulx, formerly of the National Historic Sites of Canada, and David Weber of Southern Methodist University. Drs. Billings and Weber generously reviewed our introductory essay, which also benefited from thoughtful, critical readings by three scholars at the Smithsonian's National Museum of American History: Dr. James Gardner, Associate Director for Curatorial Affairs; Dr. Rayna Green, Curator of Home and Community Life; and Harry Rubenstein, Chair, Division of Politics and Reform. We also learned from a helpful research essay on Québec provided by Mathieu d'Avignon of Laval University.

At the Virginia Historical Society, Jeffrey Ruggles, Curator of Prints and Photographs, procured the images for this book. Exhibition Assistants Dr. Kelly Spradley-Kurowski and Celine Carayon prepared drafts of picture captions. Ms. Carayon also handled much of the French correspondence with lenders and sources of graphics. Dr. Muriel Rogers, Curator of Special Projects, prepared the checklist of the exhibition. Dr. Nelson Lankford, Director of Publications and Scholarship, and Dr. Paul Levengood, Managing Editor of the *Virginia Magazine of History and Biography*, prepared the manuscript for publication. Thanks also are due to AnnMarie Price, Registrar, and Dale Kostelny, Exhibit Production Manager.

At the Smithsonian National Museum of American History, Nanci Edwards, Project Manager for the exhibition, gracefully coordinated all aspects of this complex, collaborative undertaking. Gretchen Jennings, Director of Education for Interpretation and Visitor Experience, provided thoughtful input and suggested the final comparative architecture of the exhibition. Registrar Jeanne Benas, Deputy Registrar Tom Bower, and Project Assistant Matt Kontor tirelessly negotiated a daunting array of loans. James Gardner, Rayna Green, and Harry Rubenstein helped shape the exhibition and corrected our errors through various drafts. Many other staff generously shared their collections and expertise with us, including Joan Boudreau, Associate Curator of Graphic Arts; Dr. Richard Doty, Curator of Numismatics; David Miller, Associate Curator of Military History and Diplomacy; Steve Velasquez, Associate Curator of Home and Community Life; and Helena Wright, Curator of Graphic Arts. Our thanks also go to Hugh Talman, Photographer, and La'Kecia Graham, Special Assistant to the Director.

For work on this catalogue we are grateful to our editor at Smithsonian Books, Caroline Newman, and freelance designer Robert L. Wiser.

At the Canadian Museum of Civilization, we are especially indebted to Dr. Jean-Pierre Hardy, Historian and Assistant Director, Archaeology and History, whose impressive exhibition *Once in French America* introduced us to objects that also appear here. Dr. Hardy's script provided much of the material for object captions pertaining to New France. We thank him also for suggesting essayist Gilles Proulx to us. Dr. Hardy reviewed, corrected, and improved our picture captions, as did his supervisor, Dr. David Morrison, Director of Archaeology and History. Jean-Pierre Chrestien, Curator,

Québec Archaeology, provided leads to relevant historical artifacts that have enriched the exhibition. From the time of our first visit in March 2005, we have received encouragement from Sylvie M.-A. Morel, Director General, Exhibitions and Programs, and Dr. Stephen Inglis, Director General, Research and Collections. The project has also benefited enormously from the assistance of Jennifer Elliott and Nicolas Gauvin, Exhibition Planning Officers.

In New Mexico, our gratitude goes especially to Palace of the Governors Director Dr. Frances Levine and Senior Curator Louise I. Stiver, whose efforts and expertise have enhanced the project immeasurably. Thank you as well to Deputy Director John McCarthy, Assistant Director René Harris, Curator of Historic Photography Cary McStay, and Librarian Tomas Jaehn. Ellen J. Landis of Albuquerque also provided artifact leads.

Among the lenders and graphic providers, we express appreciation to Georgia Barnhill, Andrew W. Mellon Curator of Graphic Arts at the American Antiquarian Society; Margaretha Talerman, Curator of the American Swedish Historical Museum, Philadelphia; Julie Fournier, Archiviste, Direction du Centre de Québec, Bibliothèque et Archives nationales du Québec; Doreen Crowe, Registrar, Tucson Main Museum, Arizona Historical Society; Bly Straube, Senior Curator, and Catherine Dean, Curator of Collections, Association for the Preservation of Virginia Antiquities; Jeffrey R. Ray, Senior Curator, Atwater Kent Museum of Philadelphia; Barbara O'Connor, Loans Registrar, and Robert Davies, Assistant Loans Manager, The British Library; Susan Danforth, John Carter Brown Library; Patrice Rémillard, Manager, Loans and Transport, Canadian Museum of Civilization; André J. Delisle, Executive Director and Curator, and

Patrick Blass, Archivist, Château Ramezay Museum, Montréal; Donald Smith, Executive Director, and Carol Smith, Consulting Archivist and Curator, Christ Church Preservation Trust, Philadelphia; Karen Rehm, Chief Historian, and Klydie Thomas, Colonial National Historical Park, National Park Service; Marianne C. Martin of Colonial Williamsburg; Laura Paulick, Associate Registrar, Exhibitions, Denver Art Museum; Lucie Boivin, Responsable collections archéologiques et laboratoire, Département d'histoire, Cité Universitaire (Québec City); Shane Culpeper and Dana Yarborough at the Gilcrease Museum; Warren Woods, Collections Manager, and Maclyn Hickey, Assistant Registrar at The Historic New Orleans Collection; Dr. Terry Martin, Curator and Chair of Anthropology, Illinois State Museum; Deborah Garcia, Registrar, International Museum of Folk Art, Santa Fe; Dr. Richard Luckett, Keeper of the Old Library, and Aude Fitzsimons, Magdalene College, University of Cambridge; Manon Roch, Chief Curator, Maison Saint-Gabriel; Kimberly Peters, Deputy Director, and Meredith Vasta, Registrar/Collections Manager, Mashantucket Pequot Museum and Research Center; Anne E. Bentley, Curator of Art/Acting Registrar, Carrie Supple, and Peter Drummey, Massachusetts Historical Society; Christian Vachon, Head, Collections Management, McCord Museum of Canadian History; Suzanne Flynt, Curator, Memorial Hall Museum, Pocumtuck Valley Memorial Association; James H. Willcox, Jr., Merchant's Hope Episcopal Church, Prince George County, Virginia; Claudine Giroux, Responsable des sites et des collections archéologiques du Québec, Direction du Patrimoine, Ministère de la Culture et des Communications; Mr. and Mrs. J. Roderick Moore; André Delpuech,

Conservateur en chef du patrimoine, Responsable des collections et de la muséographie des Amériques, Musée du Quai Branly, Paris; Sylvie Dauphin, Chef, Service des collections, Musée Stewart au Fort de L'Île Sainte-Hélène, Montréal; Anita K. McNeece, Curator of Collections, Museum of Indian Arts & Culture/Laboratory of Anthropology, Museum of New Mexico; Bill Field, Director, Museum of Spanish Colonial Art; John Vincler, Reference Assistant, and Catherine Gass, Photographer, The Newberry Library; Sonia Dingilian, Loans Coordinator, New York Public Library; Nelson Foss, Registrar, Palace of the Governors; Minora Collins, Registrar for Outgoing Loans, Peabody Essex Museum; Susan Conley, Museum Registrar, Colorado Springs Fine Arts Center, Taylor Museum; Michael Hironymous, University of Texas at Austin; Dee DeRoche, Chief Curator; Keith Egloff, Assistant Curator; and Melba Myers, Conservator, Virginia Department of Historic Resources; and Mary Herbert-Busick, Associate Registrar, Wadsworth Atheneum Museum of Art. For their expert knowledge we thank Dr. Ann McMullen, Curator, Dr. Patricia Nietfeld, Collections Manager, and Erik Satrum, Assistant Registrar for Loans, National Museum of the American Indian, Smithsonian Institution.

The extent of these acknowledgments testifies to the extraordinary debts incurred by curators who venture into wide-ranging and comparative historical topics such as this one. Thanks to all who aided us and whose contributions allow us to offer museum visitors a far more accurate, nuanced, and engaging exhibition than we could possibly have managed on our own.

James C. Kelly, Ph.D., Co-Curator
Barbara Clark Smith, Ph.D., Co-Curator

Page 1. Virginia Company map, manuscript on vellum, hand-colored, 1607–1609. The Phelps Stokes Collection, Miriam and Ira D. Wallach Division of Art, Prints and Photographs, New York Public Library, Astor, Lenox, and Tilden Foundations. Original at Richmond.

Pages 2–3 and 16. Matthäus Greuter, globe, paper, wood, papier mâché, and brass, c. 1632, one of the first globes to show Québec City. Stewart Museum, Montréal, Canada.

Page 4. Gourd instrument, nineteenth-century example of those fashioned by African Americans. Mr. and Mrs. J. Roderick Moore.

Pages 6 (detail), 50 (top), and back cover. Louis Hennepin, *A New Discovery of a Vast Country in America,* London, 1698. Virginia Historical Society. Original at Gatineau and Santa Fe.

Pages 8 and 64. Portrait of Captain John Smith, engraving, from *The Generall Historie of Virginia* (1st ed., 1624), German ed., c. 1630. Virginia Historical Society.

Page 10. Bartholomew Gosnold trading with Native people, published in Theodor de Bry, *America,* part 13 (1634), plate II. Reproduction. Virginia Historical Society.

Page 11. Astrolabe, bronze, dated 1603; may have belonged to Samuel de Champlain. Reproduction. Catalogue photograph © Canadian Museum of Civilization, no. 989.56.1, by Merle Toole, image no. s91–2191.

Page 12, top. Crossbow bolt heads, iron, c. 1540, found at Puaray archaeological site, New Mexico. Palace of the Governors, The New Mexico History Museum, Museum of New Mexico, Department of Cultural Affairs.

Page 12, bottom. Aztec Indians with smallpox, c. 1577, reproduction from Bernardino Sahagún, *Historia General de las Cosas de Nueba España.* Biblioteca Medica Laurenziana, Florence, Italy.

Page 13. Robert Johnson, *Nova Britannia: Offering Most excellent fruites by Planting in Virginia,* 1609. Virginia Historical Society. Richmond only.

Page 14, top. Earthenware pot, c. 1550, from the St. Lawrence Iroquois. National Museum of the American Indian, Smithsonian Institution (6/8429).

Page 14, bottom. Huron wampum belt, c. 1612, concerning a treaty made with the Iroquois on the Ottawa River. National Museum of the American Indian, Smithsonian Institution (1855).

Page 15. Moccasin embroidered with porcupine quills, Huron or Iroquois, c. 1721, from the upper St. Lawrence region, traditionally associated with "Emigré d' Esclignac." Catalogue photograph © Musée du Quai Branly, Paris, by Patrick Gries/Valérie Torre. Gatineau only.

Page 17. Hand-forged iron shears, seventeenth century, collected in New Mexico. Museum of Spanish Colonial Art, Collection of the Spanish Colonial Arts Society, Inc.

Page 18, top. Hand-forged English anvil, dated 1645, found at Falling Creek, Virginia. Smithsonian National Museum of American History, Kenneth E. Behring Center.

Page 18, center. English breastplate, iron, c. 1620–35, from Jordan's Journey settlement, Prince George County, Virginia. Virginia Department of Historic Resources.

Page 18, bottom. Halberd, iron and wood, seventeenth century, from Jamestown. National Park Service, Colonial National Historical Park.

Page 19. Shield, painted bison rawhide, c. 1750, Southwest United States. Denver Art Museum Collection, Gift of James Economos, 1973.216.

Page 20. Giovanni Battista Ramusio, *La Nuova Francia,* 1556, map based on the voyage of Giovanni Verrazzano. Reproduction. John Carter Brown Library at Brown University.

Page 21, top. Brass bells, c. 1654–81, from Native settlement in Onondaga, New York. National Museum of the American Indian, Smithsonian Institution (19/1577).

Page 21, bottom. Glass bead necklace, probably eighteenth century, used in New France. Musée du Quai Branly, Paris. Richmond and St. Louis only.

Page 22. Sculpture of a bear, basalt, sixteenth century, made at Pawtucket, Massachusetts. Peabody Essex Museum, Salem, Massachusetts.

Page 23, left. Portrait of John Winthrop, oil on canvas, c. 1630–91. American Antiquarian Society, Bequest of William Winthrop. Richmond and St. Louis only.

Page 23, right. Ralph Hamor, *A True Discourse of the Present Estate of Virginia and the success of the affaires there till the 18 of June, 1614,* manuscript, 1615. Reproduction. Virginia Historical Society.

Page 24. *The Inconveniencies that have Happened to Some Persons which have transported themselves from England to Virginia,* broadside, 1622. Smithsonian National Museum of American History, Kenneth E. Behring Center.

Page 25, top. Jesuit medal, brass, c. 1650–1700, France. National Museum of the American Indian, Smithsonian Institution (10/4182).

Page 25, bottom. Jesuit ring, brass, late 1600s, France. National Museum of the American Indian, Smithsonian Institution.

Page 26. "Prise De Possession De La Louisiane Et Du Fleuve Mississipi Par Cavelier De La Salle . . . 1682," lithograph by Bocquin, c. 1850. Reproduction. The Historic New Orleans Collection acc. 1970.1.

Page 27. Pipe tomahawk, copper alloy, of French manufacture. Illinois State Museum.

Page 28. Wheel-lock pistol, steel, c. 1620, Germany. Smithsonian National Museum of American History, Kenneth E. Behring Center.

Page 29, top. Matchlock musket, seventeenth century, France. Stewart Museum, Montréal, Canada.

Page 29, bottom. Spur, iron, sixteenth century, Spain or Mexico. Museum of Spanish Colonial Art, Collections of the Spanish Colonial Arts Society, Inc.

Page 30. Claude de Chauchetière, "Confirmation is given for the first time," drawing, c. 1680. Reproduction. Archives départamentales de la Gironde, Bordeaux, France.

Page 31. Mission bell, bronze, eighteenth century, New Mexico. Fred Harvey Collection of the International Folk Art Foundation Collection in the Museum of International Folk Art, Museum of New Mexico, Department of Cultural Affairs.

Page 32, top. Sword, early seventeenth century, found at Jamestown. National Park Service, Colonial National Historical Park.

Page 32, center. Scrap copper, early seventeenth century, traded at Jamestown. APVA Preservation Virginia and Historic Jamestowne.

Page 33. *Virginia, Discovered and discribed by Captayn John Smith,* 1606, engraved map with text by William Hole, 1624 (1st ed., 1612). Virginia Historical Society. Various editions of the map rotate.

Pages 34–35. Christian devotional belt of cylindrical shell beads, or wampum, from upper St. Lawrence or Great Lakes region of New France. Formerly in the French royal collection. Catalogue photograph © Musée du Quai Branly, Paris, by Patrick Gries/Valérie Torre. Santa Fe only.

Page 35, bottom. Sickle, after 1641, used at Kingsmill. Virginia Department of Historic Resources.

Page 36. John Simon, "Sa Ga Yeath Pieth Ton, King of the Magua," mezzotint on laid paper, 1710, after John Verelst, London. Reproduction. Massachusetts Historical Society.

Page 37. James Revel, *The Poor Unhappy Transported Felon's Sorrowful Account of his Fourteen Years Transportation at Virginia, in America,* mid-seventeenth-century account, published in London, c. 1791. Virginia Historical Society, Gift of Mrs. Beverley Randolph Wellford. Original at St. Louis and Gatineau.

Page 38. "The Heart of a Seigneury 1730," modern illustration by Andrée Héroux.

Page 39. Fragment of deed of Sir George Yeardley to Abraham Persey for Flour de Hundred, 1624. Virginia Historical Society, Gift of John Dunn of Petersburg, through the courtesy of Joseph Bragg Dunn of Richmond. Richmond and Santa Fe only.

Page 40. Shackle, early to mid-seventeenth century, from Jamestown. National Park Service, Colonial National Historical Park.

Page 41, top. Iroquois tumpline, eighteenth century, for binding captives or carrying loads. National Museum of the American Indian, Smithsonian Institution (19/6329).

Page 41, bottom. Joseph-Marie Chaumonot, drawing, 1666, showing an Onondaga (Iroquois) warrior and a captive bound by a tumpline. Reproduction. Centre historique des Archives nationales, Paris.

Page 42. Belt of cylindrical shell beads, or wampum, possibly to commemorate an agreement between the Huron and the Jesuit missionaries for the construction of the first wooden church on Huron lands in 1638. McCord Museum of Canadian History, Montréal.

Page 43. Arosen's gifts to the brother of Deerfield captive Eunice Williams: deer hide and porcupine quill bullet pouch, leather and quill tobacco bag, prehistoric red slate gorget, and wool, hemp, and bead sash, early eighteenth century. Pocomtuck Valley Memorial Association, Massachusetts.

Page 45. "Aboriginal people and African slaves in Louisiana, 1735," from Alexander de Batz, *Drawings of Savages from Several Nations.* Reproduction. Peabody Museum of Archaeology and Ethnology, Harvard University, Photographic Collection.

Page 46. Captain John Underhill, engraving of 1637 English attack on Pequot fort at Mystic, published in Underhill's *Newes from America,* 1638. Catalogue photograph by Bob Halloran © copyright Mashantucket Pequot Museum and Research Center.

Page 47. French dagger/bayonet, used in King Philip's War in New England, 1675–76. Pocomtuck Valley Memorial Association, Massachusetts.

Page 48. Weathervane, 1699, from William Penn's gristmill in Chester County, Pennsylvania. Historical Society of Pennsylvania Collection, Atwater Kent Museum of Philadelphia, Catalogue photograph by Gavin Ashworth.

Page 49, top. Swedish helmet, c. 1650–80, excavated near Philadelphia. Historical Society of Pennsylvania Collection, Atwater Kent Museum of Philadelphia.

Page 49, bottom. Swedish chest, c. 1650–70, brought to the Delaware Valley by Broer Sinnexson of Sweden in 1683. Collections of the American Swedish Historical Museum, Philadelphia, Pennsylvania.

Pages 50–51. Spanish sword, late seventeenth or early eighteenth century, found near Oraibi, Hopi Third Mesa, Arizona. Palace of the Governors, The New Mexico History Museum, Museum of New Mexico, Department of Cultural Affairs.

Page 51, top. Maria de Jésus de Agreda, engraving. Benson Latin American Collection, University of Texas at Austin.

Page 52. *Veuë du camp de la concession de Monseigneur Law, au Nouveaux Biloxy, coste de la Louisianne, designee par Jean Baptise Michel Le Bouteux le dixe Decembre 1720 de l'ordre de Mr. Elias St. Huteus, directeur general.* Reproduction. The Newberry Library, Chicago.

Page 53. Perhaps workshop of John Symonds, Salem, chest of drawers, oak and white pine with maple and walnut molding, late seventeenth century. Massachusetts Historical Society.

Pages 54–55. Guillaume de L'Isle, *Carte de Louisiane et du cours de Mississipi,* 1730 edition of c. 1700 original. Alderman Library, University of Virginia.

Pages 56 (detail) and 82. Portrait of William Randolph, oil on canvas, c. 1695. Virginia Historical Society, Bequest of Kate Brander (Harris) Mayo Skipwith Williams.

Page 58. Tile, tin-glazed ceramic, seventeenth century, found at Jamestown. APVA Preservation Virginia and Historic Jamestowne.

Page 59. Simon van de Passe, portrait of James I, engraving, early seventeenth century. Virginia Historical Society.

Page 60. *Anglorum in Virginiam adventus,* published in Theodor de Bry, *America,* part I (Frankfurt, 1590), plate II. Virginia Historical Society, Bequest of Paul Mellon. Original at Richmond and Washington.

Page 61. Cornelius Janssen, portrait of Sir Dudley Digges, oil on canvas, c. 1616. Virginia Historical Society.

Page 62. Herbert Luther Smith, portrait of Sir George Percy, oil on canvas, before 1854, copy of the seventeenth-century original. Virginia Historical Society, Gift of Conway Robinson.

Page 63. Manuscript map, "Draughte of Robarte Tindall of Virginia: Anno 1608." The British Library, Maps Department. Original at Richmond.

Page 65, left. Jack-of-plate fragment, quilted body armor of wool and iron, 1620–35, excavated at Jordan's Journey settlement, Prince George County, Virginia. Virginia Department of Historic Resources.

Page 65, right. Broadsword hilt, iron with damascened silver-wire inlay, c. 1620–35, from Jordan's Journey settlement, Prince George County, Virginia. Virginia Department of Historic Resources.

Page 66, top. Pipe with incised decoration, c. 1608, made by Robert Cotton at Jamestown. APVA Preservation Virginia and Historic Jamestowne.

Page 66, bottom. Powhatan tobacco pipe, seventeenth century. APVA Preservation Virginia and Historic Jamestowne.

Page 67, top. List of first members of House of Burgesses, 1619. Reproduction. The National Archives, Kew, Richmond, Surrey, United Kingdom.

Page 67, bottom. Lottery broadside issued by the Virginia Company, c. 1615. Reproduction. Society of Antiquaries, London.

Page 68, top. "Powhatan/Held this state and fashion when Capt Smith/was delivered to him [as a] prisoner," from John Smith's map of Virginia, engraving, 1612. Reproduction. Virginia Historical Society.

Page 68, bottom left. Shell-tempered ceramic pot fragments, made by Native people in Virginia. APVA Preservation Virginia and Historic Jamestowne.

Page 68, bottom right. Gold button, perhaps from band of hat Pocahontas wore when she was presented to King James I. Virginia Historical Society, Gift of Mrs. Hugh Blair Grigsby Galt and Margaret Purviance Hastings.

Page 69, top. Simon van de Passe, portrait of Pocahontas, engraving, 1616, published in John Smith, *The Generall Historie of Virginia,* 1624. Virginia Historical Society.

Page 69, bottom. Anne Fletcher, portrait of Pocahontas, oil on canvas, c. 1929, copy of Booton Hall portrait based on Simon van de Passe's engraving. Virginia Historical Society, Bequest of Mr. and Mrs. Alexander Wilbourne Weddell.

Page 70. The 1622 uprising of the Powhatans, engraving, published in Theodor de Bry, *America,* part 13 (1634), plate VII. Virginia Historical Society.

Page 71. Silver badge, engraved "Ye King of" and "Patomeck" [Potomac], 1662, used for passage into English settlements. Virginia Historical Society, Gift of John Pratt.

Page 72. Reverend Patrick Copland, *Virginia's God be Thanked, or A Sermon Of Thanksgiving For The Happie success of the affayres in Virginia this last yeare* (London: I/D. for William Sheffard and John Ballamie, 1622). Virginia Historical Society. Richmond only.

Page 73. Pitchfork, seventeenth century, used at Jamestown. National Park Service, Colonial National Historical Park.

Page 74. Wooden toolbox, 1670–1725, excavated at Church Neck Wells, Northampton County, Virginia. Virginia Department of Historic Resources.

Page 75. Indenture or contract, signed by Richard Lowther of Bedfordshire, England, to enter the service of Edward Lyurd, an ironmonger in Virginia, 1627. Virginia Historical Society, Gift of Preston Davie. Original at St. Louis and Gatineau.

Page 76. Census of Virginia, March 1619 [modern, 1620], recording the presence of Africans in Virginia. The Master and Fellows of Magdalen College, University of Cambridge.

Page 77, top. Narrow hoe, used at Kingsmill settlement. Virginia Department of Historic Resources.

Page 77, bottom. Broad hoe, used at Causey's Care settlement. Virginia Department of Historic Resources.

Page 78, top. Drawing of Bruton Parish Church, Williamsburg, 1702. Reproduction. Colonial Williamsburg Foundation.

Page 78, bottom. Silver baptismal basin, made by Joseph Smith of London, 1733–34, used at Jamestown. Episcopal Diocese of Virginia.

Page 79. Bible, c. 1639–40, used since 1657 at Merchant's Hope Episcopal Church, Prince George County, Virginia. Merchant's Hope Episcopal Church, Prince George County, Virginia.

Page 80. Printing block, c. 1675, and modern tobacco label for "R. Mascall's Best Virginia in As[h]ford Kent" printed from it. Virginia Historical Society.

Page 81. Attributed to Sir Peter Lely, portrait of Sir William Berkeley, oil on canvas, c. 1670. Reproduction. By permission of Mr. John Berkeley, Berkeley Castle, England.

Page 83. Portrait of Mary (Isham) Randolph, oil on canvas, c. 1735. Virginia Historical Society, Bequest of Kate Brander (Harris) Mayo Skipwith Williams.

Page 85. Window casement, Bacon House, Curles plantation, marked "1647 John Mason of Bristol fecit." Virginia Department of Historic Resources.

Page 86, top. Iron grenades, two exploded and one intact, 1676, from Bacon's Rebellion. APVA Preservation Virginia and Historic Jamestowne.

Page 86, bottom. Silver frontlet, 1677, given by Charles II of England to Cockacoeske, "queen of the Pamunkey," in Virginia. APVA Preservation Virginia and Historic Jamestowne.

Page 87. John Cotton, "Bacon's Epitaph Made by His Man," eighteenth-century copy of now-vanished manuscript, c. 1676. Virginia Historical Society, transferred from Massachusetts Historical Society. Original at Santa Fe and Washington.

Page 88. Gold wedding band, inscribed "Time shall tell, I love thee well," c. 1650–75, fragment found at Poquoson. Virginia Department of Historic Resources.

Page 89. Punch bowl, silver, 1692, made by John Sutton, London, descended in the family of Severn Eyre of Virginia's Eastern Shore. Anonymous loan.

Page 90. *Nova Belgii Novaeque Angliae Nec Non partis Virginiae Tabula,* hand-colored engraving, issued by Nicolaas J. Visscher I, Amsterdam, 2d state, 1655. Smithsonian National Museum of American History, Kenneth E. Behring Center. Several editions rotate.

Page 91. Court cupboard, Virginia, white oak and yellow pine, c. 1660. Wadsworth Atheneum Museum of Art, Hartford, Connecticut, Wallace Nutting Collection, Gift of J. Pierpont Morgan.

Page 92. Iron bill, a type of polearm, perhaps one of the group James I released from his armory in 1622. APVA Preservation Virginia and Historic Jamestowne.

Page 93. Armorial plaque of King William III and Queen Mary II, from Christ Church, Philadelphia. Christ Church Preservation Trust, Philadelphia. Catalogue photograph by Tom Crane.

Pages 94 (detail) and 109. Saint-Marc Moutillet, presumed portrait of Marie-Charlotte Denys de la Ronde, wife of Claude de Ramezay, oil on canvas. Château Ramezay Museum, Montréal, Quebéc.

Page 96. Théophile Hamel, oil on canvas, before 1870, after Balthazar Moncormet, c. 1654, fake portrait of Samuel de Champlain. Reproduction. Library and Archives of Canada, Ottawa.

Page 97. Samuel de Champlain, "Carte geographique de la nouvelle Franse," 1612, published in *Les Voyages du Sieur de Champlain Xaintongeois* (Paris, 1613). Reproduction. The Newberry Library, Chicago.

Page 98. Henry IV of France, engraving, c. 1870. Virginia Historical Society.

Page 99. Pair of Montagnais child's snowshoes, wood frame and animal skin lacing. Catalogue photograph © Canadian Museum of Civilization, no. III-C-247 a-b, by Harry Foster, image no. D2006–08034.

Page 100. Belt of cylindrical shell beads, or wampum, representing four Huron leaders, given to Samuel de Champlain in 1611. From the French royal collection. Catalogue photograph © Musée du Quai Branly, Paris, by Patrick Gries. Gatineau only.

Page 101. Cotton and glass bead bag, probably Huron, c. 1721, from the upper St. Lawrence/Great Lakes region. Musée du Quai Branly, Paris. Richmond and St. Louis only.

Page 102. Henri Chatelaine, detail of beavers from *Carte tres curieuse,* engraving, from *Atlas historique,* vol. VI (Amsterdam, 1719). Smithsonian National Museum of American History, Kenneth E. Behring Center.

Page 103. Samuel de Champlain, *Carte geographique de la nouvelle Franse,* 1612, detail of a Native woman holding an ear of corn and a squash. Reproduction. The Newberry Library, Chicago.

Page 104. Samuel de Champlain and Native allies fighting Mohawks, engraving, from *Les Voyages du Sieur de Champlain Xaintongeois* (Paris, 1613). Reproduction. The Newberry Library, Chicago.

Page 105, top. War club, from the upper Great Lakes region. Catalogue photograph by Bob Halloran © copyright Mashantucket Pequot Museum and Research Center.

Page 105, center. Religious medal given to Native converts, copper, France. Collections archéologiques de la ville de Québec.

Page 105, bottom. Guillaume de L'Isle, *Carte du Canada ou de la Nouvelle France,* engraving by Guerard, Jr., Paris, 1703, detail of a priest preaching to Native people. Smithsonian National Museum of American History, Kenneth E. Behring Center.

Page 106. Document recording the hiring of a four-year-old servant, Québec, 9 October 1703. Reproduction. Bibliothèque et Archives nationales du Québec, Montréal.

Page 107. Immigrant chest, pine and iron, c. 1650, France. Catalogue photograph © Canadian Museum of Civilization, no. 91–38, by Ross Taylor, image no. S93–2720.

Page 108. Portrait of Claude de Ramezay, oil on canvas. Château Ramezay Museum, Montréal, Québec.

Page 110, left. Wheeled plow, Québec, eighteenth century. Musée Québécois de Culture Populaire, Collection Robert-Lionel Séguin, Trois-Rivières, Canada.

Page 110, right. French axe, eighteenth century, found in a cave on the St. Lawrence River, Québec. National Museum of the American Indian, Smithsonian Institution (22/7317).

Page 110, bottom. Canoe, a modern version built in traditional style by the Attikamek Nation of Québec. Catalogue photograph © Canadian Museum of Civilization, III-P-21a, image no. D2005–10388.

Page 111. Deed of emancipation of a black slave, Québec, 1744/45. Reproduction. Bibliothèque et Archives nationales du Québec, Montréal.

Page 112. Wood cup used by a *voyageur* or *coureur des bois,* eighteenth century. Château Ramezay Museum, Montréal, Québec.

Page 113. *Map of the Discovery Made in the year 1673 in North America,* showing the upper Mississippi River, based on a drawing by Father Jacques Marquette, 1681. Reproduction. The Newberry Library, Chicago.

Page 114. Painted bison hide, given to Father Jacques Marquette by the Illinois Nation in 1673 or 1674. Catalogue photograph © Musée du Quai Branly, Paris, Photograph by Patrick Gries/Valérie Torre. Gatineau only.

Page 115. Beaver hunting hooks. National Museum of the American Indian, Smithsonian Institution (24/1612).

Page 116. Claude François, portrait of Jean Talon, oil on canvas, 1671–72. Reproduction. Musée des Augustines de l'Hôtel-Dieu de Québec.

Page 117. *Justaucorps,* or man's coat, early eighteenth century, from New France. Stewart Museum, Montréal. Two coats rotate.

Page 119. Copper kettle, seventeenth century, excavated at Place Royale, Québec City. Laboratoire et Réserve d'archéologie du Québec, Ministère de la Culture et des Communications, Québec.

Page 121, left. View of the second residence, or *habitation,* of Samuel de Champlain in Québec, from *Les Voyages du Sieur de Champlain Xaintongeois* (Paris, 1613). Reproduction. The Newberry Library, Chicago.

Page 121, right. Tobacco pipe, from the second *habitation* of Champlain. Ministère de la Culture et des Communications, Québec.

Pages 122–23. "View of the City of Québec in Canada, New France, Capital of America," c. 1721. Reproduction. Edward Ayer Collection, The Newberry Library, Chicago.

Page 124. Armchair in Louis XIII style, wood, fiber, and brass, late seventeenth century, made in New France. Catalogue photograph © Canadian Museum of Civilization, no. A-3455 a-b, Photograph by Merle Toole, image no. S93–3463.

Page 125. Native ceremonial headdress, horsehair, horn, porcupine quills, and glass beads, eighteenth century, Great Lakes region of New France. From the French royal collection. Catalogue photograph by Patrick Gries/Bruno Descoings © Musée du Quai Branly, Paris. Washington only.

Page 126, left. Reliquary of Jacques Le Ber, c. 1706. Maison Saint-Gabriel, Montréal, Québec.

Page 126, right. Child's toilet chair, pine and iron, c. 1700–1800. Catalogue photograph © Canadian Museum of Civilization, no. 978.161.6, by Merle Toole, image no. S93–3324.

Pages 129 and 164 (detail). Native-painted hide robe imitating Louis XIV style, eighteenth century, from St. Lawrence region. From the French royal collection. Catalogue photograph © Musée du Quai Branly, Paris, by Patrick Gries/Valérie Torre. Washington only.

Page 130. Bronze bell, from Beauport Chapel, 1666. Bibliothèque et Archives nationals du Québec, Centre d'archives de Québec.

Page 131. Playing card showing a Native of Virginia, designed to instruct young Louis XIV, c. 1644. Virginia Historical Society.

Page 132. Copper coin, a *sou,* 1722, perhaps used for trade with Natives. The Historic New Orleans Collection acc. 1978.137.

Page 133. Louis Nicolas, watercolor of a stallion sent to New France by Louis XIV, c. 1670. Reproduction. Thomas Gilcrease Institute, Tulsa, Oklahoma.

Pages 134 (detail) and 142. Juan Correa or his workshop, *The Assumption of the Virgin,* oil on canvas, c. 1700, Mexico. Palace of the Governors, The New Mexico History Museum, Museum of New Mexico, Department of Cultural Affairs.

Page 136. Detail of New Mexico, from Giovanni Battista Ramusio, *Universale della parte del mondo nuovamente,* 1556, map of the Western Hemisphere showing North and South America. Reproduction. John Carter Brown Library at Brown University.

Page 137. Family tree of the Martínez de Montoya family, manuscript, late eighteenth to early nineteenth century. Palace of the Governors, The New Mexico History Museum, Museum of New Mexico, Department of Cultural Affairs.

Page 138, top. Portrait of Philip III, engraving, from Gil Gonzalez Davila, *Teatro de las grandezas de la villa de Madrid* (Madrid, 1623). Reproduction. Marsden Collection Add. G7, Foyle Special Collections Library, King's College, London.

Page 138, bottom. Tewa polychrome ceramic soup bowl. Museum Excavation, LA 38 Cuyamungue. Museum of Indian Arts and Culture, Laboratory of Anthropology, Museum of New Mexico, Department of Cultural Affairs.

Page 139. John K. Hillers, photograph of Taos Pueblo, 1880. Reproduction. Palace of the Governors, The New Mexico History Museum, Museum of New Mexico, Department of Cultural Affairs.

Page 140, left. Italian breastplate, steel, sixteenth century, used by the Spanish in New Mexico. Palace of the Governors, The New Mexico History Museum, Museum of New Mexico, Department of Cultural Affairs.

Page 140, right. Comb helmet of Italian manufacture, steel, late sixteenth century, found near Grants, New Mexico. Palace of the Governors, The New Mexico History Museum, Museum of New Mexico, Department of Cultural Affairs.

Page 141. Carved wooden cross, probably eighteenth century, New Mexico. Colorado Springs Fine Arts Center, Taylor Museum.

Page 143. Map of New Mexico, oil on canvas, c. 1760, based on a rendering by Bernardo Miera y Pacheco. Palace of the Governors, The New Mexico History Museum, Museum of New Mexico, Department of Cultural Affairs.

Page 144. Ceramic chamber pot. Museum Excavation, LA 95 Quarai. Museum of Indian Arts and Culture, Laboratory of Anthropology, Museum of New Mexico, Department of Cultural Affairs.

Page 145. Lieutenant Joseph de Urrutia, plan of Santa Fe, 1766. The British Library, Maps Department. Original at Washington only.

Page 146, top. Palace of the Governors in Santa Fe, photograph, 1868. Reproduction. Palace of the Governors, The New Mexico History Museum, Museum of New Mexico, Department of Cultural Affairs.

Page 146, bottom. San Francisco Street, Santa Fe, photograph, c. 1865. Reproduction. Palace of the Governors, The New Mexico History Museum, Museum of New Mexico, Department of Cultural Affairs.

Page 147. Tewa polychrome ceramic bowl. Museum Excavation, LA 4451 Santa Fe, Palace of the Governors. Museum of Indian Arts and Culture, Laboratory of Anthropology, Museum of New Mexico, Department of Cultural Affairs.

Page 148. Priest's chair, New Mexico, pine, last quarter of eighteenth century. Museum of International Folk Art, Museum of New Mexico, Department of Cultural Affairs.

Page 149. Crucifix, silver, late seventeenth or early eighteenth century, made in Spain or Mexico. Museum of Spanish Colonial Art, Collections of the Spanish Colonial Arts Society, Inc.

Page 151, top. Sheep grazing. Photograph by Central Photographic Studio, Santa Fe. Palace of the Governors, The New Mexico History Museum, Museum of New Mexico, Department of Cultural Affairs.

Page 151, bottom. *Almud* (dry measure), pine with steel rim, c. 1850. Palace of the Governors, The New Mexico History Museum, Museum of New Mexico, Department of Cultural Affairs.

Page 152, top. Six-piece *chocolatera* set consistent with those brought to New Mexico in the colonial era. Palace of the Governors, The New Mexico History Museum, Museum of New Mexico, Department of Cultural Affairs.

Page 152, bottom. Table, pine, early nineteenth century, New Mexico. Museum of International Folk Art, Museum of New Mexico, Department of Cultural Affairs.

Page 153. Edward Curtis, photograph of the Acoma pueblo that Juan Oñate attacked in 1598. Palace of the Governors, The New Mexico History Museum, Museum of New Mexico, Department of Cultural Affairs.

Page 154, top. Spanish *escopeta* (Miguelet carbine or light musket), used in 1700s by Spanish and Pueblo allies fighting the French and French-armed Native people. Arizona Historical Society, Southern Division.

Page 154, bottom. Spanish dagger, iron, late seventeenth century, found among the Apache people of northern Mexico. Palace of the Governors, The New Mexico History Museum, Museum of New Mexico, Department of Cultural Affairs.

Page 155. Franciscan B, *St. Anthony of Padua,* painting on tanned hide, c. 1650–1750. Smithsonian National Museum of American History, Kenneth E. Behring Center. Not at Santa Fe.

Page 156, top. Ceramic figurine of a cat and mouse. Museum Excavation, LA 625 Pecos. Museum of Indian Arts and Culture, Laboratory of Anthropology, Museum of New Mexico, Department of Cultural Affairs.

Page 156, bottom. Pueblo pottery bowl decorated with a cross, from the archaeological site of Kuaua. Museum Excavation, LA 187 Kuaua, Museum of Indian Arts and Culture, Laboratory of Anthropology, Museum of New Mexico, Department of Cultural Affairs.

Page 157. Chest, colored leather, eighteenth century, New Mexico. Colorado Springs Fine Arts Center, Taylor Museum.

Page 158. Clifford Fragua, statue of Pópé of San Juan, in the U.S. Capitol. Photograph Architect of the Capitol, Washington, D.C.

Page 159, top. Beam or viga, painted wood, c. 1640–c. 1800, from a ceiling at the Pecos mission in New Mexico. Museum of Indian Arts and Culture, Laboratory of Anthropology, Museum of New Mexico, Department of Cultural Affairs.

Page 159, bottom. Photograph of the Pecos mission in ruins. Reproduction. Palace of the Governors, The New Mexico History Museum, Museum of New Mexico, Department of Cultural Affairs.

Page 160. *La Conquistadora,* wooden statue, seventeenth century, photograph by Robert H. Martin, 1948. Palace of the Governors, The New Mexico History Museum, Museum of New Mexico, Department of Cultural Affairs.

Page 161. Portrait of Don Diego de Vargas, after original dating to 1660s, now in a private chapel in Madrid. Palace of the Governors, The New Mexico History Museum (Gift of Manuel Cabrera Kabana), Museum of New Mexico, Department of Cultural Affairs.

Pages 162–63. Hide painting of last stand of Pedro de Villasur expedition in 1720. Palace of the Governors, The New Mexico History Museum, Museum of New Mexico, Department of Cultural Affairs, Photograph by Blair Clark.

THE FOLLOWING OBJECTS ARE NOT ILLUSTRATED

1. Wolfgang Kilian, "Discovery of the New World," engraved copper plate, plate 6 from *Platius, Nova typis transacta navigatio,* 1621. Smithsonian National Museum of American History, Kenneth E. Behring Center.

2. William Crashaw, *A Sermon Preached in London before the right honorable the Lord Lavvarre [De la Warr],* 1610. Virginia Historical Society, Bequest of Paul Mellon. St. Louis and Gatineau only.

3. Edward Waterhouse, *A Declaration Of The State of the colony and affaires in Virginia* (London, 1622). Virginia Historical Society, Bequest of Paul Mellon. St. Louis and Gatineau only.

4. Alexander Whitaker, *Good Newes From Virginia,* 1613. Virginia Historical Society, Bequest of Paul Mellon. Santa Fe and Washington only.

5. *A True Declaration of the estate of the Colonie in Virginia,* 1610. Virginia Historical Society, Bequest of Paul Mellon. Santa Fe and Washington only.

6. Claude de Chauchetière, "The First Six Indians of La Prairie Coming from Oneida over the snow and ice" [to Montréal, wearing snowshoes], drawing, c. 1680. Reproduction. Archives départementales de la Gironde, Bordeaux, France.

7. Map of settlements of New France. Modern graphic.

8. An explorer using an astrolabe; from Juan de Escalante de Mendoza, *Itinerario de navegacíon de los mares y tierras occidentales,* engraving, 1775. Reproduction.

9. Viceregal instructions, advising Governor Pedro de Peralta of New Mexico to "settle or found the villa" of Santa Fe, 30 March 1609. Reproduction. Archivo General de los Indies, Seville, Spain.

10. Glass bead necklace, c. 1680–1700, found along the Rappahannock River in Virginia. National Museum of the American Indian, Smithsonian Museum, used by permission of the Rappahannock Nation.

11. Belt of cylindrical shell beads, or wampum, Mohawk or Huron, from New France. Formerly in the French royal collection. Washington only.

12. "Virginiani," detail from *Nova totius Americae descriptio: Auct. F. de Wit, Amsterdam,* c. 1690. Reproduction. Smithsonian National Museum of American History, Kenneth E. Behring Center.

13. Map of Lake Ontario, 1688, showing location of Iroquois Five Nations. Reproduction. Bibliothèque nationale de France, département des cartes et plans, Paris (Ge. D. 8043. Négatif: 66. D.6261).

14. A Canadian militiaman in winter dress, c. 1690. Modern illustration and copyright by Francis Back, 1992.

15. French bayonet, 1675–76, used in King Philip's War in New England. Pocomtuck Valley Memorial Association, Massachusetts.

16. Illuminated manuscript commission, 1761, given by the French to Oconostata, chief of the Cherokee Nation. Reproduction. National Archives, Washington, D.C.

17. Supposed burial suit (*traje a la medida*) of Diego de Vargas, conqueror of Santa Fe, excavated from St. Francis Cathedral, Santa Fe. Collections of the Museum of International Folk Art and the Archdiocese of New Mexico and the Museum of New Mexico, Department of Cultural Affairs, Photograph by Blair Clark.

18. *Goncola de Céspedes y Meneses, Historia de Don Felipe IIII Rey de las Españas,* 1634, one of many titles in library of Diego de Vargas. Fray Angélico Chávez History Library, Palace of the Governors, The New Mexico History Museum, Museum of New Mexico, Department of Cultural Affairs.

19. Patent of land adjoining Flowerdew Hundred awarded as headrights, 1690. Virginia Historical Society. St. Louis and Gatineau only.

20. Printing block, c. 1700, and modern tobacco label for "I. G. Best Virginia" printed from it. Virginia Historical Society.

21. Printing block, c. 1675, and modern tobacco label for "T. Maulden's Virginia" printed from it. Virginia Historical Society.

22. Beaver pelt (modern). Provided by Dr. J. Frederick Fausz, St. Louis, Missouri.

23. *Voyageurs* or *coureurs des bois* (woods roamers). Modern illustration and copyright by Francis Back, 2002.

24. Hides (modern) from New Mexico.

25. Corn and pine nuts (modern) from New Mexico.

26. "The Old Plantation," watercolor, eighteenth century, showing a gourd instrument being played in a slave quarter. Reproduction. Abby Aldrich Rockefeller Folk Art Center, Williamsburg.

27. Land office patent, manuscript on parchment, issued 26 March 1666 to Robert Taliaferro and Lawrence for 6,300 acres in Old Rappahannock County (now Fredericksburg and Spotsylvania counties), Virginia. Virginia Historical Society. Richmond and St. Louis only.

28. Patent issued to Captain Ralph Wormeley, manuscript, 1675. Virginia Historical Society, Gift of Mrs. Peleg W. Chandler and Mrs. J. Chauncy Williams. Gatineau and Santa Fe only.

29. Man's shoe sole, found at Jamestown. National Park Service, Colonial National Historical Park.

30. "Description De La Pêche, Habille-ments, Habitations, Manières De Vivre, Superstitions, Et Autre Usages Des Indiens De La Virginie," French engrav-ings of Virginia Natives, from Henri Chatelaine, *Atlas Historique*, 1719. Virginia Historical Society.

31. Map of pueblos and Spanish settlements of New Mexico, c. 1650. Modern graphic.

32. Fragment of ceramic candlestick. Museum Excavation LA 95 Quarai. Museum of Indian Arts and Culture, Laboratory of Anthropology, Museum of New Mexico, Department of Cultural Affairs.

33. Ceramic soup bowl. Field Collection. Museum of Arts and Culture, Laboratory of Anthropology, Museum of New Mexico, Department of Cultural Affairs.

34. William Henry Jackson, photograph of *camino real* at Chihuahua City, Mexico, c. 1883. Reproduction. Palace of the Governors, The New Mexico History Museum, Museum of New Mexico, Department of Cultural Affairs.

35. Bacín or chamber pot, Mexican majolica, early eighteenth century. Houghton Sawyer Collection, Museum of International Folk Art, Museum of New Mexico, Department of Cultural Affairs.

36. Spanish coin, eight *reales*, Mexico, 1621–65. Chase Manhattan Collection, Smithsonian National Museum of American History, Kenneth E. Behring Center.

37. Spanish coin, one *real*, Mexico, 1643–53. Smithsonian National Museum of American History, Kenneth E. Behring Center, Gift of Leopoldo Cancio.

38. Spanish coin, eight *reales*, Bolivia, 1685. Smithsonian National Museum of American History, Kenneth E. Behring Center, Gift of J. Patterson.

39. String of glass rosary beads, probably eighteenth century, from New France. National Museum of the American Indian, Smithsonian Institution (25/3635).

40. Bishop St.-Vallier, title page of *Catéchisme du Diocèse de Québec* (Paris, 1702). Reproduction. Archives de la Compagnie de Jésus, St. Jérôme, Canada.

41. Claude de Chauchetière, "Several people embrace virginity and continence," drawing, c. 1680. Reproduction. Archives départementales de la Gironde, Bordeaux, France.

42. Claude de Chauchetière, "Portrait of Kateri Tekakwitha," drawing, c. 1680. Reproduction. Collection of the Saint Francis Xavier Mission, Kahnawake, Québec.

43. Ceramic chalice or bell fragment. Gift of William R. Sanderson, Jr., LA 4451 Santa Fe, Post Office Site. Museum of Indian Arts and Culture, Laboratory of Anthropology, Museum of New Mexico, Department of Cultural Affairs.

44. St. John or St. Anthony of Padua in Franciscan habit, painting on tanned hide, 1680–1700. Museum of International Folk Art, Museum of New Mexico, Department of Cultural Affairs, Santa Fe. Santa Fe only.

45. Peter Pelham, portrait of Cotton Mather, oil on canvas, 1727. American Antiquarian Society, Gift of Josephine Spencer Gay. Gatineau and Santa Fe only.

46. Portrait of Increase Mather, oil on canvas, c. 1720. American Antiquarian Society, Gift of Hannah Mather Crocker. Washington only.

47. Philip, alias Metacomet of Pakanoket, leader of the Wampanoag, published in James Wimer, *Events in Indian History*, 1843 (1st ed., 1841). Virginia Historical Society.

48. Indian belt, string and porcupine quills, from the Great Lakes region. Musée du Quai Branly, Paris. Richmond and St. Louis only.

49. Birch bark box with lid design of por-cupine quills, eighteenth century. Musée du Quai Branly, Paris. Santa Fe only.

50. Painted skin bag with tassels, decorated with porcupine quills, Great Lakes region of New France. Musée du Quai Branly, Paris. Santa Fe only.

51. "La permission au Sieur de La Salle," 1678, document signed by Louis XIV giving Robert Cavelier [La Salle] permis-sion to explore the western part of New France. Reproduction. Bibliothèque nationale de France, Paris.

52. Cypress log from Fort de la Boulaye, 1700–1707. The Historic New Orleans Collection acc. 1952.25.

Notes

INTRODUCTION

1. The New Mexico colony began in 1598, but the date of the founding of Santa Fe is disputed because of terminology. In this book, essayist David Weber uses 1608, when Martínez de Montoya made a settlement at the foot of the Sangre de Cristo Mountains. Montoya never took up his duties as governor, however, and his successor, Pedro de Peralta, carried instructions to found a chartered *villa*. He elevated the status of Santa Fe to town and capital, and our contributing partner, The Palace of the Governors, The New Mexico Museum of History, uses the date of 30 March 1609 as the founding of Santa Fe.

2. The Spanish settlement in St. Augustine, Florida, was established in 1565. We have not given extensive attention to this earlier settlement because, although it was the base from which various expeditions ventured into the interior, and although Spanish Catholics made missionizing efforts there, by the end of the seventeenth century St. Augustine had spawned no additional permanent settlements but remained an isolated outpost of the Caribbean world. See David J. Weber, *The Spanish Frontier in North America* (New Haven, 1992), 31–38, 42–45, 49–59, 87–91.

3. Alan Taylor, *American Colonies* (New York, 2001), xi.

4. On "invasion" as an appropriate term, see James Axtell, "Invading America: Puritans and Jesuits," *Journal of Interdisciplinary History* 14 (1984): 635–46. James H. Merrell, "Some Thoughts on Colonial Historians and American Indians," *William and Mary Quarterly* (hereafter *WMQ*), 3d ser., 46 (1989): 94–112, notes difficulties in the term "peopling" when applied to European arrival in the Americas. Taylor, *American*

Colonies, synthesizes work that explores the complexity of the era's interactions. See also Colin G. Calloway, *New Worlds for All: Indians, Europeans, and the Remaking of Early America* (Baltimore, 1997).

5. Ira Berlin, *Many Thousands Gone: The First Two Centuries of Slavery in North America* (Cambridge, MA, 1998), 17–19.

6. D. W. Meinig, *The Shaping of America: A Geographical Perspective on 500 Years of History*, vol. 1, *Atlantic America, 1492–1800* (New Haven, 1986), 38–39, 51. On Ireland, see Nicholas Canny, *Kingdom and Colony: Ireland in the Atlantic World, 1560–1800* (Baltimore, 1988).

7. Berlin, *Many Thousands Gone*, 29–46.

8. Neal Salisbury, "The Indians' Old World: Native Americans and the Coming of Europeans," *WMQ*, 3d ser., 53 (1996): 435–58.

9. James H. Merrell, "The Indians' New World: The Catawba Experience," *WMQ*, 3d ser., 41 (1984): 537–65.

10. Daniel K. Richter, *Facing East from Indian Country: A Native History of Early America* (Cambridge, MA, 2001).

11. Karen Ordahl Kupperman, remarks made at "Concluding Observations" session of the conference "The Atlantic World and Virginia, 1550–1624," Omohundro Institute of Early American History and Culture, Williamsburg, Virginia, 7 March 2004.

12. Taylor, *American Colonies*, 57. See also James Ivey, "An Uncertain Founding: Santa Fe," *Common-Place* 3, no. 4 (July 2003), http://www.common-place.org/vol-03/no-04/santa-fe (accessed 7 March 2006).

13. Edmund S. Morgan, *American Slavery, American Freedom: The Ordeal of Colonial Virginia* (New York, 1975), 71–91.

14. Peter N. Moogk, *La Nouvelle France: The Making of French Canada—A Cultural History* (East Lansing, MI, 2000).

15. Morgan, *American Slavery*, 46–48.

16. Denys Delâge and Mathieu d'Avignon, "We Shall Be One People: Québec," *Common-Place* 3, no. 4 (July 2003), http://www.common-place.org/vol-03/no-04/quebec-city (accessed 7 March 2006).

17. Meinig, *Shaping of America*, 11–17, 109–17, 144–50.

18. Richard White, *The Roots of Dependency: Subsistence, Environment, and Social Change among the Choctaws, Pawnees, and Navajos* (Lincoln, NE, 1983).

19. On changes that the beaver trade brought, see Richter, *Facing East*, 50–53; William Cronon, *Changes in the Land: Indians, Colonists, and the Ecology of New England* (New York, 1983). On the shortage of French immigrants and laborers, see Moogk, *La Nouvelle France*, 87–120, and Peter N. Moogk, "Reluctant Exiles: Emigrants from France in Canada before 1760," *WMQ*, 3d ser., 46 (1989): 463–505.

20. On the meanings of conversion among Pueblo peoples, see Ramón A. Gutiérrez, *When Jesus Came, the Corn Mothers Went Away: Marriage, Sexuality, and Power in New Mexico, 1500–1846* (Stanford, CA, 1991), 3–94, esp. 85–94. On Jesuit accounts of religious change among the Montagnais in New France, see Kenneth E. Morrison, "Baptism and Alliance: The Symbolic Mediations of Religious Syncretism," *Ethnohistory* 37, no. 4 (1990): 416–37. On gender aspects of French efforts to convert Montagnais and Hurons to new beliefs and ways of life, see Karen Anderson, *Chain Her by One Foot: The Subjugation of Native Women in Seventeenth-Century New France* (New York, 1991).

21. Morgan, *American Slavery*, 99.

22. Delâge and d'Avignon, "We Shall Be One People."

23. Rebecca Ann Bach, *Colonial Transformation: The Cultural Production of the New Atlantic World, 1580–1640* (New York, 2000), 21.

24. Cronon, *Changes in the Land*.

25. See Robin Blackburn, "The Old World Background to European Colonial Slavery," *WMQ*, 3d ser., 54 (1997): 65–102. Dirk Hoerder notes that by the seventeenth century, Europeans had come to see Africa as providing "a reservoir of labor" for New World ventures. See Hoerder, "From Euro- and Afro-Atlantic to Pacific Migration System: A Comparative Migration Approach to North American History," in *Rethinking American History in a Global Age*, ed. Thomas Bender (Berkeley and Los Angeles, 2002), 201.

26. Berlin, *Many Thousands Gone*, 7–8.

27. Alan Gallay, *The Indian Slave Trade: The Rise of the English Empire in the American South, 1670–1717* (New Haven, 2002).

28. Brett Rushforth, "'A Little Flesh We Offer You': The Origins of Indian Slavery in New France," *WMQ*, 3d ser., 60 (2003): 777–808. See also Brett Rushforth, "Slavery, the Fox Wars, and the Limits of Alliance," *WMQ*, 3d ser., 63 (2006): 53–80.

29. Morgan, *American Slavery*, 295–315. See also Edmund S. Morgan, "Slavery and Freedom: The American Paradox," in *Virginia Reconsidered: New Histories of the Old Dominion*, ed. Kevin R. Hardwick and Warren R. Hofstra (Charlottesville, 2003), 48–72.

30. Guillaume Aubert, "'The Blood of France': Race and Purity of Blood in the French Atlantic World," *WMQ*, 3d ser., 61 (2004): 439–78.

31. Morgan, *American Slavery*, 316–37.

32. On earlier warfare in Virginia, see J. Frederick Fausz, "An 'Abundance of Blood Shed on Both Sides': England's First Indian War, 1609–1614," *Virginia Magazine of History and Biography* 98 (1990): 3–56.

33. Joe S. Sando, *Popé, Architect of the First American Revolution, August 10, 1680* (Sante Fe, 1998).

34. Gutiérrez notes that migration into New Mexico was so limited in the seventeenth century that by 1680 "nearly 90% of the Hispanic populace were natives of the province." See Gutiérrez, *When Jesus Came*, 103.

35. See Karen Ordahl Kupperman, "International at the Creation: Early Modern American History," in *Rethinking American History*, 103–22.

JAMESTOWN

I dedicate this essay to my students, past and present, whose lives Hurricane Katrina changed forever and to the hope that New Orleans becomes better than it was but loses none of the qualities that made it the most enchanting city in the nation.

1. David B. Quinn, *England and the Discovery of America, 1481–1620* (New York, 1974), 3–194; K. R. Andrews, Nicholas P. Canny, and P. E. H. Hair, eds., *The Westward Enterprise: English Activities in Ireland, the Atlantic, and America, 1480–1650* (Liverpool, 1978).

2. Entry on Richard Hakluyt by Anthony Payne, *Oxford Dictionary of National Biography* (Oxford, 2004), http://www.oxforddnb.con/view/article/ 11892 (accessed 20 August 2005); Richard Hakluyt, *The Principall Navigations Voiages & Discoveries of the English Nation: a Facsimile of the edition of 1589, with an introduction by D. B. Quinn and R. A. Skelton and with a new index by Alison Quinn*, 2 vols., Hakluyt Society, extra series, 39 (Cambridge, 1965).

3. Samuel M. Bemiss, ed., *The Three Charters of the Virginia Company of London, with Seven Related Documents, 1606–1621*, Jamestown 350th Anniversary Historical Booklet 4 (Williamsburg, VA, 1957).

4. Warren M. Billings, *Jamestown and the Founding of the Nation* (Gettysburg, PA, 1990), chap. 1.

5. Helen C. Rountree, *The Powhatan Indians of Virginia: Their Traditional Culture* (Norman, OK, 1989); Helen C. Rountree, "The Powhatans and the English: A Case of Multiple Conflicting Agendas," in Helen C. Rountree, ed., *Powhatan Foreign Relations, 1500–1722* (Charlottesville, 1993), 173–205.

6. J. Frederick Fausz, "An 'Abundance of Blood Shed on Both Sides': England's First Indian War, 1609–1614," *Virginia Magazine of History and Biography* (hereafter *VMHB*) 98 (1990): 3–56.

7. Camilla Townsend, *Pocahontas and the Powhatan Dilemma* (New York, 2004); Helen C. Rountree, *Pocahontas, Powhatan, Opechancanough: Three Indian Lives Changed by Jamestown* (Charlottesville, 2005).

8. William L. Shea, *The Virginia Militia in the Seventeenth Century* (Baton Rouge, 1983).

9. Wesley Frank Craven, *The Dissolution of the Virginia Company: The Failure of a Colonial Experiment* (New York, 1932), 148–336; Warren M. Billings, John E. Selby, and Thad W. Tate, *Colonial Virginia: A History* (White Plains, NY, 1986), 41–45; Theodore K. Rabb, *Jacobean Gentleman: Sir Edwin Sandys, 1561–1629* (Princeton, 1998), 353–89; and Thomas Cary Johnson, ed., *By the King: A Proclamation for Settling the Plantation of Virginia* (Charlottesville, 1946).

10. Warren M. Billings, "Vignettes of Jamestown," *Virginia Cavalcade* 45 (1996): 164–79.

11. Warren M. Billings, *A Little Parliament: The Virginia General Assembly in the Seventeenth Century* (Richmond, 2004), 247, n. 2.

12. James B. Lynch, Jr., *The Custis Chronicles: The Years of Migration* (Camden, ME, 1993), 135–39.

13. Warren M. Billings, "The Law of Servants and Slaves in Seventeenth-Century Virginia," *VMHB* 99 (1991): 45–63; T. H. Breen and Stephen Innes, *Myne Owne Ground: Race and Freedom on Virginia's Eastern Shore, 1640–1676* (New York, 1980).

14. Warren M. Billings, *Sir William Berkeley and the Forging of Colonial Virginia* (Baton Rouge, 2004), 48–57, 96–99.

15. Edward L. Bond, *Damned Souls in a Tobacco Colony: Religion in Seventeenth Century Virginia* (Macon, GA, 2000).

16. Billings, *Sir William Berkeley*, 1–79.

17. Ibid., 79–113.

18. Ibid., 113–23; Billings, *A Little Parliament*, 25–35.

19. Billings, *Sir William Berkeley*, 136–63.

20. Ibid., 174–210.

21. Ibid., 210–32.

22. Ibid., 232–48.

23. Ibid., 248–65.

24. Ibid., 266–73.

25. Billings, *A Little Parliament*, 49–62.

26. Billings, *Jamestown and Founding the Nation*, 99–104; Billings, *A Little Parliament*, 141–49. The dates when Nicholson served as lieutenant governor overlapped from 1690 to 1692. At that time he filled in for Effingham, whose illness in England prevented his return to Virginia.

27. William M. Kelso and Beverly A. Straube, *Jamestown Rediscovery* (Richmond, 1995–2004).

QUÉBEC

This essay is a translation from the original written in French by Gilles Proulx.

1. Between 1600 and 1760, according to the average tonnage recorded, commercial ships were from 40 to 120 feet long (with keels from 35 to 100 feet), from 16 to 27 feet wide with a hold of between 7½ and 12 feet. Most of them, the 100- to 200-ton ships, with keels of between 55 and 65 feet, were three-masted ships. Under 100 tons were most often two-masted ships—brigantines or schooners—and one-masted ships. See Gilles Proulx, *Between France and New-France* (Toronto, 1984), 20–27, and Gilles Proulx, *Fighting at Restigouche* (Ottawa, 1999), 34–44. For the description of a Basque-type boat circulating on the St. Lawrence River, see also the edition of Raymonde Litalien and Denis Vaugeois, eds., *Champlain, La naissance de l'Amérique française* (Quebec, 2004), 104.

2. Litalien and Vaugeois, *Champlain*, 176. Information on Champlain and the commercial companies comes mainly from this great collective work on the birth of French America.

3. For a critical apparatus of the remarks on the fur trade, see Gilles Proulx, *Témiscamingue et la traite des fourrures: l'implantation française* (Ottawa, 1988).

4. H. P. Biggar, *The voyages of Jacques Cartier* (Ottawa, 1924), 52–53.

5. Ibid., 233.

6. Population figures for Québec and New France are taken from Rémi Chénier, *Quebec: A French Colonial Town in America, 1660 to 1690* (Ottawa, 1991), 183, and Yvon Desloges, *A Tenant's Town: Quebec in the Eighteenth Century* (Ottawa, 1991), 21–23. These numbers do not include the floating population of sailors, soldiers, and nonresident merchants who were temporarily in Québec for short periods.

7. Litalien and Vaugeois, *Champlain*, 199.

8. Gilles Havard, *Empire et Métissages: Indiens et Français dans le Pays d'en Haut, 1660–1715* (Québec, 2003). This study describes all the problems of the meeting between the Native peoples and the French.

9. In France the male and female religious communities worked in primary schools and occupied the entire field of secondary and college education. Lay instructors also taught in primary school, especially in the countryside. Male or female religious communities, regardless of the sex of the patient, assumed hospital care for the sick. The same model existed in Québec and all of New France. See Roger Magnuson, *Education in New France* (Montreal, 1992), 4–15.

10. Before the arrival of foreigners, Native peoples had never been exposed to European infectious diseases such as smallpox, typhus, cholera, yellow fever, measles, chicken pox, or gonorrhea. Without immunological defenses, they fell victim to four epidemics in the 1630s. Half of the Huron population disappeared in a few years. See Alain Beaulieu, *Convertir les fils de Cain: Jésuites et Amérindiens nomades en Nouvelle-France, 1632–1642* (Québec, 1994), 118–21.

11. Marcel Trudel, *Histoire de la Nouvelle-France III La seigneurie des Cent-Associés 1627–1663*, 3 vols. (Montreal, 1963), 1:155.

12. Allana Gertrude Reid, "The Development and Importance of the Town of Quebec, 1608–1760," Ph.D. diss., McGill University, 1950, 32–33.

13. Ibid., 375–77.

14. John Hare, Marc Lafrance, and David Thiery Ruddel, *Histoire de la ville de Québec 1608–1871* (Montreal, 1987), 45–57.

15. Trudel, *Histoire de la Nouvelle-France III*, 1:231–32.

16. *Dictionnaire Biographique du Canada* (hereafter *DBC*), vol. 1, "Biographie de Jean Talon par André Vachon." References to triangular trade can also be found in the biographies of Jean Bourdon, Jean-Paul Godefroy, and Antoine-Denis Raudot in vols. 1 and 2 of the *DBC*.

17. Reid, "Development and Importance of Quebec," 174–202.

18. Ibid., 232–61.

19. Hare, Lafrance, and Ruddel, *Histoire de la ville de Québec*, 23–25.

20. Trudel, *Histoire de la Nouvelle-France III*, 1:163.

21. It must be specified that in view of the distance, the orders were transmitted directly from France to Plaisance, the Ile Royale, or Louisiana. This considerably reduced the influence of the authorities in Québec.

22. Havard, *Empire et Métissages*, 273.

23. Chénier, *Quebec*, 116–23.

24. Yves Zoltvatny, "Esquisse de la Coutume de Paris," *Revue d'Histoire de l'Amérique Francaise* 25, no. 3 (1971): 317–84.

25. Havard, *Empire et Métissages*, 459–60.

26. Reid, "Development and Importance of Quebec," 11–12.

27. Hare, Lafrance, and Ruddel, *Histoire de la ville de Québec*, 16–17.

28. Lucien Campeau, "La première mission des Jésuites en Nouvelle-France (1611–1613)" and "Les commencements du Collège de Québec (1626–1670)," in *Cahier d'histoire des Jésuites* 1 (Montreal, 1972), 83.

29. Quoted in Chénier, *Quebec*, 47.

30. Quoted in Hare, Lafrance, and Ruddel, *Histoire de la ville de Québec*, 57.

31. Quoted in Reid, "Development and Importance of Quebec," 55.

32. Chénier, *Quebec*, 157–59.

33. Starting in 1694, a garbage cart came by once a week, but in winter the service was interrupted until spring cleaning. Hare, Lafrance, and Ruddel, *Histoire de la ville de Québec*, 80–83.

34. André Charbonneau, Yvon Desloges, and Marc Lafrance, *Québec: ville fortifiée du XVIIe au XIXe siècle* (Québec, 1982), 20–22.

35. Marcel Trudel, *Histoire de la Nouvelle-France Le Comptoir, 1604–1627*, 312.

36. The Iroquois killed several French families in the village of Lachine on Montréal Island early in August 1689.

37. In 1685 three ships brought soldiers, craftsmen, the new governor Denonville, Bishop St.-Vallier, and their retinue to Québec. The *Diligente* arrived without difficulty after a seven-week trip; the *Fourgon*, which landed two weeks later, lost sixty-three passengers during its crossing. One month later the *Mulet* arrived. See Noel Baillargeon, *Le Séminaire de Québec de 1685 à 1760* (Québec, 1977), 14–15.

38. Marcel J. Rheault, *La Médecine en Nouvelle-France. Les Chirurgiens de Montréal 1642–1760* (Québec, 2004), 42–52.

39. Jeanne-Françoise Juchereau de St.-Ignace and Duplessis de Ste.-Hélène, *Les Annales de l'Hotel Dieu de Québec, 1636–1716*, ed. Dom Albert Jamet (Québec, 1939), preface.

40. Serge Lambert, *Entre la crainte et la compassion: Les pauvres à Québec au temps de la Nouvelle-France Quebec* (Sainte-Foy, Québec, 2001), 58–59.

41. Rheault, *La Médecine en Nouvelle-France*, 31.

42. Trudel, *Histoire de la Nouvelle-France Le Comptoir*, 318.

43. Hare, Lafrance, and Ruddel, *Histoire de la ville de Québec*, 90–92.

44. Magnuson, *Education in New France*, 42–63.

45. Campeau, "La première mission des Jésuites en Nouvelle-France," 86.

46. Elisabeth Gallat-Morin and Jean-Pierre Pinson, *La vie musicale en Nouvelle-France* (Québec, 2003), 372–77.

47. Gilles Proulx, "Loisirs québécois: des livres et des cabarets" (Québec, 1987) and "Les Québécois et le livre," 1–150.

48. Quoted in Reid, "Development and Importance of Quebec," 390.

49. To foster a community spirit among the French colonists, to excite the imagination and impress the Natives, and to provide distraction from day-to-day difficulties, Montmagny never missed an opportunity to organize a festival. Religious ceremonies and processions on fixed dates were often followed by secular celebrations. Cannon shots, musket shots, and fireworks provided impressive displays. The governor introduced to New France the custom of planting a maypole on the first of May outside the door of someone who was to be honored. This was not yet the public maypole, for the trees were planted in front of the church and the fort of St.-Louis. Some holidays, in particular New Year's Day, were also the occasion for visits and for exchanges of wishes and gifts among the governor, the clergy, and prominent citizens.

Montmagny also introduced the theater to New France. The first play was shown in 1640 by his secretary, Martial Piraube, on the occasion of the birth of the future king, Louis XIV. In 1646 the spirit of chivalry was celebrated by the presentation of *Le Cid* by Pierre Corneille, a fellow student of Montmagny at Laflèche. The Jesuits' reserve regarding the presentation of secular plays proves the governor's spirit of independence from his former teachers (*DBC*, vol. 1, article by Jean Hamelin, "Charles Huault de Montmagny," 383–84; Jean-Claude Dubé, *Le chevalier de Montmagny, 1601–1657* (Saint-Laurent, Québec, 1999).

50. Gilles Proulx, "Loisirs québécois," 1–135.

The author extends special thanks to Fran Levine, director, Palace of the Governors in Santa Fe, and to Jake Ivey, research historian, Resources Management Program, Intermountain Region, National Park Service, for their scholarship and generosity.

1. Lansing B. Bloom and Ireneo L. Chaves, trans., "Ynstrucción a Peralta por Vi-Rey," *New Mexico Historical Review* (hereafter *NMHR*) 4 (1929): 178–87, reproduces the viceroy's orders of 30 March 1609 in Spanish and in an English translation. The orders also appear in an English translation only in George P. Hammond and Agapito Rey, eds. and trans., *Don Juan de Oñate: Colonizer of New Mexico, 1595–1628,* 2 vols. (Albuquerque, 1953), 2:1087–91. The founding of an earlier settlement at the site, named Santa Fe, first came to historians' attention through France V. Scholes, "Juan Martínez de Montoya, Settler and Conquistador of New Mexico," *NMHR* 19 (1944): 340–41. Scholes reported on a collection of documents then in private hands. One of those, a "Certification of Services," dated 6 October 1606 at San Gabriel, New Mexico, and notarized in 1785, outlined Martínez's services while in New Mexico and was signed by Oñate's secretary, Juan Gutiérrez Bocanegra. In the second document, dated 10 August 1608 at San Gabriel and also notarized in 1785, Martínez asks Cristóbal de Oñate to certify additional exploits and grant him permission to leave New Mexico. In the second document Martínez refers to "haber hecho plasa [plaza] en Santa Fe." Plaza in this sense means little more than a village, and I have translated it as village to avoid confusing it with its better known meaning in English, a town square. The documents are now in the Angélico Chávez Library in the Palace of the Governors, Santa Fe, kept as the Juan Martínez de Montoya Collection. I am grateful to Tomás Jaehn, who furnished me with a photocopy of the page where that quotation appears. See, too, Marc Simmons, *The Last Conquistador: Juan de Oñate and the Settling of the Far Southwest* (Norman, OK, 1991), 182.

2. Quoted in David J. Weber, *The Spanish Frontier in North America* (New Haven, 1992), 82, which also provides context.

3. The viceroy's acceptance of Oñate's resignation, and his appointment of Martínez, both dated 7 February 1608, are published in English translation in Hammond and Rey, *Don Juan de Oñate,* 2:1051–53.

4. Simmons, *Last Conquistador,* 180–84, sees Oñate as behind the decision to settle Santa Fe, because it does not seem likely that an individual would have attempted to found a new *villa* and provincial capital without Oñate's permission. James Ivey, "An Uncertain Founding: Santa Fe," *Common-Place* 3 (2003): 7, http://www.common-place.org/vol-03/no-04/santa-fe (accessed 5 April 2006), portrays Martínez, operating on his own, as the leader of the disgruntled faction. Much hinges on the word "villa," the term that the viceroy used to refer to the settlement that Martínez had begun, and on whether Martínez recognized Oñate's authority.

5. Instructions of 30 March 1609 to Pedro de Peralta from Viceroy Velasco in Bloom and Chaves, "Ynstrucción a Peralta," 178–79 (" *Villa que se pretende*"). Santa Fe's claim to continuous occupation rests on the inclusion of a thirteen-year period, 1680 to 1693, when Native rebels held it.

6. Velasco to Peralta, 30 March 1609, in Hammond and Rey, *Don Juan de Oñate,* 2:1084.

7. Velasco to the king, 13 February 1609, in ibid., 2:1080.

8. John L. Kessell, *Spain in the Southwest: A Narrative History of Colonial New Mexico, Arizona, Texas, and California* (Norman, OK, 2002), 91.

9. James Axtell, *The Invasion Within: The Contest of Cultures in Colonial North America* (New York, 1985), 131–33.

10. Velasco to Peralta, 30 March 1609, in Hammond and Rey, *Don Juan de Oñate,* 2:1085. For the urgency of founding the *villa,* see also Bloom and Chaves, "Ynstrucción a Peralta," 179, 187.

11. John W. Reps, *Town Planning in Frontier America* (Princeton, 1969), 35.

12. Gilbert R. Cruz, *Let There Be Towns: Spanish Municipal Origins in the American Southwest, 1610–1810* (College Station, TX, 1988), 25.

13. Alonso de Benavides, *The Memorial of Fray Alonso de Benavides, 1630,* eds. and trans. Frederick Webb Hodge, Charles Fletcher Lummis, and Mrs. Edward E. Ayer (Chicago, 1916), 23.

14. Frances Levine, "Down Under an Ancient City: An Archaeologist's View of Santa Fe," in David Grant Noble, ed., *Santa Fe: History of an Ancient City* (Santa Fe, 1989), 19–26, summarizes what was then known from the archaeological record. Cordelia Thomas Snow, "Dispelling Some Myths of Santa Fe, New Mexico, or Santa Fe of the Imagination," in Bradley J. Vierra and Clara Gualtier, eds., *Current Research on the Late Prehistory and Early History of New Mexico* (Albuquerque, 1992), 215–20, explains how promoters fabricated a large pueblo on the site of modern Santa Fe.

15. On the springs, see Cordelia T. Snow, "A Hypothetical Configuration of the Early Santa Fe Plaza Based on the 1573 Ordenances or the Law of the Indies," in Linda Tigges, ed., *Santa Fe Historic Plaza Study I: With Translations from Spanish Colonial Documents* (Santa Fe, 1990), 56–57.

16. See ibid., 55–73, for the case of Santa Fe.

17. Bloom and Chaves, "Ynstrucción a Peralta," 180–81.

18. For early irrigation, which remains speculative, see Marc Simmons, "Spanish Irrigation Practices in New Mexico," *NMHR* 47 (1972): 138–39.

19. Boyd C. Pratt, "The Santa Fe Plaza: An Analysis of Various Theories of Its Size and Configuration, a Look at Several Crucial Documents, and a Comparison with Other Spanish Colonial Towns," in Tigges, *Santa Fe Historic Plaza Study I*, 37–53; a map on page 76 shows the location of the marshland, or *ciénega,* in relation to present-day downtown Santa Fe.

20. Snow, "Hypothetical Configuration," 58; Kessell, *Spain in the Southwest*, 98, and 394, n. 3.

21. Peter Gerhard, *The North Frontier of New Spain* (Princeton, 1982), 316–17; Cruz, *Let There Be Towns*, 36–45.

22. Henry Putney Beers, *Spanish and Mexican Records of the American Southwest* (Tucson, 1979), 24.

23. For conjectures on the southern edge, see Stanley M. Hordes, "The History of the Santa Fe Plaza, 1610–1720," in Tigges, *Santa Fe Historic Plaza Study I*, 6, and Pratt, "Santa Fe Plaza," 38. For the eastern edge, see David H. Snow, "La Plazuela de San Francisco: A Possible Case of Colonial Superposition," in Thomas J. Steele, Paul Rhetts, and Barbe Awalt, eds., *Seeds of Struggle/Harvest of Faith: The Papers of the Archdiocese of Santa Fe Catholic Cuarto Centennial Conference on the History of the Catholic Church in New Mexico* (Albuquerque, 1998), 81.

24. This sketch may be seen in many sources, including Max L. Moorhead, *The Presidio: Bastion of the Spanish Borderlands* (Norman, OK, 1975), 148–49, who translates its legend.

25. Joseph P. Sánchez, "The Peralta-Ordóñez Affair: And the Founding of Santa Fe," in David Grant Noble, ed., *Santa Fe: History of an Ancient City* (Santa Fe, 1989), 33.

26. Benavides, *Memorial,* 23 and 105. For the year of Benavides's arrival in New Mexico, see Alonso de Benavides, *Fray Alonso de Benavides' Revised Memorial of 1634*, eds. and trans. Frederick W. Hodge, George P. Hammond, and Agapito Rey (Albuquerque, 1945), 2; Sánchez, "Peralta-Ordóñez Affair," 30–31.

27. Benavides, *Revised Memorial,* 68. In his *Memorial* of 1630, Benavides noted that the church as a "hut," but in the 1634 version he claimed that it had "collapsed" by the time of his arrival and that Santa Fe lacked a church entirely until he intervened.

28. Antonio de Otermín to Fray Francisco de Ayeta, 8 September 1680, in Charles Wilson Hackett, ed., *Revolt of the Pueblo Indians of New Mexico and Otermín's Attempted Reconquest, 1680–1682*, trans. Charmion Clair Shelby, 2 vols. (Albuquerque, 1942), 1:101.

29. John L. Kessell, *The Missions of New Mexico Since 1776* (Albuquerque, 1980), 37–43.

30. Carrie Forman Arnold, "The Palace of the Governors," in David Grant Noble, ed., *Santa Fe: History of an Ancient City* (Santa Fe, 1989), 130–34, who also noted competing theories as to the palace's precise location. Quotation on page 134.

31. For the Tlaxcalans, see Marc Simmons, "Tlascalans in the Spanish Borderlands," *NMHR* 39 (1964): 108.

32. Kessell, *Missions of New Mexico,* 48–55.

33. Ibid., 44–48.

34. Eleanor B. Adams and Fray Angélico Chávez, eds. and trans., *The Missions of New Mexico, 1776: A Description by Fray Francisco Atanasio Domínguez* (Albuquerque, 1956), 40.

35. Richard L. Kagan, *Urban Images of the Hispanic World, 1493–1793* (New Haven, 2000).

36. Marc Simmons, "Settlement Patterns and Village Plans in Colonial New Mexico," in David J. Weber, ed., *New Spain's Far Northern Frontier: Essays on Spain in the American West, 1540–1821* (Albuquerque, 1979), 102–103. As early as 1609, Viceroy Velasco expressed the hope that Indians could be reduced to large settlements for defense (Bloom and Chaves, "Ynstrucción a Peralta," 182–83).

37. Scholes, "Juan Martínez de Montoya," 340; Weber, *Spanish Frontier*, 124–25.

38. Gerhard, *North Frontier of New Spain*, 317–18.

39. Viceroy Velasco to Governor Peralta, in Bloom and Chaves, "Ynstrucción a Peralta," 183.

40. The Marqués de Guadalcazar to Governor Juan de Eulate, Mexico, instructions sent on 5 February 1621, in Lansing B. Bloom, ed. and trans., "A Glimpse of New Mexico in 1620,"

NMHR 3 (1928): 366–67, 368–69, in Spanish transcription and English translation. Heather B. Trigg, "The Ties that Bind: Economic and Social Interactions in Early-Colonial New Mexico, A.D. 1598–1680," *Historical Archaeology* 37, no. 2 (2003): 67–69.

41. Max L. Moorhead, *New Mexico's Royal Road: Trade and Travel on the Chihuahua Trail* (Norman, OK, 1958), 32–35.

42. John O. Baxter, *Las Carneradas: Sheep Trade in New Mexico, 1700–1860* (Albuquerque, 1987), 2–12.

43. France V. Scholes, "Civil Government and Society in New Mexico in the Seventeenth Century," *NMHR* 10 (1935): 82–85; David M. Brugge, "Captives and Slaves on the Camino Real," in Gabrielle G. Palmer and Stephen L. Fosberg, eds., *El Camino Real de Tierra Adentro, vol. 2* (Santa Fe, 1999), 104–105; James F. Brooks, *Captives and Cousins: Slavery, Kinship, and Community in the Southwest Borderlands* (Chapel Hill, 2002), offers fresh insights into captive-taking in both Indian and Spanish societies.

44. Cordelia Thomas Snow, "'A Headdress of Pearls': Luxury Goods Imported over the Camino Real during the Seventeenth-Century Mission Trade on the Camino Real," in Gabrielle G. Palmer, comp., *El Camino Real de Tierra Adentro* [vol. 1] (Santa Fe, 1993), 69–76; Donna Pierce and Cordelia Thomas Snow, "'A Harp for Playing': Domestic Goods Transported over the Camino Real," in Gabrielle G. Palmer and Stephen L. Fosberg, eds., *El Camino Real de Tierra Adentro*, 2 vols. (Santa Fe, 1999), 2:72, 74, 76, 80. From this second article, I have noted only items that come from seventeenth-century sites, and from one of the few documentary sources, a 1660 inventory of the household possessions of Francisco

Gómez Robledo, which Pierce and Snow describe. For *Don Quixote,* see Scholes, "Civil Government and Society in New Mexico," 103.

45. Trigg, "The Ties That Binds," 69–70; Heather B. Trigg, "Food Choice and Social Identity in Early Colonial New Mexico," *Journal of the Southwest* 46 (2004): 223–52; Heather B. Trigg, *From Household to Empire: Society and Economy in Early Colonial New Mexico* (Tucson, 2005), 128–30; 200–201; Ramón A. Gutiérrez, *When Jesus Came, the Corn Mothers Went Away: Marriage, Sexuality, and Power in New Mexico, 1500–1846* (Stanford, 1991), chaps. 5, 6.

46. Simmons, *Last Conquistador*, 145–56; Kessell, *Spain in the Southwest*, 84; Weber, *Spanish Frontier*, 85–86.

47. Benavides, *Memorial*, 22.

48. Benavides, *Revised Memorial*, 68.

49. The 1660s may have seen the zenith of Spanish population in New Mexico, with some decline in the 1670s as conditions deteriorated. For the conventional wisdom, see Scholes, "Civil Government and Society in New Mexico," 96, and Kessell, *Spain in the Southwest*, 110. Known for his exaggerations, Benavides gives a figure of nearly two hundred fifty Spanish males for Santa Fe and a thousand Spaniards in all (Benavides, *Memorial*, 22–23, and Benavides, *Revised Memorial*, 68). Andrew L. Knaut, *The Pueblo Revolt of 1680: Conquest and Resistance in Seventeenth-Century New Mexico* (Norman, OK, 1995), 132–35, argues for a smaller Spanish population than have previous scholars, but he appears to discount Hispanicized Indians.

50. Weber, *Spanish Frontier*, 96–98.

51. James E. Ivey, "Seventeenth-Century Mission Trade on the Camino Real," in Palmer, *El Camino Real,* 1:41, 46.

52. Weber, *Spanish Frontier*, 115–17.

53. James E. Ivey, "Convento Kivas in the Missions of New Mexico," *NMHR* 73 (1998): 121–52, explains that the friars went so far as to permit Indians to construct kivas within the walls of the mission compounds at Pecos Pueblo and at the cluster of eastern pueblos known today as the Salinas, allowing pagan kivas to coexist alongside Christian chapels.

54. In the decades before the Pueblo Revolt, the ecclesiastical headquarters moved to Isleta in 1630, back to Santo Domingo in 1661, then to Santa Fe in 1664, and finally to Jemez in 1672 (Gerhard, *North Frontier of New Spain*, 318).

55. Sánchez, "Peralta-Ordóñez Affair," 27–38, summarizes these events; Weber, *Spanish Frontier*, 129–30.

56. Elinore M. Barrett, *Conquest and Catastrophe: Changing Rio Grande Pueblo Settlement Patterns in the Sixteenth and Seventeenth Centuries* (Albuquerque, 2002), 55–58, 64–65.

57. Ibid., 67–80.

58. Weber, *Spanish Frontier*, 133–34; James E. Ivey, "'The Greatest Misfortune of All': Famine in the Province of New Mexico, 1667–1672," *Journal of the Southwest* 36 (1994): 76–100. For recent reviews of the causes of the revolt, see David J. Weber, ed., *What Caused the Pueblo Revolt of 1680?* (Boston, 1999); for insights from oral history and archaeology, see Robert W. Preucel, ed., *Archaeologies of the Pueblo Revolt: Identity, Meaning, and Renewal in the Pueblo World* (Albuquerque, 2002), 307.

59. Weber, *Spanish Frontier*, 134–36.

60. Archaeological and documentary evidence leaves much room for interpretation of the details, but it seems

to reveal this general picture. See Pratt, "Santa Fe Plaza," 37–53; Arnold, *Palace of the Governors*, 133–36.

61. For a fine overall survey of New Mexico material culture of the colonial era, see Donna Pierce and Marta Weigle, eds., *Spanish New Mexico: The Spanish Colonial Arts Society Collection*, 2 vols. (Santa Fe, 1995), vol. 1. For what no longer remains from the 1600s, see especially 1:30, 62, 108, and for medals and jewelry, 1:94.

62. Diego de Vargas to the viceroy, 13 October 1693, in John L. Kessell, Rick Hendricks, and Meredith D. Dodge, eds., *To the Royal Crown Restored: The Journals of don Diego de Vargas, New Mexico, 1692–1694* (Albuquerque, 1995), 384.

63. Weber, *Spanish Frontier*, 139.

64. David J. Weber, *The Mexican Frontier, 1821–1846: The American Southwest Under Mexico* (Albuquerque, 1982), 1–6.

65. For late nineteenth- and twentieth-century Santa Fe architecture, see Chris Wilson, *The Myth of Santa Fe: Creating a Modern Regional Tradition* (Albuquerque, 1997), and for its Hispanic residents, see Charles H. Montgomery, *The Spanish Redemption: Heritage, Power, and Loss on New Mexico's Upper Rio Grande* (Berkeley, 2002), and John M. Nieto-Phillips, *The Language of Blood: The Making of Spanish-American Identity in New Mexico, 1880s–1930s* (Albuquerque, 2004). Henry Jack Tobias and Charles E. Woodhouse, *Santa Fe: A Modern History, 1880–1990* (Albuquerque, 2001). Susan Hazen-Hammond, *A Short History of Santa Fe* (San Francisco, 1988), provides a short, comprehensive treatment of the city's entire past.

Montréal, *38, 41, 42,* 48, 97, 100, 124, *126,* 127; administration of, 117, 118; founding of, 96, 103, 108, 123; and trade, 113

Morgan, Edmund S., 42

Morning Star bowl, *88*

Moussart, François du, 128

Mystic, Connecticut, *46*

Nahumkeke, 22

National Park Service, 92

Native peoples, *68, 125;* and captives, *41,* 150; conquest of, 12; and encounter with Europeans, 15, 26, 27, 44, 53, 96–97, *131;* and English, 27, 66, 69, 71, 74, 84, 92, 102; and foreign diseases, 11, *12,* 22, 27, 29, 99, 127, 157; and French, 22, 27, 28, 53, 97, *99,* 101, *108, 117,* 118, 119, 127–28, *129;* and land, 36, 44; medical practices towards, 23, 127; and religious conversion, 22, 23, 29, 44, 52, 53, 103, *105,* 127–28, *138,* 141, 147, 149, 150, 154, 156, 159, 160; and slavery, 39–40, 42, 108; and Spanish, 17, 28, 141, 144, 150, 153, 154; trade with, *11,* 20, *21,* 27, 71, 96–97, 102

Navajos, 42, 139, 150, *156*

Nebraska, *163*

Néré, Levasseur de, 125

New Amsterdam, *90*

New England, *11, 12,* 102; establishment of colonies in, 23, *46;* Native peoples in, 44

Newfoundland, 58, 61, 97, 115, 117

New France, *12,* 25, 26, 34, *35, 42,* 44, 48, 52–53, *9, 100,* 124, 131, *131;* administration of, 107, *108,* 115, *116,* 118–19; agriculture in, 98, *110,* 115, 116, 120; colonization of, 98, 108, 128; control of, 101, 104, 108, 109, 112, 131, 132; establishment of, 22, *126,* 127; immigration to, *99, 104;* Native peoples in, 112, 118, *125, 129;* population of, 100, 103, 104, 107, *116,* 132; religion in, 118; slavery in, 41, *110;* trade in, *21,* 99, 109, 112–13, 115–16, *132;* troops in, 104, 116–17, 118, 127

New Mexico, *12, 17, 19,* 36, 52, 53, 138, 139, 140, *148,* 149, 162; administration of, 136, 143–44, 149–50; colony of, *138,* 139, 140–41; Native peoples in, 26, 34, 36, 44, 47, *138,* 144, 150, 154, 156, 160; religion in, 23, 25, 29, *31,* 34, 36, 53, *138,* 141, *141, 149,* 154, *155,* 156, 159, 160; and Santa Fe, 136, *142,* 144; slavery in, 40–41; and trade, 34, 150, *151, 152*

New Netherland, *49*

New Netherland Company, *90*

Newport, Christopher, 62, 63

New Spain, 17, 52, 141, *142,* 145, 162

New Sweden, *49*

New World, colonies, 12, *25,* 28, *60;* conflicts in, 25, 27; freedom in, 12, 40; life in, 34, 35, *36, 102;* view of, 26, *96;* religion in, 25, 44, *51*

New York, 27

Nicholson, Francis, 92

Nipissings, 22

Nipmuc, 23

Normandin, Laurent, 131

North America, *55, 115,* 127; colonization of, 10–11, 12, 15, 17, 20, 25, 47–48, 58, 61, *63,* 81, 132, 138; exploration of, 97; labor in, 39, 44, *68, 110;* population of, 11

Northampton County, Virginia, *74*

North Carolina, *60,* 61

Notre Dame de la Recouvrance, 120

Nuestra Señora de la Luz, 148

Ohke, 138

Oklahoma, 138

Old World, 12, 48; conflicts, 25, 47; diseases from, *12,* 27; immigration from, 11, 27, 34, 53, 74

Oñate, Cristóbal, 140

Oñate, Juan de, 17, 23, 138, 139–40, 141, 144, 149, 152, 153, 154, 157

Oneida, *36*

Onondaga, *36, 41*

Onondaga, New York, 21

Ontario, 42

Ontario, Lake, *14, 26,* 109

Opechancanough, 34, 44, 69, 71, 74, 77

Oraibi, *51*

Ordinances of 1573, 143, 145, 148

Ordóñez, Fray Isidro de, 156

Ossossané, 42

Otermín, Antonio de, 160

Ottawa River, *14*

Ottawa Valley, *11*

Outaouais, 100

Pacific Ocean, 17, *21,* 61, *63,* 100, 101, 138

Palace of the Governors, *146, 147*

Pamunkeys, 26, *86*

Paris, 26

Parral, 150

Paspahegh, 62

Pawtucket, 22

Pecos Pueblo, *142, 156, 158*

Penn, William, 48

Pequot War of 1637, *46*

Peralta, Pedro de, 136, 138, 140, 141, 149, 150; and Ordóñez, 156; and Santa Fe, 142, 143, 144, 145, *146, 147*

Percherons, *132*

Percy, George, *62*

Persey, Abraham, *39*

Peru, 12, 141

Philadelphia, *49*

Philip III of Spain, 25, 53, *138*

Phips, William, 124

Pilgrims, 22

Pimas, 52, 162

Piraube, Martial, 131

Place Royale, *119*

Plaisance, 115, 118

plantations, 74, 81, *83,* 84, 88; establishment of, 12, 34, 35, 36, *39;* slavery on, 41

Plymouth, England, 61

Plymouth, Massachusetts, 22

Pocahontas, 22, 23, *65, 68,* 69, *69*

Poor House, 127

Popé of San Juan, 47, *158,* 159, 160

Poquoson, York County, *88*

Portuguese, ships, 11

Powhatan, *32, 33,* 66, *68,* 69

Powhatans, 26, 44, *58,* 66, *66,* 69, *70,* 71, *71;* English policies towards, 12, 23, 71